The Art of Poetry

Stop this day and night with me and
you shall possess the origin of all poems,
You shall possess the good of the earth
and sun, (there are millions of suns left,)
You shall no longer take things at second
or third hand, nor look through the eyes
of the dead, nor feed on the spectres in
books, You shall not look through my
eyes either, nor take things from me,
You shall listen to all sides and filter
them from your self. —Walt Whitman

THE ART OF POETRY

How to Read a Poem

Shira Wolosky

OXFORD
UNIVERSITY PRESS

2001

OXFORD
UNIVERSITY PRESS

Oxford   New York
Athens   Auckland   Bangkok   Bogotá   Buenos Aires   Cape Town
Chennai   Dar es Salaam   Delhi   Florence   Hong Kong   Istanbul   Karachi
Kolkata   Kuala Lumpur   Madrid   Melbourne   Mexico City   Mumbai   Nairobi
Paris   São Paulo   Shanghai   Singapore   Taipei   Tokyo   Toronto   Warsaw

and associated companies in
Berlin   Ibadan

Copyright © 2001 by Oxford University Press

Published by Oxford University Press, Inc.
198 Madison Avenue, New York, New York 10016

Oxford is a registered trademark of Oxford University Press

Library of Congress Cataloging-in-Publication Data
Wolosky, Shira, 1954–
The art of poetry : how to read a poem / Shira Wolosky.
    p.   cm.
Includes bibliographical references and index.
ISBN-13 978-0-19-513870-2
ISBN 0-19-513870-8
1. English language—Versification.   2. Poetics.   3. Poetry.   I. Title.
PE1505 .W55 2001
821.009—dc21   00-057493

9 8
Printed in the United States of America
on acid-free paper

For my children,

Talya,

Elazar,

Tamar,

Nomi

Preface

This is a study of poetry in the English tradition, and specifically of poems written in Modern (i.e., post-Medieval) English. In it, I consider great, short lyrics in English from the Renaissance into the twentieth century. The reader will thus be introduced in the course of this book to a core of significant lyric poems that makes up the English tradition. The book, however, is not organized according to chronology. Instead, its structure is topical and cumulative, intending to have the effect of building blocks or progressive overlays. I begin with the smallest integral unit of poetry, the individual word and its selection; then move to the poetic line; then to the fundamental images of simile and metaphor, as these in turn are used as basic structural elements that build larger poetic organizations. The fourth chapter considers the role of metaphor in building the sonnet. The fifth gives a condensed history of the sonnet, showing how verse forms are themselves dynamic historical accumulations as well as flexible, articulate organizations of meanings. I then progressively turn to central elements that organize both small and large units of poetic composition: the figure of personification; questions of poetic voice and of address to an audience; questions of gender. Toward the end, I treat such traditional topics of poetics as meter, sound, and rhyme, followed by a consideration of the role of rhetoric and further tropes in poetic construction, as well as what I call incomplete figures (such as symbols) and the situation of the reader.

Each chapter carries forward, and assumes, the elements of poetry introduced earlier. At times I also glance back at poems discussed in terms of a particular element to add a further layer of interpretation. My method has been to offer readings, in each chapter, of a group of poems, focusing discussion as much as possible through the specific topic, or interest, to which the chapter is devoted. The poems illuminate the topic, and the topic illuminates the poems. I do not offer lists of examples of specific figures or techniques, as is often done in poetry handbooks. Nor do I provide comprehensive lists of kinds of verse, or of technical terms. I have instead approached poetry as a dynamic interaction between numerous formal elements, with the text itself a field of historical reference and change, and addressed to an audience. To do this, I follow the course of a specific element—diction, or syntax, simile or other rhetorical figures—through a single text, to show how it is developed within that text and is vital to its construction. When I return to a poem discussed earlier, I do so from a different angle, in terms of a different element of poetic construction, in order to show how the different features combine and contribute to the effect of the poem as a whole. The result is like the layering of, say, different organ systems in the human body, charting each one but then superimposing one over the other to give an image of the whole. I have reserved for the end the more technical aspects of poetic analysis, such as meter, since I believe these only are meaningful when they are placed within the greater complex of poetic effects, that is, within the full experience of a poem in its many aspects.

Some chapters in this book are concerned mainly with stylistics. Some are more historical; some, more theoretical. This book sets out to re-examine the relationships between these traditional divisions of poetics, often combining them so that each may illuminate the other. It undertakes, first, to historicize formal analysis. Style, format, pattern, convention, and language in poetry are seen as taking shape under conditions of historical change and in the context of widely varying experiences and pressures. Without sacrificing the status of the poem as text and an emphasis on the design of its language, this book treats the poem as a dynamic arena in which elements from outside as well as inside collide and reassemble, in which poets address audiences under particular conditions and in terms of varied cultural interests and understandings. The poetic text emerges as a site of cultural interaction, whose language is open to, and registers, the cultural worlds that situate it and that it in turn interprets and represents. But it is a self-conscious site, a field in which the operations of language become visible. Poetry thus offers a strange and marvelous mirror for seeing how language itself works in shaping our world.

Above all, I have set out to break the closed frame of the poem, to see the poem as an intensive, volatile, transformative site in which many different sorts of language come into a special, self-conscious interaction. In a final section I offer bibliographical backgrounds, to place my own arguments within the context of ongoing poetic discussion.

Acknowledgments

I would like gratefully to acknowledge Harold Bloom, Geoffrey Hartman, and John Hollander, who developed my sense of poetry as a language of figures; Robert Fagles, Joseph Frank, and Emory Elliott, who gave me a historical sense of literature as dynamic, evolving form; and Sacvan Bercovitch, whose sense of literary and historical interplay has been a deeply felt model and whose encouragement has been a precious support. I wish to thank friends whose discussions have helped shape parts of this book, especially Beverly Haviland, Michael Kramer, Cris Miller, Jeffrey Perl, Gail Berkeley Sherman, and Susanne Wofford. I also want to thank David Kazhdan for his encouragement and comments. I wish to express my deepest personal gratitude to my parents, Blanche and David Wolosky; my sister, Rickey Wolosky Palkovitz; my husband, Ariel Weiss; and my children, Talya, Elazar, Tamar, and Nomi, who have given me a new future and a new past, and for whom this book was in many senses written.

I would finally like to thank the Dean's Office of the Humanities of the Hebrew University of Jerusalem, and the Hebrew University Authority for Research and Development, for contributing funds toward the permissions costs incurred by this book.

Excerpt from Elizabeth Bishop's "Songs for a Colored Singer" from *The Complete Poems 1927–1979* by Elizabeth Bishop. Copyright © 1979, 1983 by Alice Helen Methfessel. Reprinted by permission of Farrar, Straus and Giroux, LLC.

Emily Dickinson is reprinted by permission of the publishers and the Trustees of Amherst College from *The Poems of Emily Dickinson*, ed. Ralph W. Franklin. Cambridge, Mass.: Belknap Press of Harvard University Press. Copyright © 1998 by the President and Fellows of Harvard College. Copyright © 1951, 1955, 1979 by the President and Fellows of Harvard College.

Excerpt from T. S. Eliot's *Old Possum's Book of Practical Cats*, by T. S. Eliot, copyright 1939 by T. S. Eliot and renewed 1967 by Esme Valerie Eliot,

reprinted by permission of Harcourt, Inc. Permission also granted by
Faber and Faber, Ltd. Excerpt from *Murder in the Cathedral*, by T. S.
Eliot, copyright 1935 by Harcourt, Inc., and renewed 1963 by T. S. Eliot.
Reprinted by permission of the publisher. Permission to reproduce from
Murder in the Cathedral also granted by Faber and Faber, Ltd. Excerpt
from *Collected Poems 1909–1962*, by T. S. Eliot, copyright 1936 by Harcourt,
Inc., copyright © 1964 by T. S. Eliot, reprinted by permission of the
publisher. Permission also granted by Faber and Faber, Ltd.

Robert Frost's "Desert Places," "Stopping by Woods on a Snowy Evening,"
"Design," and "Fire and Ice" from *The Poetry of Robert Frost*, edited by
Edward Connery Lathem. Copyright © 1969. Reprinted with permis-
sion of the estate of Robert Frost and Random House, Jonathan Cape,
publisher. "Desert Places" and "Stopping by Woods on a Snowy
Evening" from *The Poetry of Robert Frost*, edited by Edward Connery
Lathem. Copyright 1936, 1951 by Robert Frost, 1964 by Lesley Frost
Ballentine, 1923, 1969 by Henry Holt and Co. Reprinted by permission
of Henry Holt & Co., LLC.

H.D. is reprinted from from *Collected Poems, 1912–1944*, by H.D. Copyright
© 1982 by the Estate of Hilda Doolittle. Reprinted by permission of
New Directions Publishing Corp. H.D. is also reproduced with the
kind permission of Carcanet Press Limited.

Excerpt from John Hollander's "Blank Verse," from *Rhyme's Reason: A
Guide to English Verse*. New Haven, Conn.: Yale University Press, 1981.
Copyright 1981 by John Hollander. Reprinted with permission of Yale
University Press.

Marianne Moore is reprinted with permission of Scribner, a Division of
Simon & Schuster, from *The Collected Poems of Marianne Moore*. Copyright
© 1941 by Marianne Moore; copyright renewed 1969 by Marianne Moore.
Faber and Faber, Limited, grants permission to reproduce the "The Paper
Nautilius," from *The Complete Poems of Marianne Moore*. Copyright 1935,
renewed 1970, by Marianne Moore.

Sylvia Plath's "The Applicant" is reprinted from *Collected Poems*, by Sylvia
Plath. Reprinted with permission of Faber and Faber, Ltd. Copyright
1960, renewed 1981 by Ted Hughes. All lines from "The Applicant" from
Ariel by Sylvia Plath. Copyright © 1963 by Ted Hughes. Copyright
renewed. Reprinted by permission of HarperCollins Publishers, Inc.

Ezra Pound is reprinted from *Personae*, by Ezra Pound. Copyright © 1926
by Ezra Pound. Reprinted by permission of New Directions Publishing
Corp. Permission to reproduce Pound is also granted by Faber and
Faber, Ltd.

Henry Reed is reproduced with permission of Curtis Brown Ltd., London,
on behalf of the Estate of Henry Reed. Copyright the Estate of Henry
Reed.

Wallace Stevens is reprinted by permission of Faber and Faber, Ltd.,
publisher of *The Collected Poems of Wallace Stevens*, by Wallace Stevens.
Also from *Collected Poems* by Wallace Stevens. Copyright © 1954 by
Wallace Stevens. Reprinted by permission of Alfred A. Knopf, a Division
of Random House Inc.

William Carlos Williams is reprinted from *Collected Poems: 1909–1939, Volume I*, by William Carlos Williams. Copyright © 1938 by New Directions Publishing Corp. Reprinted by permission of New Directions Publishing Corp. Williams is also reproduced with the kind permission of Carcanet Press Limited.

W. B. Yeats is reprinted with the permission of Scribner, a Division of Simon and Schuster, from *The Collected Poems of W. B. Yeats*, revised, second edition edited by Richard J. Finneran. Copyright © 1928 by Macmillan Publishing Company, renewed 1956 by Georgie Yeats. Permission to reprint Yeats is also granted by A. P. Watt Ltd. on behalf of Michael B. Yeats.

The Art of Poetry

Contents

Poetry can be many things. Poetry can be philosophical, or emotional, or sentimental. It can paint pictures, in a descriptive mode, or tell stories, in a narrative one. Poetry can also be satirical, or funny, or political, or just informative. Yet none of these activities is specific to poetry, or reveals how poetry differs from other kinds of writing or speaking.

A definition that underscores what makes poetry distinctive might be: poetry is language in which every component element—word and word order, sound and pause, image and echo—is significant, significant in that every element points toward or stands for further relationships among and beyond themselves. Poetry is language that always means more. Its elements are figures, and poetry itself is a language of figures, in which each component can potentially open toward new meanings, levels, dimensions, connections, or resonances. Poetry does this through its careful, intricate pattern of words. It offers language as highly organized as language can be. It is language so highly patterned that there is, ideally, a reason or purpose (or rather, many) for each and every word put into a poem. No word is idle or accidental. Each word has a specific place within an overarching pattern. Together they create meaningful and beautiful designs.

Learning to read poetry is, then, learning the functions of each word within its specific placement in the poem: why each particular word is put into each particular position. Why that word? What is it doing there? How does it fit into the poem, and into what the poem is doing? In poetry there are multiple reasons for choosing and placing words. There is not one single pattern in a poem, but rather a multiplicity of patterns, all of which ideally interlock in wider and larger designs. There are in fact many designs on many levels, where each meaningful word and element points to the next one, in an endless process of imaginative possibility. These intricate patternings of poetry are what generate the essential nature of poetry: its intense figurative power, to always point beyond one meaning or possibility to further ones. This book will identify and explore these figural possibilities and their patterns. It will work from smaller to larger units of organization until the poem stands complete, a building you can enter (and note: stanza means "room" in Italian) and understand in terms of the architecture of its diverse parts, as each contributes to the whole.

Individual words stand as the first, elemental units of poetic patterning (although words themselves are made up of sound units). On this first level, poetry is an art of word choice, made up of chosen words. This art of selecting words is called *diction*. There are in fact various reasons for choosing and including particular words in a poem, each of which will be considered in turn. Words in poetry are chosen partly for their sound: a poem's high organization of language certainly also takes the sounds of the words into account, as part of the pattern of the poem. This will include sounds of consonants and of vowels, and the even tighter sound repetitions of rhyme, which themselves work through a range of relationships: half-rhymes and full-rhymes, with unrhymed or thorn words variously mixed in, in rhyming patterns that also can vary widely.

Besides the sound patterns of poetic words there are metrical patterns: the rhythm of the words, so that the poem has a melody or beat, like music. English poetry relies very much on patterns of rhythm, which may even be said to have a foundational role in the history and development of English verse. Yet, in another sense, metric seems the driest, most mechanical aspect of poetry. To appreciate more fully metrical function, grasping other systems of patterning is essential. Only within the complex construction of the poem as a whole can it become clearer how patterns of rhythm contribute to building the poem's overall design, and the ways in which poets can use rhythm for emphasis, or delay, or for pure musical affect.

Sounds and rhythms in turn take their immediate place within another fundamental pattern of a poem's words: the pattern of syntax. Diction has to do with word choice, selecting the individual words that make up the poem. Syntax has to do with the basic grammar that organizes the words into phrases or sentences. A poem, like any piece of language, must of course put its words into grammatical order. Yet a poem has particular freedom in the way it constructs its grammar, related to the fact that a poem can give to grammar, as to everything it handles, a special meaning in the patterns and design of the poem.

The first chapters of this book will be concerned with elemental levels of design in poetry: diction, that is, individual word selection, and syntax, the word order as it makes poetic use of grammar. Only later will sound and rhythm be examined, in that they are, perhaps surprisingly given their sensuous material, in certain ways the most difficult poetic patterns to grasp. We will also consider larger organizational units of the poem: images, and how they together build poetic structure; verse forms such as the sonnet, as conventional modes of organization; other poetic conventions and their uses; rhetorical patterns, including special games poets play with word order; point of view, or the question of who is seeing and who is speaking in the poem, which can in fact control diction, imagery, and rhetoric; and the question of address—who the poem is speaking to, or ways in which it involves the reader. In the end, all of these patterns intersect and build upon each other, making a whole design in which every word has its place.

The first element of poetry we will examine, then, is diction: the basic unit of the word and how it is selected. In fact, in the history of poetry, diction has played, again and again, a revolutionary role. Almost every revolution in poetry makes diction a rallying cry. Understanding why this should be the case requires a backward look at poetic tradition. In its history from Greek times and in the codification of classical literature in the sixteenth and seventeenth centuries, poetry (and indeed literature in general) was defined in part by conventions governing kinds of texts or genres and the materials considered "suitable" to them. There was, accordingly, a high literature, such as epic and tragedy. In high literature, the subject was kings, nobility, or great heroes, those who were engaged in great, public, momentous events, such as wars (events in which only great personages served as central actors). Corresponding to such elevated subjects was an elevated language: beautiful, lofty sounding words, words formal and polite, or stately words only to be heard in a king's court or in literature dealing with it. In contrast, there was a low literature that could feature lowly characters, such as servants or common people. And it could treat events that were not of great significance but had instead to do with everyday life, without great and grand implications, events that could even be funny. Indeed, this was a literature of comedy. In this literature, you could use everyday language, colloquialisms, vulgarities, and slang: words so informal that today they might not even be admitted to some dictionaries.

Diction, then, is the selection of individual words in terms not only of a word's meaning but of its level or type. Is it a polite, formal, elevated word, grand sounding, which would be used only in the society of kings? Or is it an everyday word, simple, informal; or even a low, rude word? The range can be seen in, for example, the difference between: "Gimme that," "May I please have," and "Would you be so kind as to pass the."

Formal contexts (and their social-historical situation) therefore are one arena for establishing word levels through diction. But there are many other "contexts" for words as well. Words have what might be called an address, a place where they ordinarily live. When you hear a word, or see it in a poem, you are aware of the ordinary context in which this word would be encountered. When used in a poem, it carries into the text its implicit context, which then can be put alongside other contexts brought in by other words. "Plié" is a word that belongs to ballet class; "quarterback" belongs to football. "Have a nice day" is a phrase of everyday American politeness. "Checkbook" evokes banking; "docent," museums. The disparities between different words' associations may be comic, or perhaps ironic. *Irony* is defined as a disparity between different levels or terms within a text. This can mean a disparity between points of view, levels of understanding, or, as here, of decorum. Generally speaking, classical irony involves a disparity between degrees of *knowledge*. One figure—say the reader or another character— knows more than another figure does, say a character in a play. Romantic irony differently involves a disparity between levels of *consciousness*. In this case, some signal is given in a text that it *is* a text, a work of art. This does not involve knowing, for example, that Oedipus is a murderer before he does. Instead, it involves the text signaling the fact that all its action is taking place in a play, rather than really happening. This is often the effect of a "mouse- trap" play within a play, where the viewer becomes more con- scious of the power of theater itself to frame and represent how we understand things. There is also what I would call linguistic irony, where the uses of language make the reader aware of how language itself formulates and influences our understanding and experience. This could be the effect of a poem that mixes diction, where the different language levels play off each other, making us aware of their different social contexts, or their different purposes or functions or claims.

Or, a poet may carefully select words that all belong to one particular context, or level of language. Eighteenth-century poetry tried to do this. At certain times, poetry has been thought to be poetry only if it used very formal, elevated, grand language. Then along would come some young poet who would decide that this was too limiting and that it kept out of poetry too many things that he (or she) wanted to include. If you cannot use everyday words, then you cannot introduce everyday experience into your poem. So the poet would decide to break the rules and start putting everyday words of common life into poems. In that case, more than the words in the poem would change. The whole scene of the poem—the very material of the poem, what the poem could be about and how the poem could be about it—would also shift. That is why diction has been, again and again, a revolutionary force in poetry. Thus, William Wordsworth announced his Romanticist revolution in his "Preface to the Lyrical Ballads" as "a selection of the real language of men in a state of vivid sensation." Ezra Pound launched his Modernist experiments by denouncing the nineteenth century as a "rather blurry, messy sort of period" and calling for a poetic idiom that would "be harder and saner."

Appreciating kinds of diction of course requires some sense of language-levels. You would have to be able to distinguish between a formal word and an informal one. One can watch for and identify the sudden introduction into a poem of a scientific word, a word whose context is the world of science; or of a slang word, a word whose context is the street; or of a city word, rather than the gentle words of nature; or of a mechanical word, or a technological one (can a screwdriver really fit into a poem? it depends on what you think poems can properly include); or a military word, which traditionally set a level of high diction but in modern times has become, as we will see in our first poem, a language of low diction instead— with all that this implies about changing attitudes toward experience as well. Each of these words belongs to a specific context. Each introduces a specific level of elegance or high language, or of deflationary or low language.

It may be helpful to think of a jigsaw puzzle, or a collage, where each piece is made out of a specific material—stone and wood and plastic and paper. When they are pieced together, the textures of these materials remain quite recognizable set into the completed collage and contrasting among the other pieces.

To see how diction can work in a poem we must turn to examples. Only then can it become clear how in some poems, word choice from different contexts, "levels" of speech, plays a dramatic role, as it does in "Today We Have Naming of Parts" by Henry Reed (1914–1968).

Today we have naming of parts. Yesterday,
We had daily cleaning. And tomorrow morning,
We shall have what to do after firing. But today,
Today we have naming of parts. Japonica
Glistens like coral in all of the neighbouring gardens,
      And today we have naming of parts.

This is the lower sling swivel. And this
Is the upper sling swivel, whose use you will see of,
When you are given your slings. And this is the piling swivel,
Which in your case you have not got. The branches
Hold in the gardens, their silent, eloquent gestures,
      Which in our case we have not got.

This is the safety-catch, which is always released
With an easy flick of the thumb. And please do not let me
See anyone using his finger. You can do it quite easy
If you have any strength in your thumb. The blossoms
Are fragile and motionless, never letting anyone see
      Any of them using their finger.

And this you can see is the bolt. The purpose of this
Is to open the breech, as you see. We can slide it
Rapidly backwards and forwards: we call this
Easing the spring. And rapidly backwards and forwards
The early bees are assaulting and fumbling the flowers:
      They call it easing the Spring.

They call it easing the Spring: it is perfectly easy
If you have any strength in your thumb: Like the bolt,
And the breech, and the cocking-piece, and the point of
      balance,
Which in our case we have not got, and the almond-blossom

Silent in all of the gardens, the bees going backwards and
   forwards,
For today we have naming of parts.

This is a poem constructed around, and in a sense even about,
diction. Of course it is also about the scenes it describes: the con-
trast between the world of the army camp and the world of nature.
Each stanza of the poem contrasts the instructions of an implied
army officer against some activity in a garden. In the first part of
each stanza we are instructed, as becomes gradually clear through
the course of the poem, how to assemble and fire a gun. The end of
each stanza switches abruptly into the garden world, opposing its
beauty to the grim tedium of the camp.

This opposition works on many levels. The army-camp world
of the gun is piecemeal—as is dramatized in the act itself of nam-
ing parts. Each part makes its appearance in a choppy sequence
that reflects the task of putting together a machine. It also implies
how the world of the machine is a world itself in parts, mechani-
cally composed and controlled. The very experience of time and
of life is divided into separate units that don't flow together into
any kind of wholeness: A "Today," a "Yesterday," a "tomorrow"—
or, most ominously, "after firing." Here we already see how the
syntax of the poem contributes to this dramatization of parts
(all the patterns of the poem are at work at once). Sequences of
short, choppy, phrases or sentences recount the naming of the
parts of the gun, followed by longer, flowing sentences about the
garden. This is a world not of parts but of continuous, life-giving
processes. Each stanza then concludes with a short, choppy repeti-
tion that returns to the gun.

Syntactic contrast thus contributes to the oppositions this poem
represents and explores. Nevertheless, the art and strength of this
poem, through which the contrast between the worlds of the army
and the garden is dramatically felt, is centered in its diction. The
world of the army camp is presented to us through the language of
an army instruction manual, but the world of the garden is a world
of exotic, lustrous language, in striking contrast to the dry, abortive
words naming the parts of the gun. Thus, in the first stanza, against
the almost blank "naming of parts," the phrase: "Japonica glistens
like coral" leaps out in its specificity (Japonica is a tropical flower),
its sensuous color, it shining imagery.

This pattern of contrasts in diction repeats from stanza to stanza. "The lower sling swivel," the "upper sling swivel" hang there, pieces unconnected to whatever they are part of, unconnected even to their uses ("whose use you will see of, when you are given your slings"). Again the syntax reinforces this sense of truncation, of disconnection, leaving its prepositions incomplete ("whose use you will see of"). But again, the most striking feature is the very words used—the techanical words of swivels and slings. And then, from a different language-world, come "branches" in their "silent, eloquent gestures." These are all words of high diction. They are formal words, lyrical words, words we would expect to find in a poem—as are the phrases "glistens like coral" or "blossoms fragile and motionless;" but unlike "safety-catch," and "bolt," and "breech," words we would expect to find in an army manual, but not in a poem.

Other things happen in this poem, too. Eventually we are naming not only parts of the gun, but parts of ourselves, our own bodies—yet always and only in parts: thumb and finger, but without a hand or arm or person attached to it (this naming by part is called *synecdoche*). And there are parts we do not name, at least not directly. Yet they, too, intrude into the poem—ultimately through plays with diction. When the second to last stanza talks about the bees "assaulting and fumbling the flowers," a new kind of language enters the poem: the language of sexuality. The poem develops this through the pun on "Easing the Spring"—at once part of a gun and the moment in nature of reproductive energy. The last stanza powerfully confronts these two usages. They are now no longer separate from each other, but rather are doubles (or inversions) of each other. The spring of the gun doubles the Spring of bees and flowers; but so do the bolt and "cocking-piece" of the gun, and the "breech" that goes "backwards and forwards," all words that pick up the sexual implications of the fertility of the garden. In the gun, however, they are worse than sterile. They are deadly. Against it stands only the fragile, eloquent, exotic word "Almond-blossom."

In the end it does not matter whether this poem's syntax, or imagery, or diction is most striking. In any case the poem's word choices serve an important role in contrasting the worlds it examines. And a poem called "Naming of Parts" is certainly aware of the importance of how we name things, what names we give them, what words we choose.

Another poem that uses artful diction to accomplish its design is "Design" by Robert Frost (1874–1963):

I found a dimpled spider, fat and white,
On a white heal-all, holding up a moth
Like a white piece of rigid satin cloth—
Assorted characters of death and blight
Mixed ready to begin the morning right,
Like the ingredients of a witch's broth—
A snow-drop spider, a flower like froth,
And dead wings carried like a paper kite.

What had that flower to do with being white,
The wayside blue and innocent heal-all?
What brought the kindred spider to that height,
Then steered the white moth thither in the night?
What but design of darkness to appall?—
If design govern in a thing so small.

Again, many things go on at once in this poem. For now, we will focus on the kind of language Frost includes in it. On the one hand, there is the title, "Design." This is a title of quite high diction. It is a philosophical word, a word that recalls what is known in philosophy as the "argument from design," one of the traditional proofs of God's existence which claims that, given the wonderful design of the creation, it must have had a creator. It is also an aesthetic word, evoking the very notion of pattern, of design, in the work of art.

Yet, the poem's diction is taken from very different spheres than the high philosophical or high aesthetic. Just to mention a few: "Dimpled" is a word associated with children. "Assorted characters . . . mixed ready to begin the morning right" is a whole phrase that could be drawn from a recipe book, or, even more, from an advertisement for breakfast cereal. "Paper kite" is again a child's phrase. All of these, that is, suggest the world of childlike play or everyday experience. And we must ask: what are these words of low diction doing in a poem that announces itself in its title as a text of high seriousness, a poem not about childlike play but rather about divine or artistic design?

But of course that is what the poem also is about, as its final couplet (the last two rhyming lines) emphasizes. "What but design of darkness to appall" is a line of high dignity and diction, one of formal elevated language and syntax (this line would not be spoken in ordinary conversation). Its dignity extends as well into the image pattern. Darkness/appall is a sophisticated word play of contradiction. It puts together darkness and light—appall means to make pale, to whiten—in a contradictory figure that is called an *oxymoron*. But the last line returns to the world of ordinary language and small things, challenging both the high discourse and grand claims of design: "If design govern in a thing so small."

I have so far chosen my examples from more recent poets, since I think it is easiest to hear the registers of diction that are close to our own speech usage; while it is difficult to recognize what may be mixed or contrived diction in language very removed from our own. We can hear, even today, some of John Donne's innovation in diction and natural speech phrasing in his remarkably complex verse forms. When in "The Sunne Rising" he calls the sun "Busy old foole" and "saucy pedantic wretch," even we notice the disparity and strain between his level of language and the elevated heavenly planet. However, even if we grant that Wordsworth launched a revolution in diction by returning poetry to ordinary language, to our ear the language of his poetry is, I think, rather elegant and poetic. But with modern poetry we can rely on our own sense of ordinary and extraordinary language to feel the orchestrations of diction. Therefore, modern poems are especially useful for exercises in diction—noting that the move into Modernism, rather like the Romantism against which the Modernists were rebelling, was also defined in part in terms of diction. The Modernists, as Ezra Pound (1885–1972) put it, wanted to write in a language that was hard and clear and direct, as opposed to what they saw as blurry, vague, and sentimental Romantic language. Pound's poem "The Lake Isle" is specifically written in parody of an (early) poem by William Butler Yeats (1865–1939) called "The Lake Isle of Innisfree." In this phase of his writing, Yeats dreams of escape to a lake isle in language that is gorgeous and evocative:

I will arise and go now, and go to Innisfree,
And a small cabin build there, of clay and wattles made:
Nine bean-rows will I have there, a hive for the honeybee,
And live alone in the bee-loud glade.

But Pound's poem goes:

O God, O Venus, O Mercury, patron of thieves,
Give me in due time, I beseech you, a little tobacco-shop,
With the little bright boxes
piled up neatly upon the shelves

And the loose fragrant cavendish
and the shag,
And the bright Virginia
loose under the bright glass cases,
And a pair of scales not too greasy,
And the whores dropping in for a word or two in passing,
For a flip word, and to tidy their hair a bit.

O God, O Venus, O Mercury, patron of thieves,
Lend me a little tobacco-shop,
or install me in any profession
Save this damn'd profession of writing,
where one needs one's brains all the time.

This poem stages a scene of Modernism in many ways. It insists on an everyday, urban setting as the proper place for poetry, and on everyday and even sordid matters as poetic. But one way it realizes this insistence is by introducing the low diction of an everyday, unelevated world. The poem does so in a particularly pointed way, since it opens in a grand style of invocation to the Gods, including the very formal *vocative* address, "O." The poet even offers a kind of catalogue, something routinely found in epics. But this is a catalogue naming specific kinds of tobacco. And the milieu of the poem is far from the gods of ancient Greece. Into its language the words of the corner shop find their way, the "little bright boxes," the neatly piled shelves, the glass cases, and "a pair of scales not too greasy." The poem even opens its diction to the socially marginal "whores" passing "for a flip word" in the (poetically) marginal language of slang.

Just how seriously to take this elevated frame of addressing the gods followed by such deflating linguistic gestures is of course a question the poem itself is asking. But the power of the poem, as a poem, has to do with the distances its language is willing to travel between high and low, remote and near. This is true as well of T. S.

Eliot (1888–1965), whose talent resides not least in his command of diction levels. In his late, meditative poem "East Coker" in *Four Quartets*, for example, he writes:

> Our only health is the disease
> If we obey the dying nurse
> Whose constant care is not to please
> But to remind of our, and Adam's curse,
> And that, to be restored, our sickness must grow worse.
>
> The whole earth is our hospital
> Endowed by the ruined millionaire,
> Wherein, if we do well, we shall
> Die of the absolute paternal care
> That will not leave us, but prevents us everywhere.
>
> (East Coker)

This text reviews in its own way the dogma of Good Friday, the day of Christ's Passion, in which suffering is shown to be the path of redemption as long as it is accepted in true humility as penitential and purifying. But Eliot has transposed the terms of this basic Christian pattern into the most modern language. The Church is a "dying nurse," Adam is a "ruined millionaire," and the earth on which we suffer is "our hospital." While these transpositions may seem strained, they offer one example of Eliot's commitment to modern terms for even ancient and sacred matters. This command of diction is equally present in his earlier, more secular texts, such as "The Love Song of J. Alfred Prufrock":

> And indeed there will be time
> For the yellow smoke that slides along the street
> Rubbing its back upon the window-panes;
> There will be time, there will be time
> To prepare a face to meet the faces that you meet;
> There will be time to murder and create,
> And time for all the works and days of hands
> That lift and drop a question on your plate;
> Time for you and time for me,
> And time yet for a hundred indecisions,
> And for a hundred visions and revisions
> Before the taking of a toast and tea.

In the room the women come and go
Talking of Michelangelo.

This verse mixes diction levels to great effect. There is on the one hand the high, intoning speech level of: "There will be time to murder and create / And time for all the works and days of hands." Murder and creation are momentous events; and the construction "works and days of hands" is prophetic, biblical in its word choice and phrasing—works here meaning the great works of creation or destruction. The repetition of "there will be time" has a similarly elevating, incantatory effect. But this elevated language is set alongside diction that is not only ordinary, but trivial: "That lift and drop a question on your plate." We are not in the world of prophesy, but of "the taking of a toast and tea," whose very terms introduce us into a salon, at tea-time, with all its trivial formality. We are not considering great acts of creation and destruction, but the wavering insecurity of "a hundred indecisions." The very terms are taken from social psychology. What then, is the relation between great deeds and trivial, even sordid conditions? That is what the poem is asking, not least in the famous concluding couplet, where trivial "women come and go" but talk, in the elevated language of culture, of art, of "Michelangelo."

Part of Eliot's greatness as a poet is his mastery of contemporary and ordinary diction, which he sets into his verse lines with great naturalness. The fact that this quoted verse, set into the larger free-verse text of "Prufrock," recalls the sonnet form in its fourteen lines and concluding couplet, as well as weaving an intricate rhyme pattern (time/time; street/meet; panes/hands; create/plate; me/tea; indecisions/revisions; go/Michelangelo), shows Eliot's modernity to extend not only to diction but to other poetic elements, whose high elegance he also naturalizes in new contexts. And it begins to suggest how poetry works through many connected patterns.

Syntax and the Poetic Line 2

The next elemental unit of poetry, building from the unit of the word, is the poetic line. Poetry's peculiar feature, that the lines stop (usually) before the end of the page, is what often announces to us that what we are reading is a poem. But the way the poetic line works depends upon many structures. One of these is metrical organization. The line extends only as long as a particular rhythm dictates. This we will postpone for later discussion. Another is syntax, the rules, units, and structures of grammar, which works in complex harmony and counterpoint with the construction and strategy of the poetic line.

Poetry, like all language, of course involves syntax. The language of poetry breaks up into familiar syntactical units (or purposely refuses to do so): phrases of various kinds, clauses, sentences, perhaps even paragraphs, depending on the poem. The individual words in the poem, which on one level are chosen for their diction or the associations they bring to the poem, also of course function in their grammatical roles as parts of speech. Words are subjects and objects, prepositions and conjunctions and verbs. In a poem, however, there is rather more freedom in word order, and even in word forms than in most other uses of language. This is tied to the fact that in poetry, even the bland, boring orders of syntax become charged with poetic meaning. It may no longer be a matter of subject / verb / object. A poet may reverse this order, in a desire to emphasize, say, the verb. Departure from the natural order of language is in fact a common way to "foreground" or draw attention to a particular word. It is a general truth in poetry that changes in ordinary procedures—twists against the expected order—attract attention. It is like putting a spotlight on the word or phrase or structure that surprises, as a dramatic gesture.

Word order in a poem also often works in ways similar to word choice in diction levels. The word order may be very formal, raising the "pitch" of a poem the way high diction does or it may be very colloquial to lower the level of diction. Or, word order may conform to normal grammar; but the way the phrases are broken up can strongly affect the impression the poem makes. And, of course, where the sentences come to completion is always very important.

It is this question of grammatical phrasing and ending that orchestrates relationships between syntax and the poetic line. Sometimes a sentence, or phrase, or clause comes to an end as the line does, so that the rhythm and syntax work together. But sometimes a sentence, or phrase, or clause spills over the end of the line, into the next line. This is called *enjambment*: the excess of syntax over the boundaries of the poetic line. With enjambment, line and syntax do not match together; each one instead goes its separate way. Great poets are masters at using these coincidences and departures, correspondences and breaks, to attain particular effects in their verse. When Milton's Satan, for example, first addresses Eve in tempting her to Fall, he says to her: "Thee all things living gaze on, all things thine / By gift" (*Paradise Lost* Book IX 539–540). The syntax of the line proves to be incomplete; the full sense of the phrase "all things thine" is only filled in by the next phrase in the next line. In fact, as so often in Satan's speeches, the next line not only completes but reverses the meaning of the line as left suspended and enjambed on its own. It is almost completely opposite to tell Eve that all she sees and who see her belong to her, as her possession and command; as against admitting that creation is in fact hers only "By gift" of a greater Power Who commands the world and to Whom she owes gratitude. It is the difference between self-conceit and self-reference, as against putting herself in wider and generous contexts. It is of course Satan's purpose to insinuate the enjambed meaning, and to repress the completed one, as an underlying and underhanded suggestion that he hopes will bear fruit (as alas it does). Here the placement of "all things thine" at the end of the line adds further emphasis to its apparent, enjambed meaning. This art of stopping or continuing lines, of establishing line breaks, is called *lineation*.

Since it is not only difficult, but impossible, to follow a discussion of poetic syntax in abstract terms, let us turn at once to examples. In the last chapter, we already touched on poetic syntax in discussing "Today We Have Naming of Parts." The piecemeal world of the army camp, reflected in the language of the army manual, was also realized through a syntax of short, abrupt, and truncated phrases and sentences. The phrasing contributed as well to the low diction level, especially in its colloquial use of prepositional phrases ("whose use you will see of," which ends with the preposition) as well as word order and dependent clauses ("Which in our case we have not got"). The enjambing, or cutting-off of lines in mid-sentence, where the pause is not expected, similarly intensified the sense of disjunction and lack of connection between experiences in the army camp ("And this / Is the upper sling swivel"). This clipped effect contrasted with the longer, flowing sentences of the garden, where enjambment has a different effect. "Japonica / Glistens like coral" uses enjambment to create a sense of overflowing continuity of garden life. This also is an important point. No stylistic feature has only *one* function or effect, but rather takes on its meanings within the context of the poem and as the poet employs it at a given moment.

In Robert Frost's poem "Design," the striking final lines similarly achieve their effect through syntax no less than diction. "What but design of darkness to appall" sounds formal and even stilted or contrived compared to the more ordinary speech of the poem's first part. This oddness has mainly to do with Frost's use of the infinitive (to appall), which allows a certain latitude or openness in the way the line can be interpreted. On the one hand, the line suggests that it is the purpose of the design to appall—that it is an evil design. Or it can mean that the design appalls or frightens, though not intentionally. Cause and effect thus become crossed, as does the whole question of intention which the poem is examining.

Such moments of hesitation before phrases or words that could carry more than one interpretation introduce a sense of ambiguity which can be central to a poem's art, and which poetry's syntax deploys and controls. A flexibility in the order of the words can allow them to be read in a number of different ways, each of which, however, has some significance, and which then work together in a way integral to the poem's meaning. In Milton's famous elegy "Lycidas," for example, Milton writes: "Weep no more, woeful shepherds, weep no more / For Lycidas your sorrow is not dead." Here, the syntax allows for two readings. The shepherds should not weep, because Lycidas is not dead—he is rather in Heaven, as the poem goes on to urge. Or, they should not weep, because their sorrow for Lycidas is not dead; it has, rather, produced important responses and insights. Milton often artfully controls the syntax in his poems to multiply meanings, which the reader must then assess.

Artful syntax may contribute particular effects in a poem, or may serve as the very core of the poem's art. "Leda and the Swan," by William Butler Yeats, provides an example:

> A sudden blow: the great wings beating still
> Above the staggering girl, her thighs caressed
> By the dark webs, her nape caught in his bill,
> He holds her helpless breast upon his breast.
>
> How can those terrified vague fingers push
> The feathered glory from her loosening thighs?
> And how can body, laid in that white rush,
> But feel the strange heart beating where it lies?
>
> A shudder in the loins engenders there
> The broken wall, the burning roof and tower
> And Agamemnon dead.
>   Being so caught up,
> So mastered by the brute blood of the air,
> Did she put on his knowledge with his power
> Before the indifferent beak could let her drop?

This is one of the great sonnets of the twentieth century. Yeats is a poet with an especially melodic ear. He succeeds in achieving lines of poetry that are at once supremely melodious and yet also incredibly natural (he once said a good line takes a year to write, but looks as if it were written in a minute). Here, too, his phrasing is very natural and yet shows tremendous artistry.

It is, to repeat, always important to watch where the sentences fall in the poem. Here, the first quatrain (the four-line divisions of a sonnet) is also a sentence: the sentence and quatrain division coincide, by ending together. The second quatrain is composed of two questions, each extending over two lines. Then the last six lines of the poem (the "sestet" of the sonnet) is separated into two complete syntactic units. First there is a sentence, and then a question. A break in the middle of the third line shows the move from the one to the other.

But the first quatrain begins with a phrase all its own, a sharp, powerful phrase, "A sudden blow." This phrase is set off almost as a sentence fragment; and it represents a fragment of action, sudden, unsituated, plunging us into the poem without warning. It catches and suspends us, just as Leda, "the staggering girl," is caught and suspended by Zeus, who comes in the shape of a swan to rape her. But although the title identifies these two figures, neither one is identified in the poem itself. Instead, Yeats uses the general article "the" to indicate the actors: "the great wings" (a synecdoche, or part, standing for the whole swan); "the staggering girl." The two only exist as they appear within the action the poem depicts, an action, as it will show, that is momentary but momentous. All happens in an instant—"A sudden blow." But immense consequences follow.

The first lines of the poem sustain the sudden and suspended sense of that opening blow. It keeps the action in an extended present, and does so by inflecting verbs as participles in a continuous present (the ——ing form): "the great wings beating still." "Staggering" is also in participial form, although it is used as an adjective, and similarly keeps the action in the present, as if the girl continues to stagger on and on. When the poem then does introduce a past tense— "caressed," "caught"—it does so still in the sense of ongoing action, as if the poet were describing what he continues to see before him, using verbs (past participles) mainly as adjectives and not as active verbs at all.

The grammatical effect of seeming to suspend the action is made still stronger by the way Yeats arranges his lines. Here we come to a good example of the way grammar can play off against line in a poem. "Still," the word ending the first line, and "caressed," the word ending the second line, are both enjambed. The end of the line does not match the end of the grammatical unit, so that the phrases spill over from one line into the next. This leaves each end-word suspended, making the reader pause there, held, just as the girl is held. Finally, we notice that in these phrases the girl is strangely poised between serving grammatically as the subject and the object. "Her thighs" are the noun, but the adjective "caressed" places them in the passive position. The same holds for "her nape caught in his bill." "Nape" is the sentence's grammatical subject, but it is passively caught. Indeed, the girl appears only as a list of body parts—thighs, nape, and then breast. (This is not a grammatical feature, but is instead a figure of speech, or trope, that plays parts against whole metonymically or synecdochically. These will be more fully discussed in a later chapter.)

The contest between active and passive is both syntactic and strategic and continues to structure the poem as a whole. Only the swan is given an active verb—"he holds her helpless breast against his breast"; while the girl's powerlessness is also expressed in her passive grammatical treatment. In general, the girl remains the grammatical subject but in ways that make her the passive object of the swan. That she continues to be named by body parts—"vague fingers," "body laid"—emphasizes her reduction. She is the mere "body" of the god's desire, and not a free subject at all. The futility of her position, and of any resistance to it, is intensified through the question form. Questions reflect the terrible uncertainty of Leda's position. Moreover, the questions are rhetorical—that is, they answer themselves, so that they aren't even really questions at all. "How can the fingers push?" Well, they cannot. Even the seeming activity of the verb "push" disguises helplessness—the inability to push away a power much greater than herself. She is merely "laid in that white rush" and can only "feel" actions she in no way is able to influence or prevent.

In the concluding sestet, Leda as paradoxically passive subject becomes no more than a site—a "there"—suspended in enjambment at the end of the first line. She is nothing but a point of transition between the god's momentary "shudder" and its incalculable results in the "broken wall" and "burning roof and tower" of Troy. Greeks and Trojans will destroy each other over Helen, the here unnamed and unforseen offspring of Leda's rape by Zeus. The break between sentences returns us to the main action, suspending us in the passive voice of Leda's experience: "Being so caught up, / So mastered by the brute blood of the air." These phrases take form as a question, re-emphasizing the limits of Leda's understanding (she has no answers). And the poem concludes with an ultimate expression of her passive place in the action. It lets her drop.

This analysis has been somewhat technical, as syntactic analyses of texts tend to be. But it was meant to show some of the avenues of approach into the syntax of a poem, always with the poetic *function* of the grammatical patterns in mind. Here we see the importance of following the sentence units, but also of placing the phrases, noting the tenses of the verbs; of the word order of subject, verb, object; of exchanges between parts of speech, such as when verbs may serve as adjectives; and of passive and active constructions.

Yeats's "Leda" is a poem whose syntax is extraordinarily complex. William Blake (1757–1827), in contrast, wrote poems with a syntax painstakingly simple:

Tyger! Tyger! burning bright
In the forests of the night,
What immortal hand or eye
Could frame thy fearful symmetry?

In what distant deeps or skies
Burnt the fire of thine eyes?
On what wings dare he aspire?
What the hand dare seize the fire?

And what shoulder, and what art,
Could twist the sinews of thy heart?
And when thy heart began to beat,
What dread hand? and what dread feet?

What the hammer? What the chain?
In what furnace was thy brain?
What the anvil? What dread grasp
Dare its deadly terrors clasp?

When the stars threw down their spears,
And water'd heaven with their tears,
Did he smile his work to see?
Did he who made the Lamb make thee?

Tyger! Tyger! burning bright
In the forests of the night,
What immortal hand or eye,
Dare frame thy fearful symmetry?

"Tyger, Tyger" is a poem with essentially no enjambment. Phrase and line end together, often punctuated as a sentence or a question, following on the whole a straightforward word order. When there are connectors between phrases or lines, these tend to be in the most simple form of addition, using the conjunction "and": "And what shoulder, and what art, / Could twist the sinews of thy heart? / And when thy heart began to beat, / What dread hand? and what dread feet?" This sort of additive or coordinating grammar is called *paratactic* syntax, in opposition to a more complex grammar where phrases are subordinated to each other in a complex logic and through the use of subordinating conjuctions, called *hypotactic* syntax.

Blake often uses this simplified syntax in his *Songs of Innocence*, which is one way he creates an illusion of innocence. He similarly tends to use very simple diction, words that even a child could understand. But, needless to say, the poems are not nearly so simple as they seem. This is not to accuse Blake of using his syntax dishonestly. The poem demands that the reader think through the fuller implications of the relationships between phrases that are connected by the weak and unassertive "and" or that are simply juxtaposed. Making such connections is the specific challenge of this poem. In one sense, this is a poem of and about creation. It addresses—indeed, traces—how immortal (and mortal) hands and eyes construct something: the Tyger, for example. On this level, the "and," "and," "and" construction pursues, records, in fact enacts the process of creation, part by part, so that by the poem's end the whole Tyger has been put together: eyes, sinews, heart, hand, feet, brain. This Tyger is, according to the poem, the work of some creator. But the creator himself is constructed in the process as well. Each stanza names and places not only parts of the Tyger, but also the hand, eye, grasp and smile of the creator.

But the poem is about not only creation, but also destruction. The Tyger emerges as a quite violent figure: burning and fearsome. And the creator-artist is so no less, with his own dread grasp, daring, seizing, twisting. The poem does not offer this duality as incidental, but rather insists on it. "Did he who made the Lamb make thee?" We finally realize that the challenge of putting together "and," "and," "and" involves an awesome and profoundly troubling problem. What is the relationship between creation and destruction, good and evil, horror and beauty? The lack of clear relationship between the named activities in this paratactic syntax is the poem's pressing question. Within this syntactic string lurks the religious and philosophical problem of theodicy, how to explain God's goodness despite the existence of evil. As the poem suggests, the mere co-existence of creation and violence does not explain or justify evil, but rather intensifies the need to do so.

Poets use syntax to various ends and effects. The extent to which a poet can also break the rules of syntax for his or her own purposes can be seen in Emily Dickinson (1830–1886). Wordsworth might be called a poet with no diction: no word was so low as to be excluded from his poetry. One might similarly say of Dickinson that she is a poet with no syntax—a poet who so transgresses against the norms of syntax as to almost eliminate them. Indeed, her first reviewers saw little in her work beyond bad grammar. "Four Trees" is a Dickinson poem whose language is so fragmentary as to almost defy normal syntax altogether:

Four Trees—upon a solitary Acre—
Without Design
Or Order, or Apparent Action—
Maintain—

The Sun—upon a Morning meets them—
The Wind—
No nearer Neighbor—have they—
But God—

The Acre gives them—Place—
They—Him—Attention of Passer by—
Of Shadow, or of Squirrel, haply—
Or Boy—

What Deed is Their's unto the General Nature—
What Plan
They severally—retard—or further—
Unknown—

One of the most striking—if not also distracting—features of Dickinson's verse is its lack of punctuation. She omits commas, semi-colons, periods. In their stead, she introduces dashes. This lack of punctuation has to do with a general lack of grammatical media-tion between her words and phrases. Dickinson, that is, refuses to an extraordinary degree to allow the rules of grammar to regulate and order her language. And this extends beyond punctuation. In "Four Trees," the first stanza tries as hard as it can to avoid a verb. When the verb "Maintain" does at last appear at the end, it is as inactive as a verb can be; and it is made more inactive still by hav-ing no object (what, after all, is maintained here?). Throughout the poem the verbs are few in number and prevented from activity. The sun "meets" the wind in the place the acre "gives" them. Verbs, instead of articulating action in time, seem only to register place. In this, they seem to function almost as prepositions—a part of speech Dickinson strongly favors in this poem. She offers locations frozen in space rather than actions unfolding in progresive time.

What is left is a set of almost unconnected nouns: trees, sun, wind; acre, place, passer by, shadow, squirrel, boy; deed, plan. But the disconnection between things is just what the poem is about: objects which simply appear one beside or after the other, but whose relationships remain utterly unclear. There is no obvious order; no clear design; no clear action; no clear plan. A scene is given, in its stark presence. The sun rises and sets over it, an eye glances at it. But there is no hint as to its place in a wider scheme. And God, who is named in the second stanza, really does very little to tie the different items together. He appears instead as just another object, another noun, and not as an overarching, organizing figure in terms of whom all the other things fall into meaningful place. If God is present, he does not unite the scene. This remains a collection of isolated objects that do not cohere. And if at the end, the poem still seems to be seeking such order and design, this too proves to be an illusion, both in event and in syntax. "What Deed," the poem seems to ask, "what plan." But despite the interrogative "What," the final stanza turns out not really to be a question at all. The answer provided is no answer: "Unknown." At the end, what looks like a question turns out to be only a flat statement of lack of knowledge.

In this poem, then, the syntax actively expresses and even structures the radical doubt and disorder which the poem is about. The short, cut-off lines, the lack of verbs, or of punctuation, or of clear connectives, take place in both grammar and understanding. In her refusal to fulfill it, Dickinson particularly brings to view what normative grammar in fact accomplishes. Prepositions locate. Verbs project action and, above all, mediate time. Conjunctions connect, expressing relationships of logic and sequence. Dickinson helps us appreciate how much our sense of order (and not only in poetry) has to do with the kind of connections—in time, in place, in cause and effect, in logic—that the grammar of our language realizes and asserts.

The disjunctions of Dickinson's grammar reinforces and is reinforced by the sense of rupture in her whole poetic format, including line breaks. Lineation is very much a matter of syntax, organizing the poem's grammar across its lines in ways significant and central to the poem's meaning:

Between Walls

the back wings
of the

hospital where
nothing

will grow lie
cinders

in which shine
the broken

pieces of a green
bottle

In this poem by William Carlos Williams (1883–1963), lineation—that is, line distribution—is almost everything. It is worth noting that the poem is a grammatical fragment. It is missing an opening preposition which would situate the scene it presents—"[At] the back wings." But this is consistent with the whole sense of fragmentation the poem cultivates, as dramatized and constructed through its line breaks.

The way the lines are broken up becomes an active part of the images they are presenting. When we see "the back wings," we think of insects, or perhaps birds, but not of the wings of a hospital which the poem then proposes. It does so, however, after a line of delay ("of the" does nothing except make you wait to find out: of what?). "Hospital where" again leaves you waiting, which is to say leaves you imagining things that ordinarily do happen in hospitals. This is to imagine the wrong things, the things this poem will not be about. "Where / nothing." Well, that doesn't tell very much. "Where / nothing / / will grow lie." This is peculiar. There is growth in hospital; and there is "lying in," for hospitals are a place of birth (Williams himself delivered babies as a practicing gynecologist and obstetrician). But not here (or is that right?). "Lie / cinders." Now we have a better sense of where we are. We are not in the hospital, but behind it, between the wall of its back wings. And what is back there is nothing but—cinders, things thrown away and burnt out. Hospi-

tals are also places of decay, of discard, of death. "Lie / cinders //
in which shine." At last, something bright, something hopeful!
"Shine // the broken." Uh oh: something discarded, something
defeated, something ruined. "Pieces of a green." Again, something
alive, a plant perhaps, or some grass, or maybe just a leaf . . . and
then: "A green / bottle."

Where, then, does this poem leave us? The way in which Wil-
liams breaks up the poem's lines is central to our experience of it.
This dramatizes how much reading a poem is indeed a process, a
sequence, an event through time. Syntax is, finally, integral also to
the experience of reading the poem. Syntactic forms not only di-
rect the reader through the poem's word patterns. They underscore
how the process of reading itself is part of the poetic experience.
Piecing words together, working through patterns, suspending
understanding and directing attention, are experiences mediated by
the syntax.

In this particular poem, the reading process is one of mistake and
correction, and mistake again, and correction again. We go back and
forth between things that are alive and organic, as against things that
are dead and inorganic: insects (perhaps a butterfly) and buildings;
growth and cinders; green plants and bottles. Yet there is an overall
effect. We discover as we go that a place that seems doomed only
to rubbish and broken objects can become a scene of beauty; that
even an old broken bottle, given the proper attention, seen the right
way, can shine green, alive, lovely, for a moment, for a fragment of
a moment.

Syntax is inevitably a technical and dry subject: dry as bones. But,
like bones, syntax remains the understructure holding together the
poem as its more enticing imagery or logic or composition or
melodious language unfolds. In ordering and mediating both the
structure and the reading experience of the poem, syntax, like dry
bones, can awaken and rise to new and exciting poetic life.

Images: Simile and Metaphor 3

Diction and syntax are important to any kind of writing or speaking. But in poetry their use may be more conscious, more considered, and they may take on special meanings and effects—like a dancer who walks or runs, but does so with more grace, more intention, and as part of a fuller purpose of design and beauty. Imagery is another basic poetic unit, one more specific to poetry and much more obviously exciting; it is the fireworks of poetry, often thought of as poetry's defining characteristic. Actually, how large a role the kind of vivid visual picture we think of as the very stuff of poetry plays varies from literary period to period, with changes in literary taste and literary fashion. Different ages admire different things in poetry, and our admiration for certain kinds of imagery has its own specific historical context. Still, through most literary tastes and trends, the poetic image has remained a fundamental unit of poetic composition, whether as a small decorative moment in a larger argument, or as the primary organizing principle of the poem as a whole.

There is a wide and indeed surprising number of kinds of poetic image. We will begin with the most familiar images, those of likeness: that is, *simile* and *metaphor*. Both simile and metaphor are structures of comparison. They assert: this is like that, in such and such a way. In simile, the comparison is made explicit. A simile is a comparison that *tells* you it is a comparison. It openly declares "*x* is like *y*," using a word of comparison such as "like" or "as," but other words, such as "resemble" or "compare," can serve the same function. These words act as signals that a simile is taking place, and are themselves part of the image structure and effect. The open declaration of a resemblance may make simile seem simpler or clearer than other images. But it also allows the simile to be extended over any number of lines, which can lead to complex comparisons involving many terms, in which it is not always obvious at once what is being compared to what, or in what ways.

Metaphor is also a structure of comparison, a likeness. But in metaphor the likeness happens without warning, and involves its own distinctive structure. Instead of, as in a simile, stating x is like y, in a metaphor, some quality or trait or action associated with x is directly attributed to, or transferred, to y. Metaphor in fact means transfer (as Aristotle was the first to analyze in *Poetics* 21, 1457b): the transferral of some quality, or attribute, or word associated with one thing to another. It is this transferral that implies the comparison. The two different things are alike in the way that the transferred quality suggests. If we say: the moon sails in the sky, then a verb belonging to ships—to sail—is transferred to the moon. The movement of the moon, then, is compared to that of a ship, while, implicitly, the sky is also compared to a sea. You could try to reverse this comparison: the ship rises in the sea; but the result would be weak. "Rises" is not specific enough to the moon to make the comparison clear. For the metaphor to be strong, its terms must carry their associations with clarity and specificity. In "the ship rises in the sea," the ship might be like the moon, or it might be like the sun, or some other planet in its rising. Or, the ship might be simply a ship: rising up on the waves, with no transfer, no metaphor, at all. One may speak here of degrees of transfer: some words very strongly assert a transfer from one sphere to another and hence a comparison because of their very strong and specific associations. Other words may loosely or vaguely imply a comparison.

Handbooks offer you lists of examples of similes and metaphors. But of course the effects and purposes of simile or metaphor only fully emerge within the poetic texts that build upon them. Only then can their complexity and richness be appreciated, or the way in which they might extend throughout an entire poem be followed. This is the case in a simple-looking poem by William Wordsworth (1770–1850), "I Wandered Lonely as a Cloud."

> I wandered lonely as a cloud
> That floats on high o'er vales and hills,
> When all at once I saw a crowd,
> A host, of golden daffodils;
> Beside the lake, beneath the trees,
> Fluttering and dancing in the breeze.

Continuous as the stars that shine
And twinkle on the milky way,
They stretched in never-ending line
Along the margin of a bay:
Ten thousand saw I at a glance,
Tossing their heads in sprightly dance.

The waves beside them danced; but they
Out-did the sparkling waves in glee:
A poet could not but be gay,
In such a jocund company:
I gazed—and gazed—but little thought
What wealth the show to me had brought:

For oft, when on my couch I lie,
In vacant or in pensive mood,
They flash upon that inward eye
Which is the bliss of solitude;
And then my heart with pleasure fills,
And dances with the daffodils.

This poem opens with a simile: there is the "as" ready at the start to tell you a comparison is being made. The first two lines set up the first terms of the comparison: an "I" who wanders like a "cloud." People wander, and saying that clouds do compares clouds to people (the more cloudlike word for this sort of aimless movement would be, say, drift). So far, the comparison seems to have to do with movement, a kind of undirected leisurely motion. There is, however, another comparative term, introduced through "lonely." The poet is saying that the cloud, like himself, is one, alone. But only a human being can, one presumes, feel such solitariness as loneliness. Only humans can feel lonely.

The next lines introduce a metaphor, or perhaps two metaphors: "when all at once I saw a crowd / A host, of golden daffodils." The daffodils are compared to a crowd, or host, that is, to a group of people. Here number (in contrast to "lonely") seems to be the main point: there are many daffodils, all close together. The image chosen for this group is, however, a human one (a crowd or host rather than a bunch, or bouquet, of flowers) so there is also some sense that the flowers seem alive and human. Then the last line, very gently, suggests further metaphorical comparisons. "Fluttering" normally applies to flags; or perhaps butterflies; or perhaps to hearts, when they become excited. Yet "fluttering" can also apply to flowers, since it merely implies a light, waving movement that can describe petals, too. "Dancing," however, is more clearly metaphorical. Flowers dance only if you are comparing them to people. Here the motion of the flowers is definitely likened to a human activity.

This attention to the imagery is meant to show the way a comparison can be thought through. We can even go further. In the opening simile, a human person, the "I," compares himself to something inanimate, a "cloud." In the metaphor that follows, something nonhuman, the daffodils, are compared to human beings, human crowds and hosts and dancers. There has been as well a question of location. The cloud floats on high; but the daffodils are down low, "beside the lake, beneath the trees." And where is the "I?" Well, not up in the sky we suppose. Yet we picture him in some sense as "high" too, as though looking down at the daffodils from above. This play on height and location is picked up in the next stanza, through the next simile of the stars: "Continuous as the stars that shine." There is the "as" declaring the simile. Number and extension again take part in the comparison. The flowers stretch on like the numberless stars in the sky. The sky itself seems to parallel the "bay" that the flowers stretch alongside—partly because of the rhyme that connects them (milky way / bay), but mainly because of the repeating play on what is above and what is below. If flowers by a lake are like stars in the Milky Way, then flowers are like stars, and the lake is like the sky. The comparison doubles, connecting everything that appears on the two sides of the "as." Then comes the "I" again, still almost unlocated, or rather, located somewhere between the stars and the flowers: for to see ten thousand at a glance implies a quite commanding position. The stanza ends with metaphors that pick up on, and strengthen, the earlier comparison of the flowers to humans. "Tossing their heads in sprightly dance" repeats the dance image, but "tossing their heads" makes the comparison to human action even more explicit.

Thus far, the images have generally attributed human traits to the natural world, a kind of comparison called *personification*, which we will discuss more fully in chapter 8. An image personifies something nonhuman by granting, or transferring human features, or actions, or attitudes to it (the daffodils "tossing their heads"). Personification forms the central image pattern throughout this poem, which is carried forward from stanza to stanza, always with further intensification. In the next stanza, the metaphor of dancing is extended to the waves of the water of the bay. Now there is a triple comparison: the waves are like the flowers are like people dancing. And the ultimate transfer then follows: "A poet could not but be gay." The gay dancing of nature comes to find its place within the poet himself. Here, he doesn't openly announce that he is drawing a new, and indeed governing comparison: simile at this point drops out. But the whole series of comparisons to human beings is now given a location, solving the mystery of placement the poem has posed.

The whole poem has, we come to see, taken place inside the poet, in some interior space. He, the poet, is "on my couch" looking with an "inward eye." That great expanse of the opening sky with its lonely cloud is finally transferred to the interior space of the solitary heart, where the flowers also find their ultimate location: "then my heart with pleasure fills and dances with the daffodils." Here we see the metaphor completed, at which point, however, it also almost ceases to be a metaphor. The dance is finally a dance of the heart—a strange collapse in metaphorical distance, in that now the human is compared to the human: the human dance to the human heart. The poet sees himself in nature; and then he sees nature in himself. It all becomes a moment of self-reflection, the inward eye of solitude which Wordsworth here unveils as the ultimate poetic source and subject.

Detailed analyses of images can become quite intricate. What is important here is a sense of main lines of development and of how comparisons may be more complex than they first seem. Once you begin comparing one thing to another, multiple terms begin to enter into the quotient. Even the opening simile was more complex than it appeared. The comparison of the "I" to the "cloud" finally included not just wandering motion, but also questions of number (one or many) and of placement in relation to the scene viewed—the question that becomes the central one in the poem's conclusion. Or consider the lake, which in the first verse seemed merely descriptive, decorative but not essential. Yet from stanza to stanza the lake takes on more and more metaphorical power, first becoming an image of reflection for the sky—and, as is very common in Wordsworth, for the reflection in the poet's mind of what he sees—and then personified as waves dancing, like the flowers themselves. The lake thus becomes part of a whole system of comparison that takes on more and more terms as it goes along. Here we also see how a word that first appears for one purpose (decorative) may gather through the poem more and more purpose, more and more meaning, and not be an idle word at all.

This multiplicity of comparison—the fact that comparison is many-sided, so that comparing one thing to another may carry along with it any number of terms and parallels, may be seen in a poem by Edmund Waller (1606–1687) called "Song":

> Go lovely rose,
> Tell her that wastes her time and me,
>   That now she knows,
> When I resemble her to thee,
>   How sweet and fair she seems to be.
>
> Tell her that's young,
> And shuns to have her graces spied,
>   That hadst thou sprung
> In deserts where no men abide,
>   Thou must have uncommended died.
>
> Small is the worth
> Of beauty from the light retired;
>   Bid her come forth,
> Suffer herself to be desired,
>   And not blush so to be admired.
>
> Then die, that she
> The common fate of all things rare
>   May read in thee;
> How small a part of time they share,
>   That are so wondrous sweet and fair.

This poem raises a number of different issues, some of which we will return to and examine in chapter 6 when we discuss poetic conventions. But for now, we only need notice that at the center of this poem is a simile—that the whole poem is constructed as a developing simile comparing a lady to a rose. The poem is, artfully, addressed to the rose, which the poet is sending to his lady. Everything he says to the rose he then wishes to be applied to her. This kind of address to an inanimate object (or to an abstraction, an absent person, an animal, etc., as if it were present, alive, and capable of understanding) is called an *apostrophe*—a figure closely related to personification. But the message the speaker sends is constructed through an elaborate comparison between lady and rose. And although there is no "as" or even "like," the poet states: "When I resemble her to thee." "Resemble" acts as the "simile" word announcing a comparison to be at hand. This comparison is hardly original. (Waller, writing in the 1600s, wasn't so worried about originality. He was happy to use old, time-honored material—what we will later examine as *topoi*, conventional literary elements and figures. Originality becomes a major poetic ambition later, with Wordsworth, for example.) The comparison of the lovely lady to the lovely rose is, then, not the poet's invention. But in developing it in the poem, he brings out aspects of the comparison that are not immediately obvious, and are finally quite alarming.

The first feature of comparison the poet mentions is how "sweet and fair" the lady, like the rose, "seems to be." We notice the word "seems." The poet says "seems" rather than "is," and we wonder why. Perhaps he is merely discussing appearance, and so says "seems," as a way of saying that she looks a certain way. There is another word in the opening stanza that draws our attention—"wastes": "Tell her that wastes her time and me." For one thing, this word belongs to a lower diction-level than do the stanza's other words, such as "lovely" and "resemble" and "sweet and fair." It is even a bit aggressive because of the poet's bluntness; and it inserts into the poem a hint of decay.

The second stanza opens with an emphasis on life, on youth: "Tell her that's young." But this seems a bit of an aside—that is, it doesn't seem part of the main business of the stanza, which is the simile or comparison, now focusing on hiding. The lady "shuns to have her graces spied." She should instead, says the poet, heed the example of the rose, which, had it remained hidden "in deserts where no men abide," would have died without being appreciated. The comparison here takes on a little twist. Instead of saying the lady is like the rose, the poet says she ought to be like it. It is open to view; she is not, but she should be. At the end of the stanza, death is brought in again, almost as an aside, but adding a rather threatening note: "Thou must have uncommended died."

In the third stanza the poet openly declares that the lady should herself fulfill the simile, as it were, by coming forth into the light.

There is again a small change in the structure of the comparison, however. "Desired" is a rather strong word; and it applies much more to a lady than to a rose, which can certainly be admired, but is not normally "desired" with the full connotation of passion this word brings. Here, the rose is like the lady rather than the lady being like the rose, a way for the poet to express his full intentions toward her, which otherwise he can't politely say. The aggressive note in the poem, which repeatedly resurfaces, comes out here in this indirect way. It also comes out in the lineation of the poem—the way the poet arranges his lines. "Small is the worth" as a phrase standing alone is rather denigrating, a threat in fact.

This threatening element becomes the central feature of the poem's conclusion: "Then die." In the end, the lesson of the comparison is not going to be how both lady and rose are sweet and fair, but how they are both mortal—how they both share "the common fate" of death. Death here gathers earlier hints of threat in words like "wastes" and "young." It is death that forms the center of the simile, this that the lady should "read" in the rose's resemblance to her. As a simile it works; but it is not neutral. It is important to notice here not only the likeness between the two terms of the comparison, but also the pull of difference between them. This is actually the case in any simile or metaphor. The two compared terms may be alike, but they are never identical. There always remains some difference between them, some *distance* between the terms of the figure. This distance our poet now exploits. In fact, the life of a rose is much, much shorter than that of a lady. Moreover, the rose lacks something that the lady has: a soul. This is in fact the part of the lady that does not share the fate of the rose, the fate of death. For the Christian, the soul is immortal.

All of this remembrance of the Christian soul is not in the poem. Indeed, it is the strategy of the poem energetically to ignore this little question of the difference between the lady and the rose with regard to the length, and kind, of life each leads, and toward what final ends. For the poem has a particular purpose, and is a poem of a particular kind, also not invented by the poet: it is a poem of seduction, of desire. In poems of this kind, the (male) poet never mentions things like the lady's soul. He focuses instead on her body, and he asks her to do so too; to remember only that her body is mortal, and will die, and that therefore she only has a limited amount of time in which to enjoy it while she has it.

The poetry of seduction is one of the enduring genres, or kinds, of poetry. Poetry can have varied and useful functions; and seduction is apparently something worth writing poems for. Here I would just like to emphasize how the poem develops its simile of the rose and the lady, and how in doing so it focuses now on this aspect of the comparison, now on that; how what seems at first to be the main element shared in common proves not to be (or proves to be so in a different way than it at first appeared); how a quite different point of comparison (mortality), introduced first in a seemingly accidental way, becomes the real heart of the matter; and, finally, how other points of difference between the terms compared are repressed for a particular rhetorical purpose—that is, to persuade.

Thus: comparisons—similes or metaphors—can be thought through in exact and logical ways. Often the comparison will contain or imply more than one feature or aspect; X will be like Y in more than one way. In a good poem, these comparisons will often gather and build on each other and collect resonance and depth. One comparison may also connect with another as the poem unfolds. The comparison, therefore, is not static, but dynamic. It has many parts, and as it develops it modifies and brings into various relations each of the terms drawn into it. Moreover, the comparison is not neutral. It moves to convince; to elevate or deflate; or to draw attention to some specific interest or topic.

In any comparison, furthermore, there will be elements not only of likeness, but of difference. A poem may mute or conceal differences; or it may exploit difference—may play on the pull between compared terms. This case of difference, with its tensions and manipulations, is especially visible in another artful seduction poem, "The Flea" by John Donne (1572–1631).

Mark but this flea, and mark in this,
How little that which thou deny'st me is;
It suck'd me first, and now sucks thee,
And in this flea, our two bloods mingled be;
Thou know'st that this cannot be said
A sin, nor shame, nor loss of maidenhead,
   Yet this enjoys before it woo,
    And pamper'd swells with one blood made of two
    And this, alas, is more than we would do.

Oh stay, three lives in one flea spare,
Where we almost, yea more than married are.
This flea is you and I, and this
Our marriage bed, and marriage temple is;
Though parents grudge, and you, we're met,
And cloister'd in these living walls of jet.
    Though use make you apt to kill me,
    Let not to that, self-murder added be,
    And sacrilege, three sins in killing three.

Cruel and sudden, hast thou since
Purpled thy nail, in blood of innocence?
Wherein could this flea guilty be,
Except in that drop which it suck'd from thee?
Yet thou triumph'st, and say'st that thou
Find'st not thy self, nor me, the weaker now;
    'Tis true, then learn how false, fears be;
    Just so much honor, when thou yield'st to me,
    Will waste, as this flea's death took life from thee.

"The Flea," like "Song," turns on a comparison, one rather compli-
cated in its construction. It involves a lady, a man, and a flea. If you
find this a strange grouping, that is because it is strange, very strange.
It underscores the question of distance between terms in a compari-
son: how unlike the two things being compared are. Compared
terms may be more like each other, for example, a lady and rose, or
they may be more unlike each other, for example, love and a flea.
When a poet compares two quite similar things, things that seem
to go together, the unlikeness may lurk around, perhaps in a sub-
versive way. But sometimes a poet compares two things that are
very unlike. John Donne is a poet who likes to do this. It is part of
his wit, which his period prized above all. He can show how even
very unlike things have something in common: things like a flea and
a "marriage bed," or worse, a "marriage temple."

    These comparisons appear in the middle stanza of the poem: "This
flea is you and I, and this / Our marriage bed, and marriage temple
is." How can a flea be (like) a marriage bed? Well, the poet tells us:

Though parents grudge, and you, we're met,
And cloister'd in these living walls of jet.

In the first stanza, the poet described how the flea sucks blood from both himself and the lady: "And in this flea, our two bloods mingled be." Now he calls this joining a marriage bed, indeed, a marriage temple, where "we're met, and cloister'd." The body of the flea is compared to the walls of a cloister, a monastery or convent! The sucked blood, now contained in the insect, is like monks, or nuns, who live within such containing walls.

To assert such a comparison, is to overlook (to say the least) the fact that life in a cloister is above all chaste; that a cloister is a place where intimate life is lived, but without sexual activity. But here, the flea-image is purposefully sexual. The first stanza had turned on another manipulated comparison, between a flea-bite and the act of intercourse.

> It suck'd me first, and now sucks thee,
> And in this flea, our two bloods mingled be;
> Thou know'st that this cannot be said
> A sin, nor shame, nor loss of maidenhead,

In a flea-bite, as in the loss of virginity, blood is shed; while the mingling of blood is compared to the sex act itself. This is, ahem, rather far-fetched. To then extend the comparison into the realm of sacred vows, such as marriage, is more so. To carry it still further, making it an image of the sacred vows of chastity, is to stretch all credibility—as the poet knows quite well.

The outrageousness of this comparison is also due to diction. A flea just doesn't belong in the same sentence with "temple" and "cloister'd." It is an outrageousness Donne is happy to cultivate. In the last stanza, he continues the overblown religious language by suggesting that, in squashing the flea, the lady has martyred it: "Cruel and sudden, hast thou since / Purpled thy nail, in blood of innocence?" And he goes on to argue that the loss of virginity is no more significant or consequential than the death of a flea: "Just so much honor, when thou yield'st to me, / Will waste." This is, we may remark, quite faulty logic. But the poet is not all that concerned with logic. He is concerned, rather, with effect. This can be best seen, perhaps, in the most provocative comparison of all, when he compares the lady's threat to kill the flea (in the middle stanza) not only to (both) murder and suicide, but to "sacrilege, three sins in killing three." The lady/gentleman/flea become nothing less than a figure of the Trinity, and its rejection, a species of blasphemy.

This sort of extended, complex, and daring comparison is called a *conceit*, announced here by a simile-signal, "Mark but this flea," and pursued in a rapid and embedded elaboration. The conceit was very popular among the Elizabethan poets and seventeenth-century metaphysical poets, and Donne's poems provide some of the most famous examples of it. The term, derived from the Italian *concetto* (concept), underscores its display of cleverness. And if its logic does not stand up under close scrutiny, this need not weaken its rhetorical power. For, while we may not be convinced of the gentleman's right to our company by logic, we may nevertheless be persuaded, given how entertaining he shows himself to be, that he may just be worth spending time with.

Metaphor and the Sonnet 4

Word choice and the poetic line, images of comparison such as simile and metaphor, are among the primary elements that go into making a poem. They are the smaller structural components from which larger ones are constructed. To see how this works, we will now consider a verse form—that is, the overall organization of a poem—watching how smaller units fit into its larger organization. This is especially vivid in the role of metaphor in the construction of a sonnet; that is, the way the sonnet form can make use of metaphor to build its structure.

Having mentioned the sonnet, describing its form becomes unavoidable. But the abstract or prescribed form is, in the end, only given energy and meaning by the way the sonnet's elements are balanced, or developed, or opposed in dynamic ways within the sonnet's very compact and highly designed frame. But first, its formal definition. A sonnet is a poem of fourteen lines. Each line generally has, in English, ten syllables, accented in the traditional English rhythm called iambic, which is an unaccented syllable followed by an accented one. The result is a line of ten syllables with five accented beats, called iambic pentameter (te-TA, te-TA, te-TA, te-TA, te-TA). This metrical pattern will be more fully discussed in chapter 11. More important for our present interest, the sonnet's fourteen lines are divided into several possible groupings. There can be three divisions of four lines each, called *quatrains*, with each four-line grouping (quatrain) bound together by a specific pattern of rhymes. These are followed by two rhyming lines, the *couplet*, which concludes the sonnet. Or, there can be two divisions, the first of eight lines, called the *octave*, and the second of six lines, called the *sestet*. Each of these two divisions is, again, bound together by a particular rhyming pattern. The first type of sonnet, of three quatrains and a couplet, is called an English or Shakespearean sonnet

(Shakespeare especially used it). It developed out of the second type, of octave and sestet, called an Italian or Petrarchan sonnet, since it was perfected by Petrarch in the fourteenth century, then brought to England in the sixteenth by Sir Thomas Wyatt.

The next chapter will take up the history of the sonnet and features such as its typical subjects or rhetoric or modes of representation. Here we will examine metaphorical construction within sonnet structure. One exemplary sixteenth-century sonnet, constructed out of blocks of metaphor, is Shakespeare's "That time of year thou mayst in me behold" (Sonnet 73):

> That time of year thou mayst in me behold
> When yellow leaves, or none, or few, do hang
> Upon those boughs which shake against the cold,
> Bare ruined choirs where late the sweet birds sang.
> In me thou seest the twilight of such day
> As after sunset fadeth in the west,
> Which by and by black night doth take away,
> Death's second self, that seals up all in rest.
> In me thou seest the glowing of such fire
> That on the ashes of his youth doth lie,
> As the deathbed whereon it must expire,
> Consumed with that which it was nourished by.
> This thou perceiv'st, which makes thy love more strong,
> To love that well which thou must leave ere long.

This Shakespearean sonnet follows the first division described above, that of three quatrains and a couplet. Generally speaking, the poem is about aging: that is, about the passing of time, and the facing of death as it begins to press against the precious things of this life, such as love. What is important to notice is how each quatrain is organized around a metaphor: The first quatrain proposes a time of year, to which the poet compares himself; the second quatrain, a time of day; the third, a moment in the burning of a fire. Each of these metaphors the poet in turn proposes as an image of himself, that is, in comparison with himself (and therefore also implicitly with each other). The couplet then acts as a conclusion to this sequence of three related metaphors.

In the opening metaphor, the poet compares himself to a time of year, which the person addressed ("thou") can "behold" "in" the poet. Time of year here is thus compared to a time of life. What time of year is it? "When yellow leaves, or none, or few, do hang." The poet, then, is in the autumn of his life. But how does this comparison help us to understand just what the autumn of life means to him, just what it is supposed to represent? Exactly how does he present the autumn? For note, the attention of the metaphor is all on the time of year. The poet himself remains only an initial term, to which what he says about autumn will be metaphorically transferred, but without his spelling it out for us. And this transfer will not be entirely straightforward. Already in the first two lines something peculiar has occurred with regard to the image of autumn. "Yellow leaves, or none, or few do hang." Are there, then, no leaves, or few? And why put "none" before "few" rather than follow the natural sequence in which first the leaves become fewer on the trees and only afterward have finally disappeared? Looking closely at the image, we begin to feel that although it seems to be offered as a visual image ("behold"), it is really very hard to visualize.

The next image has a similar effect. "Upon those boughs which shake against the cold" seems to locate those leaves (or were there any?) on tree branches, and to indicate that the time of year is becoming (or is already?) cold. Here we again pause. What time of year exactly is "that time of year?" It seems now not to be altogether fixed: a time when autumn is turning to winter, when the cold is penetrating into the last moments of foliage.

"Bare ruined choirs where late the sweet birds sang" is obviously complicated; indeed, it presents enough problems to have excited much critical debate. Grammatically it refers to the boughs, with the fourth line introducing an additional metaphor, now tacked on to the initial one that compares the time of year to the poet. The boughs are likened to bare ruined choirs—to the empty chapels of abandoned monasteries, say, or churches. But choirs also could refer to the singers in these rooms, as a metaphor for the birds. In either case, however, the birds are no longer even there. They, like the leaves, are and are not there. They are described as already gone. And this, again, is something very difficult to visualize. Despite the invitation to "behold," the images that follow resist perceptual definition: leaves that may not be there, a season that is and isn't cold, and boughs like choirs like birds, who are gone.

The second quatrain also begins with a comparison, again based on visual likeness: "In me thou see'st." Here, syntactic repetition

helps shape and bind the sonnet's structure, marking off the qua-
train division to signal parallel instances that will also, however,
mark a development. In this quatrain, what we will "see" is not a
time of year, but a time of day. The poem is progressing, as it turns
out, from larger to smaller units of time—first the year, now the
day, and then, in the third quatrain, a single moment.

What time is it in the second quatrain? "The twilight of such day
/ As after sunset fadeth in the west, / Which by and by black night
doth take away." The poem takes two and a half lines to tell us what
time it is. But even so, we really aren't sure. Is it sunset, or not? Do
we see twilight, its fading, or the black night which engulfs them?
As in the first quatrain, which this one parallels, the time is finally
one of transition, not a fixed moment, but a moment as it ceases to
be, as it becomes something else. As autumn moves into winter in
the first quatrain, so here day moves into twilight moves into night.
It thus turns out that the two main metaphors of the first two qua-
trains are also metaphors for each other—which makes sense, since
both are metaphors for "me," to be seen in the poet. The parallel is
made even more definite by inserting again in the eighth line an-
other subordinate metaphor: "Death's second self, that seals up all
in rest." Now black night is compared to death, as its "second self"
or double, which, like death, "seals up all in rest."

The careful construction of the sonnet in parallel image-blocks is
cemented by the poem's syntax. Each quatrain is made up of one
sentence, marked by a period. And each opens with a similar invi-
tation to visual comparison. Yet each then presents an image that,
far from being visible, is instead absent or unable to be seen. The
time period each offers turns out not to be stable or fixed, but one
that is fading, a departure of something already gone. In the first
quatrain, we are asked to see birds that have disappeared; in the
second, darkness that has already descended, making everything
black. We are, therefore, repeatedly shown things we cannot see,
or that prevent us from seeing altogether.

Still, death seems only a secondary image in the second quatrain,
a metaphor for the coming of night (which is in turn somehow
metaphorical of the autumn and the poet). This will recur in the
third quatrain. There, we are again invited to see: "In me thou
see'st." There, again, we are offered a metaphor for the poet, which
turns out to be a parallel metaphor to the other metaphors in the
sonnet. But this time the time-frame is a single, intense moment:

the moment a fire goes out. "In me thou see'st the glowing of such fire / as on the ashes of its youth doth lie." Glowing mingles with ashes in a contradictory figure known as an *oxymoron*, one that, as in the second quatrain, mixes light with darkness; and perhaps also heat with cold, as in the first quatrain. And, as in the preceding quatrains, this image becomes unstable the more you gaze at it. In the end, no single fixed moment has been specified, but rather, as before, a moment of transition, a moment of disappearance. You only see the fire as the embers are becoming extinguished. Growth and decay, presence and absence are mingled, a paradox intensified in the oxymoron of the twelfth line: "Consumed with that which it was nourished by." This phrase is gently metaphorical. Consuming and nourishing are words first associated with food, belonging to the sphere of nourishment. But transferring them to fire is not a full transfer; for they are, after all, the only words we have for describing fire (this is called *catachresis*: when the only terms to describe or designate something are metaphorical ones) which is, like food, a fuel.

But between the two oxymorons (ashes/youth; consumed/nourished) comes, as in each prior quatrain, another subordinate metaphor: "As the death-bed whereon it must expire." Death comes into the poem again. Yet again it does so only as an image, a metaphor, and not as an actual event in the poem, or even a primary image. This remains the governing comparison between the poet and some time—that of a fading fire, or, as we might say, a dying fire. A dying fire, however, reminds us that here, too, we describe fire in normal usage by transferring to it a term that does not properly belong to it (catachresis) since a fire is never really alive. Shakespeare picks up on this ordinary expression and brings it to full metaphorical life, by extending the image of the ashes of a dying fire to that of a death-bed. But with "death-bed" we are fully in the language of human death. Only people expire on a deathbed.

Death till now has remained a secondary image. Only in the couplet is it revealed to be the true subject of the poem, what the poem has been talking about, describing, all along. "This thou perceiv'st, which makes thy love more strong / To love that well which thou must leave ere long." The final "vision" of the poet—what we have been beholding all along—is his own disappearance in death. That this is an invisible event—what exactly do we see when someone dies? we surely don't see death itself?—the poem has successfully presented, exactly in giving us images that we can't see, of what is no longer visible. This suggests, among other things, that metaphor does not have to rely on visual imagery, building comparisons only in terms of how things appear. Metaphor can establish a variety of likenesses or relationships on a very special plane, the plane of language, beyond what might be specifically visual.

The couplet here works in a way very typical of the English sonnet. It is a conclusion, summing up all that went before, with a further repetition of the visual invitation strengthening its place within, and reinforcing, the sonnet's syntactic units: "This thou perceiv'st." Yet it does so by a kind of turn, that is, with a surprise, not just repeating what went before but adding something new to it. In light of the couplet, we now can see that death was not merely a secondary image in the poem, but its hidden center. The couplet also picks up another powerful pattern of the poem: the mixing together of contradictory things which, however, now also prove to be intensely related to each other. To consume and to nourish; to glow and to fade; to be present and to disappear—like the fire; like the twilight; like the "late," "sweet birds" and the "yellow leaves, or none, or few"—all of this contradictory force now gathers into the end: "To love that well which thou must leave ere long." The love and the loss come together, and we feel that they have strongly to do with one another. Within our time-frame of mortal life, the precious, fragile value of love only increases in the face of an overarching black night.

In any poem, but perhaps especially in the compact territory of a sonnet, every word takes on full weight and significance. Metaphorical construction can provide both a method of organization and an avenue of development, as relationships multiply through the course of the poem. In a sonnet such as "That time of year," the metaphorical pattern acts as the backbone, the controlling pattern of the sonnet itself, further reinforced by syntactic patterns and repetitions. In the sonnet "When I have fears that I may cease to be" by John Keats (1795–1821), metaphor is used similarly to provide fundamental structure:

When I have fears that I may cease to be
Before my pen has glean'd my teeming brain,
Before high-piled books, in charactery,

Hold like rich garners the full ripen'd grain;
When I behold, upon the night's starr'd face,
Huge cloudy symbols of a high romance,
And think that I may never live to trace
Their shadows, with the magic hand of chance;
And when I feel, fair creature of an hour,
That I shall never look upon thee more,
Never have relish in the faery power
Of unreflecting love;—then on the shore
Of the wide world I stand alone, and think
Till love and fame to nothingness do sink.

This sonnet is, like the first one, a "Shakespearean" or English
sonnet. It too proceeds through three quatrains to a couplet (with
characteristic rhyme scheme). Each quatrain is again organized
around a specific metaphor, which then enters into further meta-
phoric relation to other images in the different quatrains. Thus, the
first quatrain compares the poet's "teeming brain" to a rich field;
his pen to the harvest-scythe; and "high-piled books" to a granary
holding the "full ripen'd grain" of his poetry. Note how here each
term is held in a tight, close correspondence, so that one sequence
of elements links up with a second sequence to which it is compared.
This is accomplished by a very controlled transfer between terms
normally associated with each system of reference. Thus, "field—
gleaning scythe—garners—grain" correspond with "brain—pen—
books—[written] charactery" of his poems. This is almost a conceit,
but one that is very condensed, and so rapidly accomplished as to
make its elaborate comparison seem almost effortless.

As in "That time of year," each quatrain is introduced with a par-
allel phrase marking time ("When I"), allowing the syntax to estab-
lish the comparative structure that will also be realized through the
imagery of metaphor. The second quatrain picks up the image of
writing from the first one; but this time its arena is not a field, but
the sky, which is compared, in a subsidiary metaphor, to a face:
"night's starred face." Note that "star" here can refer either to the
sky, or to the markings on a page. "Huge cloudy symbols of a high
romance" keeps up the image of the sky, with its clouds, as a book—
symbols of high romance. Yet the face hasn't entirely dropped out,
still hovering within the "I" who beholds the sky above it; the I who

is tracing these very symbols with his "hand." This "I" further connects the second quatrain to the one above it. In both, he is metaphorically a writer—as he is in fact, too.

The third quatrain again repeats the "when I" construction. Again, certain elements from before are carried forward, but with significant changes. The "romance" of the second quatrain is now clarified as this writer's own; the face in the heavens is like his beloved's face; and the harvest becomes not only one of imagination, but of love. Yet we also come to feel forcefully that the poem is not about fullness, whether on earth or in heaven, but about loss. The very act of seeing is blocked and interrupted: "That I shall never look upon thee more." We realize now that even in the first quatrain, there was no harvest. The "rich garners of full ripen'd grain" were not images of accomplishment, but of failure. The granary is empty, the teeming brain ungleaned, the books unwritten. Similarly, the second quatrain emerges as an image of obstructed vision, of clouds that prevent from seeing, of shadows in the sense of something unrealized, and of writing that has not occurred: images the poet "may never live to trace."

Because the sonnet structure is so carefully defined, departures from the expected pattern acquire special force. This is the case here, in Keats's handling of the final lines. Instead of confining his last reflective remarks to the sonnet's couplet, he begins them a half-line early, in line twelve. There, the syntactic and rhetorical signal that has marked the poem's progress—"When I"—switches to a conclusory "then," introducing the implications of the argument he has been conducting. Syntactically, the couplet seems to start before the final two lines, already in the third quatrain. And the poem again shifts ground—this time to a shore. This is a kind of border region, depicted as a place of exclusion. The "wide world" recalls the plenty the poet first evoked, but only as an image of its lack. He stands alone, not with his love. And he concludes with an image of nothingness. The fullness of mind here becomes thoughts of emptiness, which has in some sense been the substratum of this poem's mourning throughout: "Till love and fame to nothingness do sink."

The impact of this conclusion can only be fully felt by the reader familiar with—and anticipating—a conventional, or typical, sonnet ending. It in fact works against the characteristic conclusion of a sonnet, in which the sonnet itself is often celebrated as a monument against time, as something enduring, and specifically so as a way to

preserve or memorialize love and fame. This reference to the son-
net tradition goes beyond the specific question of metaphor into the
wider topic of sonnet form. Yet, wider reference is somewhat inevi-
table. Sonnets often reflect back on the sonnet form. There is even
what might be called a subgenre of sonnets that self-consciously
make the sonnet form their subject: sonnets on the sonnet. One
famous sonnet on the sonnet by William Wordsworth offers an-
other pattern of metaphor as an organizing principle, although one
not grouped by quatrain:

Nuns fret not at their convent's narrow room;
And hermits are contented with their cells;
And students with their pensive citadels;
Maids at the wheel, the weaver at his loom,
Sit blithe and happy; bees that soar for bloom,
High as the highest Peak of Furness-fells,
Will murmur by the hour in foxglove bells:
In truth the prison, unto which we doom
Ourselves, no prison is: and hence for me,
In sundry moods, 'twas pastime to be bound
Within the Sonnet's scanty plot of ground;
Pleased if some Souls (for such there needs must be)
Who have felt the weight of too much liberty,
Should find brief solace there, as I have found.

This sonnet is not English, but Italian. Its pattern falls into a first
group of eight lines, and then a second group of six: the octave and
sestet, marked by a characteristic Italian rhyme scheme. Yet even
these broad divisions are somewhat complicated. Some lines stand
almost alone; others flow into each other in unusual ways. Instead
of developing one metaphoric block in a four-line quatrain, each of
the first three lines offers a distinct term of comparison. That is,
each line proposes its own metaphorical comparison, each of
which is also offered as comparable to the others. Thus, nuns in
convent rooms, hermits in cells, and students in citadels are all
presented as if in a comparable situation (note the syntactic struc-
ture is paratactic: each example is added on to the other by "and").
Then "Maids at the wheel" gives another comparative term, but
in half a line; while "the weaver at his loom / Sit blithe and happy"
completes the line and spills over for another half-line. Finally,

"Bees that . . . murmur by the hour in foxglove bells" takes up another two lines and a half.

In this opening sequence, Wordsworth has provided a list of instances, each of which is a term of comparison. And yet, he has not yet said what he is comparing them to. Each is drawn from a somewhat different sphere: nuns and hermits from a religious life, students from a scholarly one; maids and weavers from common laboring; and bees from nature. And each proposes a restricted space in which, however, the occupant is "contented"—with that one verb form carrying across all the subsequent lines—bringing together contentment and confinement, both in space and as concentrated activity.

This list of as yet incomplete comparisons concludes the first division of the poem but strikingly fails to complete the sonnet's first division or octave. Wordsworth instead introduces the next stage of his argument in the eighth, and not in the ninth line, which properly begins the next section of the sestet.

> In truth the prison, unto which we doom
> Ourselves, no prison is: and hence for me,
> In sundry moods, 'twas pastime to be bound
> Within the Sonnet's scanty plot of ground;

This is the poem's "turn," as it is called, when the sonnet changes direction to reflect back on the material it has presented, or redirects its argument, which usually takes place (unlike here) at the opening of the sestet in the ninth line. Here Wordsworth finally begins to complete the comparison by telling us what all of these examples have been examples of, thus revealing their intention. This withheld term of comparison turns out to be ourselves, as we doom ourselves into prisons. And yet, the poem has already given us a series of corresponding images for enclosed spaces that do not simply constrain, but rather frame concentrated and contented activity. It has thus already urged that it is not restriction in space, but our attitude toward it, that imprisons. He then moves forward to the final, corresponding image, the concluding term of comparison.

This master image, of a confinement that is no confinement, is the sonnet. The sonnet itself is likened to a "scanty plot of ground," inevitably evoking a grave-plot, our ultimate constricted space that haunts us and threatens to narrow our lives into a prison of mortality. Yet, as this sonnet has just shown, the sonnet's small space remains extraordinarily flexible, in its pace of imagery and divisions between sections. And, it can include almost anything. It can extend as far as any metaphor. Metaphor can bring into the sonnet any world the poet cares to explore or invoke, through just such imagery of comparison. The sonnet can contain, and offer, a multiplicity of references, as it has done here, references which open out in many directions at once, as here. The image of the sonnet comes to include the convent and cell and citadel, with their lives of spirit and intellect; and also the practical activity of spinning and weaving (traditional images for poetry); and finally the natural activity of the bee, who, like the poet, transforms nature into a wild and intense sweetness.

What we see here, then, is some of the power of metaphor, to transfer whole realms, and bring together whole areas of experience, just by introducing a term within a structure of comparison. And, as Wordsworth shows in his sonnet's very formality, the discipline of restriction may become an avenue of power. In this, he is not alone:

> Pleased if some Souls (for such there needs must be)
> Who have felt the weight of too much liberty,
> Should find brief solace there, as I have found.

Wordsworth is joined by the company of "Souls" able, like him, to find in the sonnet the wide, sweeping world of the imagination, a world in its own way at once spiritual and practical and natural. The door of metaphor has opened this confined space to a whole territory of devotion. In the end, the sonnet even suggests that "liberty" is to be found not in formlessness, but exactly within the definition of form. The sonnet, like the images it has here drawn into itself and to which it gives structure, is the true space of freedom. The sonnet's "narrow room" becomes then a kind of release from the burden of undefined liberty; while its confinement becomes a place of comparison, which is to say a place of encounter.

Verse Forms: The Sonnet 5

In the last chapter we discussed the sonnet in relation to metaphor, focusing on how metaphor can be used to build a sonnet structure. Now we will consider the sonnet more generally as a verse form. Besides allowing a fuller examination of the sonnet itself, it will help us to begin thinking about the importance of formal features—frameworks, rules, conventions—for poetry and for the way poetry works.

The sonnet, as we saw, has a basic formal design. It has fourteen lines, each of a particular length, written in a particular rhythm, and marked by a particular order of rhymes. These lines can follow a number of patterns of division. The *English sonnet*'s fourteen lines are divided into three quatrains of four lines each and two rhyming lines, the couplet, at the end. An *Italian sonnet* instead divides into one group of eight lines, the octave, followed by a group of six lines, the sestet. The octave, however, can also play on the quatrain structure. Its eight lines may fall into two groups of four, like quatrains. The sestet, similarly, can fall into two groups of three lines each, creating two tercets. It can, quite flexibly, be divided into other line groupings as well.

Indeed: despite—or rather, within—these set forms, the sonnet as a verse form is extremely flexible. There are, to be sure, limits to such flexibility. For example, the defining rule for a sonnet is that it must be fourteen lines long. If a poem does not have fourteen lines, it is not a sonnet. This is more or less an ironclad definition. Yet a poem may refer to a sonnet, play on a sonnet, recall a sonnet, by adding or taking away a line. That is, the strict rule of fourteen lines can serve as a reference point for variations that take on meaning exactly as they point to a fixed norm. This possibility of variation is still greater in terms of the divisions of a sonnet into quatrains, octaves, sestets, or couplets. These can be varied, to some extent in

THE SONNET

Line No.	English (Shakespearean)		Italian (Petrarchan)		
1	*a*	⎫ Quatrain	*a*	⎫ Quatrain	⎫
2	*b*		*b*		
3	*a*		*b*		
4	*b*	⎭	*a*	⎭	⎬ Octave
5	*c*	⎫ Quatrain	*a*	⎫ Quatrain	
6	*d*		*b*		
7	*c*		*b*		
8	*d*	⎭	*a*	⎭	⎭
9	*e*	⎫ Quatrain	*c*	⎫ Tercet	⎫
10	*f*		*d*		
11	*e*		*d*	⎭	
12	*f*	⎭	*c*	⎫ Tercet	⎬ Sestet
13	*g*	⎫ Couplet	*c*		
14	*g*	⎭	*d*	⎭	⎭

their rhyme patterns, but certainly in their logical, syntactic, and rhetorical development and distribution. The divisions permit, and indeed generate, creative variations: like variations on a musical theme. But to vary a theme you have to first have one. The invention relies on the norm. Creativity is generated by restrictions. This paradox is central to the sonnet and has often been its subject also, as was the case in the Wordsworth sonnet "Nuns fret not at their convent's narrow room."

In the end, the sonnet's formal divisions and features such as rhyme and syntax are significant, and exciting, not as mechanical rules but because of what they do and how they work: how the divisions structure the sonnet's material by balancing its parts, developing its statement, distributing its concerns. The sonnet can be thought of as a building, with an architectural design. Its divisions are like rooms which open into each other, all shaped by use and function. For instance, in the Italian sonnet, the division into two parts often involves a "turn" or *volta*: that is, some new direction the sonnet takes in its final six lines. But such a turn can take place in the English sonnet, too, in its concluding couplet. In the Italian sonnet, moreover, some further "turn" may also occur in its last two lines, suggesting a couplet structure; while in the English sonnet, a turn in logic, or emphasis, or self-reflection may take place in the ninth line, as it would in an Italian sonnet. The two forms, in this sense, remain in a dynamic relation with each other (although they can usually be formally identified by rhyme scheme, despite their structural flexibility). Divisions may also spill over into each other, as a sentence begun in one quatrain comes to syntactic completion in the next. Even a whole sonnet may spill over in a sense, becoming part of an ongoing *sonnet sequence* that allows for more extensive treatment of the subjects each sonnet raises, and of the poet who is writing them.

There is, for example, the question of rhyme scheme. Sonnets do have them. Rhymes mark basic sonnet structures: English or Italian, quatrain divisions, couplets. But rhyme is not simply mechanical. In chapter 12 we will see how rhyme can be used in poetry in very creative ways, serving a number of poetic functions. What must be underscored is the function of rhyme: how rhymes serve to group lines or images together, the relationships they develop between words in the text. This is the case as well within set patterns, such as the sonnet's. And the sonnet's rhyme schemes can vary to a considerable degree. They can be alternating (*abab*), as they are in the English sonnet. They can be enclosing, so that the first and fourth lines of a quatrain division match, framing the second and third lines within (*abba*), as in an Italian sonnet. They can be contained within individual quatrains; or they can be interlocking from quatrain to quatrain (Edmund Spenser experimented with interlocking forms) continuously through the octave. The lines of the sestet in an Italian sonnet can follow a variety of rhyme patterns, although there is usually not a concluding couplet.

Besides these strictly formal features, the sonnet also has a number of characteristic subjects, or topics, especially love, as well as characteristic ways of handling them that developed out of earlier verse forms. In this sense, a verse form is quite dynamic. Each form is a kind of historical field, or archeological site, in which the traces of past forms remain but take on new shapes and functions. In the case of the sonnet, one origin of the form goes back to Troubador love poetry of the twelfth and thirteenth centuries. This was a courtly verse written in Provencal (a kind of old French), which then influenced later medieval Italian poets, especially Petrarch and Dante and his circle. It was addressed to a lady of the court, in admiration and even adoration of her, also (or thereby) showing the effects of this admiration and worship on the writer.

In this sense, it is a perfectly valid riddle to ask: how is love like a sonnet? In attempting to reflect the experience of love (as it was then conceived) the sonnet took on certain features. Love, for example, was thought of as a malady, with carefully described symptoms, so you could tell whether or not you really had the disease, and how badly. Many sonnets therefore include imagery of illness. Thus Dante in his *Vita Nuova* (1294) speaks of how "Love takes hold of me so suddenly / My vital spirits I am near to lose." Sir Thomas Wyatt, whose translations of Petrarch brought the sonnet to England, speaks in "I Find No Peace" (from Petrarch's *In Vita* Sonnet XC) of how "I burn and freeze like ice; . . . I desire to perish, and yet I ask health" (1557). Sir Philip Sidney, in Sonnet 6 of *Astrophel and Stella* (1591), unmasks such imagery as already habitual to sonneteering:

> Some lovers speak, when they their Muses entertain,
> Of hopes begot by fear, of wot not what desires,
> Of force of heavenly beams infusing hellish pain,
> Of living deaths, dear wounds, fair storms, and freezing fires;

Here, too, is already apparent the sonnet's uses of paradox; for love was considered paradoxical. It elevated and lowered, it was violent and gentle, cruel and wonderful, fleeting and eternal. Therefore, the sonnet characteristically introduced self-contradictory images (*oxymoron*) and intricately balanced opposites (*antithesis*).

But this sonnet material reached into other experiences. The intense consideration of love on one level encouraged psychological introspection. Thus, the sonnet became an early form for psychological self-examination. It was one of the first literary modes for identifying and pondering the inner world of experience in all its multiple aspects. This includes sexuality, which the poets did not shy away from exploring. But on another level love raised issues not only psychological, but also religious. God, of course, was the true, highest object of love in the religious tradition. So the sonnet came to explore the relationship between the love of the lady and the love of God. This had a double effect. On the one hand, it elevated the lady, and the lover too, in regarding earthly love as a conduit to love of divine things. On the other hand, it brought divine love down to an earthly level. This could lead to a sense of harmony and continuity between things earthly and heavenly (a harmony made easier if the beloved lady died and took up residence in heaven). Or it could set up a competition between them. At this point we want to remember that the sonnet is a Renaissance form, and that in it we see issues that were coming to the surface in the Renaissance—the whole question, for example, of religious devotion and its proper object; of allegiance to the heavenly world or to the earthly one; and of the proper balance between them. Love became a battleground for the struggle between these emerging questions and allegiances; and the sonnet, as a love poem, reflects these struggles.

But the sonnet is not only addressed to the lady. It also represents the lover, that is, the poet, who is writing to his beloved. Here, too, ideas emerging in the Renaissance can be felt: a new sense of the status of the individual, influenced in part by the rediscovery of the pagan classical texts of Greece and Rome, which had been neglected or lost during the Christian Middle Ages. With this rediscovery, and this sense of the individual, came also a new sense of the status of literature and of poetry. As lover, the poet explores his inner emotional, psychological, and religious life. But he also has a new sense of himself as poet, who not only experiences, but also reflects upon this interior world through artistic consciousness.

Humanism, which broadly speaking was a revival of classical values in sixteenth-century Europe, was more specifically a program of training, especially in eloquence. The humanists intended education in rhetoric to find its true application in public discourse and political life. But the rigor and splendor of its rhetorical training also bore fruit among writers and poets, whose elegant wit was particularly cultivated in courtly life. The sonnet, certainly in England, developed and came to its most extraordinary flowering in Queen Elizabeth's court. To a large extent a courtly genre, the sonnet was intimately shaped by courtly modes of conduct—in which eloquence itself played a defining role—as well as by scenes, terms, and social structures of the court. The sonnet's imagery and forms of address; its conceptions of social relationships; its figure of the lady; and its representation of the poet, who in many ways resembles a courtier, all reflect characteristics of the court. Finally, with the recovery of the classics, literature itself became an emblem of what could survive from the past, a monument to past cultures, and past writers, as they continue to live on and to inspire cultural achievements. Literature itself, that is, became a site for immortality. The poet could gain eternal life, could defy time, by writing. This becomes a central, characteristic commitment of the sonnet.

There are other historical precedents that shaped the sonnet. As a short form, it took on certain features from the epigram—a sharp, witty saying—which can be felt in the witty conclusions of the couplet. But the epigram was not necessarily an admiring genre. It could celebrate public events and men, but it could also criticize and satirize, could act as a short, biting insult. The sonnet, too, can descend from the fine mist of adoring love to deliver a sharp, critical blow—can mix the "sweet" with the "salt," genre terms that directly enter into the diction and imagery of the sonnet itself.

The main points to be emphasized from this historical sketch are: (1) that the sonnet as a verse form involves much more than the basic formal features such as its length, rhyme schemes, and divisions—or rather, that these formal features have in the sonnet particular *functions*, which are their purpose and point; and (2) that there are aspects of the sonnet other than its formal traits: its use of paradox; its psychological depth; its balancing of earthly and heavenly claims; its wit; and finally, the way in which its principal concerns—love or devotion or glory or fame—find expression through the sonnet's particular formal progressions and construction, and the dual roles of the writer as lover and poet at once.

To see how reading a sonnet takes shape within the requirements, history, and intentions of a verse form, let us turn to an example: "My Love Is Like to Ice," by Edmund Spenser (1552?–1599).

My Love is like to ice, and I to fire:
How comes it then that this her cold so great
Is not dissolved through my so hot desire,
But harder grows the more I her entreat?
Or how comes it that my exceeding heat
Is not allayed by her heart-frozen cold,
But that I burn much more in boiling sweat,
And feel my flames augmented manifold?
What more miraculous thing may be told,
That fire, which all things melts, should harden ice,
And ice, which is congeal'd with senseless cold,
Should kindle fire by wonderful device?
    Such is the power of love in gentle mind,
    That it can alter all the course of kind.

This obviously is a sonnet devoted to love. The first thing to notice is how it is constructed around paradoxes: ice/fire, heat/cold, melting/freezing. These paradoxes also reflect the notion of love as malady. They are physical conditions, fever and chill. In this sense, Spenser did not invent the image-scheme of the poem, but used a convention (the topic of our next chapter) that was already well established, not only in manuals of love, but also in earlier sonnets, especially Petrarch's. Here, that is, the originality of the imagery plays almost no role in the poem's effect. Everyone already knew that love was like an illness, causing the lover to burn and freeze in turn. But the poet's way of handling this well-worn image is of great effect: the way he develops it, both psychologically, and rhetorically, within a linguistic pattern of carefully balanced opposites.

Psychologically, the poem has considerable depth and offers a keen analysis of the lover's interior condition. It in fact goes far toward presenting the immediate experience of internal sensation. It shows the very process of love as felt from within. For this psychological state, the sonnet offers an extended simile, or really double simile, introduced in the first line with the simile-word "like." The beloved lady is said to be "like to ice"; the lover in his turn is like "to fire." The sonnet develops each likeness, proceeding through three quatrains and a couplet. That is, the quatrains here do not separate into different image systems. Instead, they progress through the development of the central simile. This basic continuity of the sonnet is further realized through its rhyme scheme, which is alternating but continuous. Spenser, in his own adaptation of sonnet form, uses the same two rhymes throughout the sonnet (until the couplet). Spenser does this often. He is a great master of the music of poetry, a truly melodious writer, with a wonderful ear for rhyme—no easy accomplishment in English, which is basically a rhyme-poor language.

But despite this fundamental continuity through the sonnet, each quatrain does mark a particular stage. In the first quatrain, the focus is on the lady: on "her cold so great" which resists all his "hot desire." The basic antithesis between ice and fire here is heightened through this image of ice that refuses to melt—refuses to allow the antithesis to relent, as it were. Instead, the opposition intensifies. The ice not only is not "dissolved" by heat; it grows even "harder." As to the simile, the lady remains cold as ice; while the fire is associated with both desire and entreaty—both with the poet's desire for the lady, and his desire to persuade her to respond to his desire.

In the first quatrain, the ice, representing the lady, intensifies, hardening rather than melting before the fire. In the second quatrain, the focus shifts from the lady to the lover, and to the intensifying figure of fire that represents him. Parallel phrasing and syntax help to define each quatrain and also to unify them in a definite structure. Before, the poet asks: "How comes it then that this her cold so great." Now he repeats "How comes it" (syntactic repetition becomes a structural principle) but this time with regard to his "exceeding heat." The quatrain as a whole plays on this reversal. Before, her ice would not melt under his fire. Now, his fire will not be cooled by her ice. Again, the oppositions are intensified rather than reconciled. Each term is only more obdurate and unrelenting in the face of the other. This quatrain further adds a physical dimension. The cold and heat acquire bodily location. Her cold is "heart-frozen." His heat is "boiling sweat." We notice here a change in diction level. Boiling sweat is much less polite than the elevated diction of the rest of the sonnet. It slaps us in the face with the fact that the poet is not only describing a psychological condition, but also a physical one. This has been implicit in the hot/cold imagery throughout, but the sexual implications of fire is here almost crudely concretized. As at the end of the first quatrain, where the fire became a double figure for both desire for the lady and the desire to persuade her; so here, too, the flames are "augmented manifold." Before, he desired both the lady, and to persuade the lady. Now he desires both in mind and in body.

The third quatrain is more reflective, looking back on the conditions and deployment of forces in the first two (this is often the function of the sestet of an Italian sonnet, almost as if Spenser were invoking the Italian sonnet form even though he does not, technically, follow it here). The poet reiterates what he has so far discovered: the strange transformation in the natures of fire and ice, such that each intensifies, rather than modifying the other. Again we are told how fire hardens ice, and ice kindles fire. Two things can be noted here. The first concerns the sonnet structure generally. The sonnet, as mentioned above, became a new arena for pshychological exploration. One format in which this new exploration took shape was through the balance between the sonnet's divisions, where the opening section(s) provide a description of the poet's condition, while the closing section(s) offers an interpretation of the condition that has been described. The sonnet's later sections, whether as sestet, as couplet, or as quatrain and couplet, reflect back on the material it has already presented. Thus, the sonnet can both record experience and analyze it, even as, in his imagery, Spenser represents the psychological territory of his internal world.

The second point concerns the role rhetoric can play in the sonnet. Although the third quatrain here seems merely to reflect and repeat what has gone before, its emphasis and evaluation has shifted. This is done mainly through the quatrain's adjectives, which begin to emphasize the power of fire and to associate it with wonder. The behavior of fire is called a "miraculous thing"; and although the miracle here is to "harden ice," we are also reminded that fire "all things melt." Ice, on the other hand, is described negatively: as "congealed," and as "senseless cold." And the quatrain's conclusion in effect subordinates cold to fire. If cold is "wonderful" here, it is so because it acts to produce more fire. The quatrain's final image is of increased kindling, giving fire the last word.

What, then, has happened, without any alteration in the sonnet's image pattern, is an alteration in its rhetoric. The balance between ice and fire has shifted, giving to fire the stronger hand. But this makes sense. The poem is after all addressed to a lady, and it has a particular purpose, seen in the first quatrain: to persuade her. It, too, is a kind of seduction poem; Spenser emphasizes the power of desire's fire, and also, the possibility of sudden change in the course of things. If the ice has stood fast until now, this does not mean it cannot melt in the future. It is this further implicit point that the couplet picks up: "Such is the power of love in gentle mind / That it can alter all the course of kind." Things, the lover reminds the lady, can change. Miracles can happen, changing the "course of kind," which also suggests that the course should be altered to one of kindness. Now, moreover, the love is not hot fire, but is "gentle." The poem, finally, combines three activities: description, analysis, and rhetorical persuasion. The ice-lady is invited, through subtle shifts in imagery and diction, to become gentle, in fact to melt, before this, the poet's entreaty.

Here we come across another feature characteristic of the sonnet: how one of its subjects tends to be the sonnet itself. The sonnet may be said to have two great overarching subjects: love and immortal fame. Love is obviously important here. But so is fame, in the sense that the sonnet itself speaks for its writer, not only as lover, but as poet. It speaks for him here in its power to persuade the lady. For this poem is itself the way he "her entreat[s]." Thus, it reflects back on its own power, representing not only love, but the lover as poet, with his ability to encapture in the sonnet form the great struggle between desire and resistance, and the great miracle of conquering but gentle love.

"My Love Is Like to Ice" is one sonnet in a long sequence (*Amoretti*) that Spenser wrote to his lady, Elizabeth Boyle, who became his second wife, a sequence that concludes with his *Epithalamion* celebrating their marriage. In Spenser, the love of the lady becomes an avenue to virtuous love, not through warfare between spiritual longing and bodily desire, but as an image of their reconciliation and mutual affirmation. The role, or image, of love and the beloved can, however, vary greatly in a sonnet. The object of love very greatly affects the kind of love explored and expressed, as well as the condition and position of the lover. Therefore, sonnets that share a common resource of imagery, rhetoric, or topical concern can approach and treat this common material in strikingly different ways. A Holy Sonnet by John Donne provides an excellent example of a poet's reworking of a body of conventional material:

> I am a little world made cunningly
> Of elements, and an angelic sprite,
> But black sin hath betray'd to endless night
> My world's both parts, and, oh, both parts must die.
> You which beyond that heaven which was most high
> Have found new spheres, and of new lands can write,
> Pour new seas in mine eyes, that so I might
> Drown my world with my weeping earnestly,
> Or wash it, if it must be drown'd no more:
> But oh it must be burnt! alas the fire
> Of lust and envy have burnt it heretofore,
> And made it fouler; let their flames retire,
> And burn me O Lord, with a fiery zeal
> Of Thee and Thy house, which doth in eating heal.

We see here strangely transformed many elements that were present in Spenser's sonnet. There are again paradoxical antitheses: this time not fire and ice, but fire and water. Again, there is an appeal to the two parts of human nature—mind and body, in their complex and difficult relation. And again, love remains the underlying concern of this poem, generating these paradoxes. But this time the love at issue is not human, but divine. Donne, between writing "The Flea" as a courtier and writing this Holy Sonnet, had become an Anglican minister. In his own life he had therefore experienced the struggle that is also one of the sonnet's characteristic concerns: the relation between divine and human love. In one sense, his taking orders marked a profound change in his notion of the relationship between these loves. In "The Flea," he displays his courtly elegance and eloquence through his witty use of terms associated with religious love for love of the most profane kind. In this Holy Sonnet, he speaks as a minister, directing all love toward devotion to God. This is a change indeed. And yet, there is genuine continuity between Donne's earlier poetic methods and his later ones. What we see here, surprisingly, is not repudiation but transformation. Now he addresses God but still makes use of the same verse conventions for very different purposes.

This sonnet follows the Italian rhyme scheme of enclosing rhymes (*abbaabba*) through the octave. And yet, it concludes with a rhyming couplet, as in an English sonnet. And, like an English sonnet, its strucural divisions seem to fall into three quatrains and a couplet. Formally, then, there seems to be a cross, or mutual reference, between the Italian and English forms in a highly dynamic and forceful use of elements from both. The question is it Italian or English becomes exactly beside the point. The poem's divisions are constructed around metaphoric blocks, as we have seen before. And, while each metaphor remains separate, there is also development and reference from metaphor to metaphor as the quatrains proceed. As is characteristic of Donne, these metaphors continue to be conceits—elaborate, sustained comparisons whose various parts are brought into a complex system of correspondences, and which contain in this system very varied and even straining degrees of likeness: a wit with considerable distance between the terms compared.

The first quatrain, then, compares the poet to a "little world." Here, Donne makes use of a traditional figure—what we will recognize in the next chapter as a *topos*, or conventional poetic unit. The comparison of the human person to a world is an ancient one. It relies on a whole structure of belief in which *microcosm*, or man as a little world, is thought to correspond to the *macrocosm*, the universe at large, in ways both philosophical and physical. Here Donne intends both orders of correspondence. He is a "little world" in a physical sense, that is, in his actual composition. Like the universe as he (and his age) understood it, he is made of matter and spirit, "Of elements, and an angelic sprite." What the sonnet examines is the relation between these two "parts" in philosophical and religious terms.

The poem begins (in complex continuity with Donne's earlier work) with a disturbed relation between body and soul. "Black sin hath betray'd" both his "angelic sprite," his spirit, and his material "elements." Through black sin, "both parts must die." What is this sin? It is exactly an improper relation between flesh and spirit. "Black sin" occurs when physicality comes to contest, or to subordinate and control, the spiritual, when one's attachment to things of this world as opposed to eternal things; to things of the body as opposed to the life of the spirit, becomes too great. The destructive result of this disorder is represented in the first quatrain's micro/cosmic imagery as apocalyptic. The personal "black sin" corresponds to a world-destroying "endless night." But these religious-metaphysical hierarchies of body and soul, matter and spirit, structure more than the poem's image patterns. They are, as we shall see, fundamental to the poem's understanding of metaphoric language itself.

This becomes evident in the second quatrain. This quatrain develops the (conventional) figure of the worlds. It begins by focusing on the greater world to which the "little world" corresponds and is compared. It is addressed to a "You": "You which beyond that heaven which was most high / Have found new spheres, and of new lands can write." This "You" intends astronomers and explorers. Astronomers had, in Donne's own unsettling scientific day, discovered "new spheres" of planets and stars infinitely beyond the closed, perfect circles that, until Copernicus and Galileo, had been thought to represent the ordered cosmos. And it is addressed to the explorers who had in similarly unsettling fashion discovered unsuspected "new lands." Donne here registers in literature the shock of the profound changes in the picture of the universe and of his world which was felt during the sixteenth and seventeenth centuries, as the geography of the earth and the skies, and indeed the very notion of place itself, was radically altered.

But the point of the quatrain is ultimately to turn attention away from this physical remapping of the world. This emerges in the use of the word "heaven" in the first line of the quatrain, which is almost, here, a pun. Seeing "heaven" after the opening mention of "black sin," we assume the poet means the word in a religious or metaphysical sense. But what he does instead is put the very meaning of "heaven" in question. "That heaven which was most high" means the highest sphere of the old Ptolemaic universe. But it has now been superseded by the "new spheres" mapped by Copernicus and made immediately vivid by Galileo's telescope.

The fact that the old highest "heaven" also had religious meaning is just the point Donne is raising, and in effect reaffirming. Donne contrasts a physical image of the universe, defined by physical place, with a religious, spiritual sense of "place" that transcends the physical, having no physical location. And he asks: is the word "heaven" a physical word or a spiritual one? If you recall that the "black sin" in the first quatrain was an imbalance between physical and spiritual states, you can see how this double meaning of the word "heaven" is of utmost importance. To refer to "heaven" only as physical space is an image of black sin. Seeing it in its proper spiritual sense will be a release from sin, from placing matter over spirit.

This is just what the sonnet, in its own language, will do. It will do this by insisting on the spiritual meanings of the images it employs. "Pour new seas in mine eyes, that so I might / Drown my world with my weeping earnestly." In the context of the new spheres and new lands, we expect these seas to be the ones just discovered and added to the new maps of the world, but they are instead seas of tears. This image continues the metaphor comparing the macrocosm and the microcosm, the world (seas) and the human (tears). But the "new seas" the poet asks to have poured in his eyes are for "weeping earnestly" in repentance for black sin. They are, that is, spiritual seas, seas in a metaphoric and not a physical sense. And they must "Drown my world." Which world? Well, that is exactly the question. The poem gives priority to spiritual experience; and the world that is drowned is therefore the world in material terms. This is, moreover, exactly what Donne in his language does. The physical "seas" are drowned by the metaphorical sea-tears of his repentance.

The water imagery is carried into the sestet (or third quatrain) where it is given an ever more intense metaphorical and spiritual meaning. "Or wash it if it must be drowned no more" is an allusion (a literary reference or echo of an earlier text): here the Bible and God's promise to Noah that there would be no more floods. It shifts the water from a destructive punishment to a cleansing purification, as in baptism. Yet the sestet will go on to insist on radical measures: "But oh it must be burnt." Now Donne shifts his vision from things of the past (the flood) and of the present (the new discoveries) to the future—to the Apocalypse, or end of the world, when things as they now are will undergo their final consummation and transformation. Moreover, although it will only take place at the end of time, Donne shows how the vision of these last things also penetrate here and now. By keeping in mind the final destruction of this world, Donne will arrive, even while in this world, at its proper image. Again, he enacts this in his language. The events of this sestet all take place entirely in the religious domain. All the images have only spiritual, interior meanings. The water is the water of penitence. The fire is the inner fire of lust and envy and also the "fiery zeal" of spiritual purgation, burning away these material attachments.

This purgatorial flame becomes the subject of the couplet, which is also part of the sestet, beginning in the second half of the twelfth line: "let their flames retire." "Retire," like "wash," promises a lessening of intensity, a move toward something gentler. Donne, however, instead brings his imagery to still greater intensity, concluding now in the paradoxes that the very sonnet form urges on him, as does his subject. "Burn me, Lord, with a fiery zeal." Nothing less than utter destruction will be enough to reorder the parts of his little world. Like the great world at the end of time, so now his little world must undergo apocalyptic fire. But this is a fire that "doth in eating heal." In destroying, it brings new health and new birth.

We conclude, then, with the deepest paradox of Christianity— that only in dying to the life of sin can you be reborn into the eternal life of grace. This sonnet attests to such transformation—not only in its religious assertions, but in its language, which constantly turns away from outward, material meanings to spiritual, inward ones. If you compare this sonnet to Spenser's, you see how the sonnet itself has been transformed. The sonnet in its earlier development often addressed a lady as an avenue toward divine love. It then became a means for introspective examination of the psychology of love. Here Donne redirects introspection back toward religious meditation. Love becomes emphatically divine love. Instead of being, as Spenser's is, addressed to a lady with persuasive wit, here the wit is brought into the service of address to God, in renunciation, humility, and devotion.

Poetry in its very name (*poiein*: to make) suggests original creativity. Yet poetry is highly conventional. Indeed, every element of poetry discussed so far can be considered in terms of poetic convention. Levels of diction, poetic syntax, the sonnet itself, and, as we shall see, verse forms in general are defined by established conventions. Even simile and metaphor, along with other figures of speech, are conventions we recognize, and indeed expect, from poetry.

What do we mean by convention? In a general sense, convention in poetry, as elsewhere, is a customary form, an accepted and therefore expected way of doing something. Whatever original material or insights a new literary work offers remain framed by expectations established through all the literature that has come before. This fact of conventionality was in the past seen as both obvious and central. A poet would begin in school. He (and, rarely, she) would study what other poets had written by translating, paraphrasing, and imitating them as models. Only after such initial training would they begin to write their own "original" compositions—an originality consciously set within a tradition. Even John Donne's startling and wild comparison of love to a flea had already received large elaboration in a collection of playfully erotic poems called *The Flea* (*La Puce*) (1582) by Catherine de Roches and her coterie in Poitiers. The notion that poetry just happens as a mode of personal expression is quite recent.

There is, however, a more specific and restricted sense of convention—what is called a *topos*. Topos in Greek means place. In its literary use, it means a place in a text that is, as it were, revisited; a place that is familiar because of (many) past occasions when it already appeared in literature and poetry. It is therefore recognizable, marked as a specific, established convention within a larger text. Yet it is not a cliché. A cliché (boringly) repeats something the same way.

A topos repeats in different ways. It is always used distinctively. It is a building block, but one that is put to different uses from text to text. It can also be a basis of parody, as a poet inverts or satirizes a convention that has grown stale and indeed become clichéd. One famous instance of such parody is Shakespeare's Sonnet 130, "My mistress' eyes are nothing like the sun," in which Shakespeare systematically overturns and controverts the conventional praises of a lady that had been exhausted by Petrarch and his imitators.

There is a great deal of range in what might be called the size of a topos—how extensive or concentrated, how elaborately or briefly it may be treated, and also in the structural roles it can play through the course of a poem. A topos can involve the way an audience is addressed, or the way a poet presents him or herself. It might be an invocation to a muse, or an apology that the poet can never adequately say what he or she means (inexpressibility topos). It can be a traditional description; or site; or event; or activity; and so on. Some kinds of poetry—the epic, for instance—come close to being defined by topoi (along with other things, to be sure). To be an "epic" at all requires that certain traditional events or figures appear. Epic adventure, for example, must sooner or later include a journey to the underworld. If a text doesn't have one, well, then, it just isn't an epic.

But we need not reach beyond the lyric to get a sense of what topoi are and how they work. Here we can build on material we have already examined. Donne's "I am a little world made cunningly," for example, introduces and develops a comparison between man and cosmos that is thoroughly conventional. It draws on the ancient idea of the world of man and the world at large corresponding to each other as microcosm and macrocosm. The "little world," then, is not original to Donne. It is a topos, which he makes particular use of. What is crucial is not merely to repeat something given, but to re-use it to new purpose and direction. We saw that in their sonnets both Spenser and Donne used features characteristic of sonnet writing, such as antithesis, and indeed introduced specific oppositions that recur from text to text and poet to poet. One of these is fire and ice. Spenser used this opposition, but it was already conventional when he did so. Let us turn now to another, later use of this topos—Robert Frost's "Fire and Ice"—to see how its conventional features can be recognized, and how this becomes part of a new form of its use.

Some say the world will end in fire,
Some say in ice.
From what I've tasted of desire
I hold with those who favor fire.
But if it had to perish twice,
I think I know enough of hate
To say that for destruction ice
Is also great
And would suffice.

Frost's poem is not a sonnet. It seems in fact quite removed from sonneteering, except in being short. It does not, for example, address a lady, or seem to concern itself with love. Instead, it is about the destruction of the world. Frost, moreover, uses extremely colloquial and informal speech here (Frost once boasted that he uses diction even Wordsworth wouldn't stoop to). Plain diction is one of the outstanding features of this text. For it is very odd that Frost uses such an informal idiom to present so momentous and disturbing a topic as the world's apocalyptic destruction.

This conjunction of the colloquial and the momentous is central to the text. It begins in the first lines. "Some say" promises to introduce the most casual hearsay or gossip. But the subject is one far greater than gossip: how "the world will end." And much more is at stake than would seem apparent in the casual difference of opinion implied in "some say fire" and "some say ice."

Colloquial diction continues to control the poem's phrasing, promising something quite insignificant. "From what I've tasted" sounds as though the topic at hand is no more important than, say, which kind of apple one prefers to use for making cider, Macintosh or Golden Delicious. "I hold with those who favor" has a similar casual and understated effect (*litotes*). Little seems at stake. It is merely a question of preference. "But if it had to perish twice" seems to say, at least in its conditional grammar (if), that no real decision is even called for. There is always a second chance, you really can have it both ways. But the verb "to perish" of course starkly contradicts this casual diction and phrasing. It even contradicts the sentence's sense: if something has perished, how can it perish again?

At this point you want to stop to ask: why this conjunction of the terribly casual and the truly terrible? This is where the topos can help. Fire and ice had represented in Spenser interior states, psychological conditions. That is also what they represent here. Frost associates fire with desire, ice with hate. Desire and hate are, like Frost's diction, very commonplace. They are all too everyday. Yet, as in Spenser, they are potent and powerful, having, as Frost wants to show, dramatic implications. Their potential for destruction in psychological terms becomes here an image for general destruction. What Frost does, then, is use a topos with a history of psychological depth to show how our commonplace experiences can have profound, even dangerous consequences. The interior spaces explored in the sonnet tradition through just such imagery is transplanted to an everyday language of everyday experience, in a verse form far more casual than the sonnet's is. But the explosive power of such inward experiences remains, now directed toward examining their consequences in ordinary life and daily experience. In this, by way of the topos, Frost re-situates the commonplace, showing the seriousness of daily actions and emotions, and how they may have profound, even disastrous consequences.

Frost's poem offers an example of a topos as a very small unit—a particular antithesis as it has been used in a variety of contexts, which therefore recall one another, importing into each other the added power and scope of a history of usages. But a topos may be more extensive. It may involve not simply a specific image, but a broader topic or structure of composition. One such topos is the approach or attitude to life called *carpe diem*, or "seize the day." This has a long history in Latin verse, as the designation "carpe diem" suggests, a history which writers in English learned and referred to. One classic example in English is "To the Virgins, to Make Much of Time" by Robert Herrick (1591–1674):

Gather ye rosebuds while ye may,
  Old time is still a-flying;
And this same flower that smiles today
  Tomorrow will be dying.

The glorious lamp of heaven, the sun,
  The higher he's a-getting,
The sooner will his race be run,
  And nearer he's to setting.

That age is best which is the first,
  When youth and blood are warmer;

But being spent, the worse, and worst
   Times still succeed the former.

Then be not coy, but use your time,
   And, while ye may, go marry;
For, having lost but once your prime,
   You may forever tarry.

As this poem shows, "carpe diem" is a way of saying: Hurry! Time is running out! Take your chance, seize your opportunity while you can, especially your opportunity for love, before your powers desert you and your decaying body ceases to be an object of desire. The poem delivers this call through a series of metaphors. The first, the "rosebuds," are images of passing time—if they are not gathered now, then tomorrow will be too late—and therefore of mortal life. More specifically, as the third line shows—"this same flower that smiles today"—the images of the rosebuds are images of the virgins called on to gather them. The word "smiles" associates the flower with the girls, who, like the flowers themselves, need to be plucked, since they too "tomorrow will by dying."

The poem goes on to propose other images of passing time: the sun whose advance also marks its descent; youth, whose warm blood precedes and hence signals an inevitable decline. But the first image should sound familiar. We have already seen this comparison of the virgin girl to a rose, urging her to learn a lesson of haste and action from its near and inevitable death. This was the central figure in the Waller's "Song," "Go lovely rose." "Go lovely rose" is not exactly cast as a "carpe diem." It doesn't state outright: "Then be not coy, but use your time," as "carpe diem" tends to do. Yet this need to make haste in the face of mortality is its implicit lesson. Once we have made the association, we recall how implicitly violent that poem was; how its act of persuasion bordered on an act of coercion, a threat. Remembering this, we return to "Gather ye rosebuds" to see whether something similar is taking place. The general nature of this poem's address makes it rather less urgent than Waller's specific address to the rose and, through it, to his lady. Here, no particular lady seems called on to act in response to a particular desire. Yet these rosebuds also blossom under the shadow of death, which they represent no less than they represent the young girls. And at the end there is a threat, mixed here with something close to a sneer. "For having lost but once your prime / you may forever tarry." The ladies here are not told that they will die, but only that they will be scorned as useless and unwanted.

"Gather ye rosebuds" can serve as introduction to what is probably the greatest expression of "carpe diem" in English, "To His Coy Mistress," by Andrew Marvell (1621–1678):

> Had we but world enough, and time,
> This coyness, Lady, were no crime.
> We would sit down, and think which way
> To walk, and pass our long love's day.
> Thou by the Indian Ganges' side
> Shouldst rubies find; I by the tide
> Of Humber would complain. I would
> Love you ten years before the Flood,
> And you should, if you please, refuse
> Till the conversion of the Jews.
> My vegetable love should grow
> Vaster than empires and more slow.
> An hundred years should go to praise
> Thine eyes, and on thy forehead gaze.
> Two hundred to adore each breast:
> But thirty thousand to the rest.
> An age at least to every part,
> And the last age should show your heart.
> For, Lady, you deserve this state,
> Nor would I love at lower rate.
>   But at my back I always hear
> Time's wingèd chariot hurrying near:
> And yonder all before us lie
> Deserts of vast eternity.
> Thy beauty shall no more be found,
> Nor, in thy marble vault, shall sound
> My echoing song: then worms shall try
> That long-preserved virginity:
> And your quaint honor turn to dust;
> And into ashes all my lust.
> The grave's a fine and private place
> But none, I think, do there embrace.
>   Now therefore, while the youthful hue
> Sits on thy skin like morning dew,

And while thy willing soul transpires
At every pore with instant fires,
Now let us sport us while we may;
And now, like amorous birds of prey,
Rather at once our time devour
Than languish in his slow-chapt power.
Let us roll all our strength, and all
Our sweetness, up into one ball:
And tear our pleasures with rough strife,
Thorough the iron gates of life.
Thus, though we cannot make our sun
Stand still, yet we will make him run.

We recognize this as "carpe diem" at once, in the title, which echoes
Herrick's "Then be not coy." And of course the concluding verse
paragraph brings the lesson home: "Now therefore, while the youth-
ful hue sits on our skin like morning dew . . . now let us sport us while
we may." The whole poem follows a rhetorical structure of argument
and persuasion: *If, but, therefore*. On this level, it is a skillful effort to
accomplish its purpose, which is the seduction of the coy mistress.
We see, in fact, that "carpe diem" is a form of seduction poem, bring-
ing together two impulses or patterns in poetry.

The poem's argument is divided into three verse paragraphs. The
first verse paragraph follows the forms of an elaborate compliment,
a courtly convention in itself, and concludes with a play on the tra-
ditional catalogue in praise of the lady's beauties, called a *blason*.
(Another example of a blason is Spenser's Sonnet 64, which cata-
logues his lady's beauty and shows the connection between such
compliments and the *Song of Songs*, that work of canonized sensual-
ity, which grants authority and precedent to the blason.) This first
paragraph works in a way comparable to the rhetorical *concession*:
it acknowledges the other side of the argument, that it might be
reasonable for the lady to wish to be coy and to delay her response
to his entreaty. But the poet makes this concession only in order
the better to defeat it.

This the second verse paragraph proceeds to do. Here the poet-
lover presents the counterargument, the heart of his own persua-
sion. "Had we but world enough and time," he conceded at the
outset, producing in his imagery vast stretches of time and place:
far India, the flood at the beginning and the conversion of the Jews

at the end of time; the temporal measures of vegetation and of empire; then ending with an ever grander temporal scale for adoring the lady's body parts. "But," he reminds us in the second verse paragraph, "at my back I always hear time's winged chariot hurrying near." He would like to take all the time in the world to court the lady, but he hasn't got it—and neither, he hurries to point out, has she. "Yonder all before us lie / Deserts of vast eternity." These deserts stretch before, and surround, the lady, himself, and indeed all mortals. He, however, focuses mostly on her.

> Thy beauty shall no more be found,
> Nor, in thy marble vault, shall sound
> My echoing song: then worms shall try
> That long-preserved virginity:
> And your quaint honor turn to dust;
> And into ashes all my lust.

Against the desert vastness of eternity he poses the increasingly small space of the body and the grave, finally reducing all to a fistful of dust and ashes.

These constrictions of space contrast severely with the great sweeps of time introduced in the first verse paragraph, ultimately acting to reduce them in the same gesture. All time and space in the end reduce to just this grave, this dust and ash. The final verse paragraph continues these processes of restriction, to drive home the poem's main rhetorical purpose: seduction. "Now therefore" picks up the argument as its logical conclusion: as though what will follow is an obvious logical deduction from the clear and self-evident points already made. In light of what has come before, the lady's "youthful hue" stands in stark contrast to the dust and ashes of the previous verse paragraph. And yet it remains qualified and even defined by the colorless dust. The "while" of "while thy willing soul transpires" has in fact been positioned as a very, very shrunken space of time. The youthful hue is no more than a bare moment, the "instant fires" are truly fiery only for an instant. There is very little time in which to act at all. And so, "now let us sport us while we may." Since we have only this moment in which to act, let us act now, in this moment. The constriction of time into an immediate "now" is matched and reaffirmed by a constriction of space into "one ball," the sexual union that carries with it, in light of the geographic ranges of the first verse paragraph, a sense that the whole world is now contained in, that is, reduced to, this one "ball" (a brief invocation of the topos of micro/macrocosm).

From here the poem moves to its swift, and seemingly irresistible, conclusion of logic: "Thus, though we cannot make our sun / Stand still, yet we will make him run." The concluding couplet alludes to the biblical Joshua, who made the sun stand still over Gideon. But the poet-lover makes the allusion work through dissimilarity. He wants to remind the lady, yet again, that the sun will not stay for her. It will not stand still. At most, she can try to keep up with the sun's unrelenting motion—or, more accurately, and in a further use of the convention of the microcosm of the "ball," she can make the sun try to keep up with her. That is, she can not really conquer the sun, which will go on in any case; but she can challenge the sun in racing against it.

So far, we have only considered the use of the convention of the "carpe diem" in our reading of the poem. We have traced how it follows this topos and fulfills its patterns. But to do this we have mainly paid attention to the poem's rhetorical conduct: had we but world and time; but we don't; now therefore; thus let us act. This rhetorical progression proposes itself in the guise of a logical argument, with the imagery introduced in terms of this effort at persuasion. The poem, however, contains other elements besides this topos of "carpe diem," haste in love. And it points in other directions than the lesson of headlong action to seize the moment. How can we locate these other impulses? One important feature of the poem that can help us to do so is its diction. Analyzing diction will allow us to notice a different pattern of imagery, directed towards a different effect, than was evident within the "carpe diem" argument. In this way, another topos at work through the poem will emerge, another conventional pattern, which acts in counterpoint and ultimately in contradiction to the first topos of "carpe diem."

The first verse paragraph, as we saw, used a language of expansion in time and place, which the second verse paragraph then controverted into ever more constricted spatial and temporal dimensions—into, in fact, the grave. The first verse paragraph closed with a catalogue of the lady's body, itself a topos or convention in praise of a lady's beauty. Here, however, the language of praise was carried to such an extreme that it bordered on the satirical ("two hundred to adore each breast"). This focus on the body is then echoed, but almost inversely, in the second verse paragraph: "then worms shall try / That long preserved virginity: / And your quaint honor turn to dust; / And into ashes all my lust." This is very strong, indeed graphic language. Its effect is not to make you feel sexy. It instead directs you to confront and to contemplate, with horror and dread, the decay of the flesh in death. This grotesque language, and this sobering effect, Andrew Marvell did not invent. It too is part of tradition and convention. The convention is called *memento mori*, the remembrance of death, within an art of meditation on dying (*Ars Moriendi*). In painting it is often introduced through an image of the death's-head, or skull, the bare skeleton without flesh, grinning its hideous smile. Often such a death's-head is depicted as the image seen in the mirror by the living subject of a portrait contemplating his own reflection. The death's-head can also be placed on a desk, for the edification of all who gaze upon it. It is intended to convey a very particular lesson: that mortality is the ultimate truth about our human condition. We will all die, and our bodies will rot in the grave. But this is not intended to lead to despair. On the contrary. Through this instruction we are meant to understand that the life of the flesh is not our true life at all; that the life of the flesh is transient and will pass, grotesquely, away; that our true life is the life of the spirit, beyond the flesh; of commitment to God and to religion, which will lead not to mortality and death in the grave, but to eternal life, to immortality, in heaven.

Now, on the whole, this sort of vivid reference to rotting flesh and the worm-eaten body is not a very good argument for seduction. If the lady is thinking about the decay of her body and the eternity of her soul, she is not so likely to jump into bed in some sinful, fleshly way. The poem, then, actually presents two arguments: one for seduction and one against it. The logic of the rhetoric admonishes us to act hastily and seize pleasure before it is too late. But the imagery and diction of the text remind us that such hasty action has very far-reaching, indeed eternal consequences, with the body but a small and doomed arena in the eternal scheme. This double message is sustained throughout the third verse paragraph. The logic of the concluding lines ("Now therefore," "thus") all argues for seduction. But what about the diction and imagery? "And now, like amorous birds of prey," for example. Comparing lovers in their lovemaking to birds of prey (say, vultures) is not, when you come to look at it, all that appealing a simile. Or take "And tear our pleasures with rough strife, / Thorough the iron gates of life." Tear, rough, strife; iron gates: these are all violent, harsh, daunting words. They do not make the act of pleasure seem all that pleasurable but, instead, make it seem aggressive and desperate. Even the concluding couplet looks, from this angle, rather different. It no longer seems to offer a way of conquering the sun (which even in the first reading proved a rather specious logic, since the conclusion asserts that conquering the sun is impossible). Instead it seems a futile challenge to a power that you can never overcome.

The poem offers, then, not one, but two topoi: the overt "carpe diem" and a subversive remembrance of death inscribed into the text alongside the call to seduction. This does not make the poem incoherent, however. Both topoi are urgent calls, calls to weigh your life to see what, in its short compass of time and space, you really can accomplish; what, in its short span, really has value; what you should be striving for. It calls on readers to face in full urgency the sun, and to see themselves in its all too passing shadow. The excruciating tension between life's possibilities and its limitations meet here as a clash between traditional representations, topoi that have, through much of history, given voice to each impulse in all its driving power.

We have had an opportunity to examine the sonnet as a verse form. We have also looked at the question of poetic conventions, seeing how these can be quite small units, such as an image that is returned to repeatedly in the history of literature (the rose); or how conventions can involve larger structures, indeed whole topics, such as love, and ways of handling them. We now can see that in a sense a verse form is itself a kind of convention, with a history that is recalled each time a poet uses the form. What is paramount in each case is how the form of the poem is significant and functional—the part it plays in the way the poet shapes the poem's material.

The sonnet is a very specifically defined verse form. But there is a wide range of verse forms, with a wide range of formal specifications. There are forms that are rather general, such as a basic stanza of four lines (ballad stanza) with an alternating rhyme scheme through all four lines (*abab*), or perhaps only in the second and fourth lines (*xaya*). There is *blank verse*, which is unrhymed verse in iambic pentameter, the basic English metrical pattern of ten-syllable lines with five strong accents. Milton wrote in blank verse, which can be organized into long verse paragraphs. Or, verse paragraphs can be written in couplets, so that every two lines rhyme. This was the pattern of Chaucer in the *Canterbury Tales*, and in Marvell's "To His Coy Mistress." Then there are poems that create their own verse forms, that is, they establish a pattern in the first stanza and then repeat it through all the stanzas that follow. Here one line may be long, another short, with all kinds of lengths and all kinds of rhyme schemes. Donne's poem "The Flea" is written this way. So is Wordsworth's "I wandered lonely as a cloud."

There are other verse forms that are much more formal, much more defined, containing repeating lines like refrains, arranged in very special orders. These forms mostly come out of the early lyric

tradition, in Old French and Italian—the lyric history out of which
the sonnet too first emerged. They include the *sestina*, a poem in
sixes: six stanzas of six lines each, followed by an *envoy* of three lines,
with repeating words throughout but not in rhymed patterns. An-
other form is the *villanelle*, a poem in tercets (three-line groups)
whose first and third lines then repeat through the last lines of a
series of (usually five) stanzas, then resuming in an end quatrain.
These are forms whose organization is rigidly defined, but which
can treat any material. There are also poems which treat particular
topics but have no specific formal requirements. These include the
alba or *aubade*, a song of dawn, usually expressions of a lover's re-
gret at parting, or the *enueg*, or song of complaint. There are as well
elegies, *odes*, and *pastorals*. And there is the twentieth-century inno-
vation of free verse: verse that has very little fixed patterning; al-
though, as T. S. Eliot remarked in "Reflections on *Vers Libre*," no
verse that is any good is entirely free. Instead, free verse often works
out of, or against, older established forms, which then hover in the
background.

The point here is not to memorize the different kinds of verse
forms, but to get a sense of how a verse form works and what it
does. For this purpose, I would like to begin with a relatively spe-
cific verse form, which had a relatively specific purpose in the hands
of the poet who used it. The poet is Emily Dickinson, and the verse
form is the hymn. Unlike most poetry, the hymn has remained ex-
tremely popular among a wide audience. Hymns are sung in
churches, and people enjoy them as part of their religious lives. The
hymn has particular stylistic features in accordance with its purpose,
which is to praise God, as part of prayer. The form is relatively
simple, regular, and accessible, since a hymn is usually written so
that it can be read or sung by a whole congregation, in unison. It is
a stanzaic form, usually with four lines to a stanza. But the lines do
not have the full ten syllables of traditional English verse. Instead,
hymns are usually written in sixes and eights—a combination of lines
with six or eight syllables (or sometimes four syllables), in which at
least the second and fourth line, and often all four lines in the stanza,
alternately rhyme.

Emily Dickinson wrote almost all of her poetry in this hymnal
verse form—but almost always for purposes other than those of the
church hymn. Dickinson's poetry more or less consistently ques-
tions, or struggles with, the claims of her religion. She repeatedly

questions God, both in his wisdom and his goodness (although she
generally assumes his power). What we want to look at is how she
uses her verse form for her own poetic purposes. For example, there
is a little poem about prayer:

Prayer is the little implement
Through which Men reach
Where Presence—is denied them—
They fling their Speech

By means of it—in God's ear—
If then He hear—
This sums the Apparatus
Comprised in prayer—

This poem works in sixes and fours rather than sixes and eights,
a sort of truncated hymnal form. But then again, it isn't very hym-
nal in other ways, either. It begins as though it will offer some defi-
nition of prayer. But, as is very characteristic of Dickinson, what it
then proceeds to do is to complicate, and eventually to unravel the
definition that the poem first seemed to promise. What exactly does
the first stanza propose? "Prayer is the little implement / through
which men reach / where Presence." Certain words in the poem at
first seem to be saying that prayer is the means for reaching up and
through to divine Presence. But to arrive at this positive declara-
tion requires ignoring some other words that make this straightfor-
ward definition less clear. First, there are the words "little" and
"implement." Prayer as "implement" seems somewhat mechanical;
while "little" seems diminutive. And yet, these hesitations are not
decisive. Prayer can be, after all, a small thing, which only makes
its ability to reach up to God the more wonderful.

But "little" is not the only qualification in the first stanza. In the
poem, prayer does not reach "To" Presence, but "Where Presence—
is denied." This denial may not be absolute. That we are on earth,
and not (yet) with God in the next world, in some sense is the very
reason for prayer. Prayer allows us to reach across the great distance
separating earth from heaven, and, despite this distance, to address
God.

The second stanza begins in a more encouraging fashion: "By
means of it in God's ear." Here we feel a moment of security. But
the poem adds: "If then He hear." The prayer does not necessarily

reach God's ear; its success at reaching the divine presence is instead left in doubt. Now all the hesitations we have been able to put aside return in force. Prayer is "little" in the sense of being weak, too weak to penetrate "where Presence" may be "denied." It is not a certain "means" of reaching "God's ear," and there is no guarantee that he does "hear" it. These suspicions are reinforced in the poem's conclusion: "This sums the Apparatus / Comprised in prayer." The "sum" here (a rather deflationary word) remains incomplete, interrupted. "Apparatus" reinforces the mechanical and trivial implication of "implement." While apparently summing up the earlier definition, the poem's conclusion dramatizes its failure to define prayer, or to declare prayer's power.

What then are we to conclude about Dickinson's use of the verse form? On the one hand, the poem is like a hymn; on the other, it pointedly fails to do what hymns are supposed to: to assert our ability, in hymn and prayer, to reach up to God. We might talk about this failure in a number of ways. With regard to the hymnal form, the poem can be called ironic. It uses the verse form for a purpose that undermines its ordinary one. This subversion of hymnal purpose reflects on some of the poem's other formal features. Unlike a hymn, but very typical of Dickinson's poetry, the syntax here is interrupted, unclear, and tricky. The lineation, too, is abrupt and choppy, causing suspensions that are then filled in with discouraging completions. If a hymn is designed for clarity and accessibility, Dickinson's writing almost willfully tries to block understanding. And yet, Dickinson's use of the hymnal form isn't simply ironic either. Dickinson is genuinely concerned with the question of reaching God—deeply concerned. She is profoundly troubled by her inability to reach her God through language. Her verse might be called a disappointed hymn. She uses a hymnal form not simply to mock it, but out of genuine desire, and genuine despair, at its not accomplishing its purpose of discourse with God.

Here, then, is one example of the way in which a poet can make use of a particular verse form and its traditions. Dickinson's handling of the hymn is caught between ironic treatment and a genuine appeal to the hymn's true function. Yet, the subversion of what we expect of a hymn is only possible, and powerful, through her very use of the hymnal form.

The hymnal form was essentially shaped by the audience for which it was written and for the specific (religious) purposes it

serves. This may be said of poetic form generally: that many for-
mal features of the poem—including syntax and diction, repetitions
and musicality, length and complexity—are essentially shaped by
the audience the poem addresses and the purposes it serves. This
intimate relationship between form and audience can be seen in
another popular poetry, the children's poem or song. Formal fea-
tures define and link the poem and its audience. How this formal
negotiation with the audience may be applied and redirected can
be seen in the *Songs of Innocence and Experience* by William Blake.
Blake consciously uses the traditions of nursery rhyme and children's
poetry in a poem such as "A Poison Tree":

> I was angry with my friend:
> I told my wrath, my wrath did end.
> I was angry with my foe:
> I told it not, my wrath did grow.
>
> And I water'd it in fears,
> Night and morning with my tears;
> And I sunned it with smiles,
> And with soft deceitful wiles.
>
> And it grew both day and night,
> Till it bore an apple bright;
> And my foe beheld it shine,
> And he knew that it was mine,
>
> And into my garden stole
> When the night had veil'd the pole:
> In the morning glad I see
> My foe outstretch'd beneath the tree.

What marks this poem so clearly in the tradition of a child's song?
First, there is its apparent simplicity. Its diction is very plain. All the
words in it could easily be understood by a child. Its syntax is also
very simple. Each phrase is short, and takes up in each instance a
single line, with no spillover (enjambment) from line to line and no
complicated extended sentences. The syntax is simple as well in its
lack of subordination. There are no inset clauses to qualify each brief
phrase. Instead the phrases are strung together, one after the other,
in a straight narrative sequence. First one thing happens, then an-
other. Actions are linked through the simplest conjunction "and,"

which asserts addition (paratactic syntax) rather than a more complex qualification or subordination (hypotactic syntax). In the same way there is a steady, almost sing-song rhythm. The metric is very regular, with no inversions or complicated play of accent. And the rhyme scheme is the simplest rhyming couplet, set in the most traditional four-line stanzas, so typical of children's verse (though not only of it).

All this formal simplicity gives to the poem a kind of momentum, as though each thing that happens in it is obvious and necessary. One thing simply follows another, as the only possible course of events. All the actions the poem recounts are also seemingly simple and uncomplicated. But the conclusion they lead to is frightening, and indeed violent. Moreover, for all the simplicity and seeming necessity of the sequence of action, the poem is about duplicity—about hidden actions, and the traps they lay. The wrath-bearing tree grows out of hidden, unspoken anger. It is "sunned with . . . smiles / and with soft, deceitful wiles." The poem further involves an acute calculation: that the foe would want to steal the deceptively bright apple, which would therefore accomplish its deadly purpose by manipulating the enemy's own evil inclination.

This poem's seemingly simple surface thus traces a progression involving hiding, calculation, and evil intent. The poem strengthens the tension between these two impulses by combining another convention with the formal elements of a child's song. The verse form recalls children's poetry, but the imagery in the poem is also conventional, introducing a specific topos. This is not the first wrath-bearing tree, not the first bright apple stolen out of evil inclination, not the first garden whose boundaries are broken with deadly result. The poem irresistibly points back to the biblical Tree in the Garden of Eden. In combination with the child's song, this topos proves particularly powerful. For here the verse form itself becomes subject to a complex combination of innocence and evil, of boundary and its penetration. The innocent song, itself a kind of garden, proves not to be innocent at all. Its sing-song rhythm and seemingly natural and irresistible course of events themselves become a mode of hiding, of duplicity. And its apparently straightforward narration, through a paratactic syntax, is revealed not to be a clear and necessary sequence. It is instead a hypnotic trick to make this sequence look necessary and natural, when the poem's action in fact pursues a course of active and evil choice.

This hidden complexity finally comes to affect, and indeed to infect, not only the "foe" in the poem but also the speaking "I." The "I" starts off presenting itself as childlike. It is "I"'s song. Yet this "I" is progressively compromised. For all its casual recounting of the tree it plants and waters, we stand at the end in a kind of horror at its deceit, its wilful ensnaring of the enemy, and its final joy at the destruction it has so carefully and casually wrought. We feel at the end that this poison tree, this tree of evil, is an outgrowth of the "I" itself. It is an image of the "I," of which the "I," however, is not entirely aware. For the "I" has presented this narrative in a most matter-of-fact way, as if one action simply and justly followed from the one before, and in apparent self-satisfaction at the deadly result the "I" has accomplished with such duplicity. But the song in this way finally implicates the reader, too. It places us in a compromised position. The poem's first-person voice invites the reader to identify with the speaker, almost as a grammatical assumption. The "I"'s self-certainty, and his confident presentation of events as justified and inevitable, further strengthens our identification with him: aren't we also childlike in our innocence and correct in our actions? But the poem's conclusion suddenly leaves us also responsible, or at least implicated, in the speaker's poisonous plot. For we have gone, sing-song, along with the poem's speaker, step by simple step.

The verse form itself is left in a somewhat ambiguous position by this poisonous conclusion. In this complication of the child's song, has Blake simply used and abused it, betraying its true function as a mask for his own purposes? Is he as poet in a position similar to the "I" of the poem, with the poem itself a poison tree? The answer to this question depends upon what a child's song actually involves. On the one hand, Blake seems to make the child's song darker, and more terrible, than is appropriate to childhood innocence. And yet, in examining the evil that can lie hidden under simple surfaces, can lie hidden in the very claim to innocence, Blake is quite concordant with what goes on in many children's stories and fairy tales. This uncovering of dark motives in a dangerous and even violent world is, in fact, quite typical of fairy tales and surely accounts, at least in part, for their power. And the poem is also a lesson: a lesson about deceit, about its destructive power, not only on those deceived, but on the deceiver himself. By exposing destructive impulses rather than hiding them, as this speaker hides his anger, the poem brings out to the light of word and image what otherwise can eat away in us like a poison.

There is then finally a kind of split between Blake and this poem's "I," despite the grammar of the first person. The "I" may practice repression and deceit, but the poet urges recognition and expression. This didactic element in the poem is of course very true to the intentions of literature for children. The poem offers after all a lesson, which comes to involve a complicated question of position: the position of the speaker, who proves to be different from the poet; and also the position of the reader, who has become involved, and even compromised, through the poem's progress. As a lesson, the poem's ultimate interest will be in the reader, to whom the lesson is addressed. We, too, become confronted with a potential split within us. We are made to ask: are we like the poet or like the speaker? What are we hiding from ourselves, to the destruction of ourselves and others? Are we really childlike and innocent, or must we achieve this state as a difficult undertaking, and as our most important adult achievement?

Blake's use of the child's poem makes its formal features fully participate in the poem's meaning and experience. It shows how verse forms, far from consisting merely of static rules and fixed procedures, are extremely dynamic. They act as a space of interaction between the author and/or speaker, and the audience of readers. The lyric, as we will explore in a later chapter, tends to be strongly identified with its speaking voice. Lyric itself seems almost defined as a poet uttering his/her intimate feelings or thoughts, and therefore as a medium almost constituted through self-consciousness. And yet, the formal features of verse are fundamentally determined by the relation to the audience. The poem is always addressed to someone (even if that someone turns out to be the poet, in a mode of meditative verse). The verse form itself can be deeply shaped by the audience it addresses. In a hymn, for example, the audience is presumably a religious one, involved in a religious devotion or service. The hymn's formal features all encourage the congregation's easy participation—the steady rhythm and rhyme, the direct progress toward praise and prayer, the straightforward syntax. Emily Dickinson assumes all of these features, which she then recasts through her own more ambivalent purposes. Yet she always recalls the original purpose of the hymn as part of her own intention. Similarly, if you are writing for a child, you must be direct in syntax and sequence, songlike in rhythm and rhyme, vivid in imagery—all conventions Blake uses to effect in his deceptively simple poem.

In the history of the sonnet form, as well as other English Renaissance poetry, the audiences of the lyric can be felt through almost every line and every word. Essentially an art of the court, the sonnet and other Renaissance verse forms reflect and apply the practices of courtiers, as well as their sense of themselves as an exclusive group. The subtlety of wit, the balancing between opposites, the adoration of the lady, and the intricacy of pattern of Renaissance verse forms derive from, concentrate, and in turn influenced aspects of courtly behavior. At court, elaborate praise, wit, and sophisticated accommodation all came into play in seeking favor from the sovereign and plotting to advance one's position. In this sense, while poetry cannot be reduced to a social function or political purpose, it nevertheless must be seen as taking shape within social contexts and interactions. Even devotional verse confirms this interactive shaping. Supremely concerned with self-examination, it is nevertheless and no less profoundly informed and fashioned towards its very particular (although variously defined) audience, God, in modes that are certainly historically and culturally various.

Just how deeply verse form is shaped by social context, and even social purpose, can be seen in the revolutions in verse that were launched by Walt Whitman (1819–1892). Writing in mid-nineteenth-century America, Whitman consciously set out to redefine the relation between poet and reader, and ultimately the audience that poetry would address. This change in poet/audience relationship is deeply reflected in his poetic medium:

I celebrate myself, and sing myself,
And what I assume you shall assume,
For every atom belonging to me as good belongs to you.

.   .   .   .

Stop this day and night with me and you shall possess the
    origin of all poems,
You shall possess the good of the earth and sun, (there are
    millions of suns left,)
You shall no longer take things at second or third hand, nor
    look through the eyes of the dead, nor feed on the spectres
    in books,

> You shall not look through my eyes either, nor take things
>   from me,
> You shall listen to all sides and filter them from your self.
>
>   (Song of Myself, 1 and 2)

Whitman here rejects most traditional poetic norms. The lines of the poem do not rhyme, nor do they follow a regulated syllable count. Verse paragraphs greatly vary in length, with each one determined as a single sentence. Each line is constructed around phrases, and each verse paragraph concludes with a period. The diction and phrasing are quite direct and natural, even conversational, if also incantatory. As to subject, the poem offers an assertion of radical equality. Certainly the poetic "I" is almost extravagantly announced, as the precious center of integrity and value. Yet this assertion of worth, of centrality and of possibility, is at once extended to the "you" that concludes the first sentence/stanza. This becomes the vital call of the second verse paragraph quoted. Each person, each reader, can realize his or her poetic potential and fulfill that poetic promise. Each reader is urged, even incited, to perceive the power to create from out of himself or herself a poetic world that is endless ("there are millions of suns left") in its reproductive energy and possibility.

If the norms and procedures of courtly verse assert and communicate a sense of privilege, subtle wit, and initiated tastes, then what is declared in Whitman's verse is a strong sense of inclusion, excitement, and invitation. The straightforward directness of his utterance is such as to deny special privilege ("You shall no longer take things at second or third hand"). On the contrary, the verse intends to initiate each individual into the possibilities of poetic creation. This, for Whitman, is a profoundly American venture. As America opens opportunity to each individual, radical and irreducible in her/his value and integrity, so his verse will awaken each individual to participate in the American promise, in a language that all can share, a diction that does not disdain even the lowest slang word, a syntax at once relaxed and propulsive, and an energy that is endlessly creative and open.

Formal features organize a poem as a textual unit. But in formalizing a relationship between artist and audience, verse forms are profoundly historical. Placing the reader in relation to the poem, and mediating his or her experience of it, verse forms shift as their social contexts change, and reflect changed conceptions both of poetry's place within an ongoing cultural life and of the poet/reader relationship. Thus, poetry's forms are not fixed abstractions. Rather, they give design to that moment of encounter between writer and audience, within terms of expectation and mutual positioning, and within a larger social organization that frames them both.

In Modernist verse, this sense of verse form as a space of encounter or negotiation between author and audience seems to have been mitigated by a new commitment to the artwork as an object, independent of context and existing in detachment from both writer and audience. Nevertheless, Modernist verse may be said to formalize a special, and perhaps especially anxious, relationship between poet and audience. Ezra Pound's "In a Station of the Metro" can illustrate:

The apparition of these faces in the crowd;
Petals on a wet, black bough.

This poem, a founding text of the Imagist movement, introduced a new conception of verse form, which it is meant to define. Pound, as theorist of this movement, urged that the basic unit of verse should be the "image" (as the term "Imagism" suggests), which Pound defined as "that which presents an intellectual and emotional complex in an instant of time" ("A Retrospect"). This poem accordingly offers a single image, but one that has the complexity of a conceit. The poem presents a comparison—between the faces in the crowd in the Metro and the "Petals on a wet, black bough." The image thus brings together two very different worlds: the mechanical world of the city subway and the organic world of nature. It also involves number: the many faces of a crowd, yet all brought together in the configuration of a single branch holding its petals. The word "apparition" suggests something ghostlike or even hallucinatory (an apparition is a haunting, disappearing vision). Together with the black bough, it gives the presented image a kind of pictorial effect of shadows and transparencies.

This, then, is a model of the imagist image: a multiplicity of effects all intersecting in one, complex representation, as the basic formal unit of the poem (here the poem in its entirety). The image stands as a composition of the various elements united within it, which are offered without introduction or explanation. In this, it moves toward a more object-like verse form, one which apparently eliminates both authorial self-reference and direct address to the reader. And yet, the Modernist verse form, in its very detachment and starkness, also heightens and accentuates the role of the reader (as of the poet) in piecing together the connections and comparisons which make up the art-object. In this poem, the word "apparition" places emphasis on appearance—on how things appear to someone. It implies that this complex, single image is constructed by someone, representing how she or he sees, which has in turn to be reconstructed by the reader. Thus, the stark presentation, without introduction or narrative or any syntactic effort to situate the image (the poem is grammatically a sentence fragment), places the burden on the reader's imaginative effort to re-construct the logic of the composition, in order to arrive at last at its complex whole.

Indeed, the question of audience, always implied in the way a verse is constructed, here becomes itself a center of poetic form— a form that dramatizes how the individual must reconstruct the poem in reading it. Radically assertive of poetic imagination, the poem insists on the reader's effort to achieve the poem's vision. This increased responsibility and demand—indeed, strain—on the reader may have developed out of a sense among early twentieth-century writers of their uncertain relationship to an audience with whom they may not have shared cultural commitments, interests, and norms, and also of art's uncertain place in the modern cultural world. Modernist poetry thus is another example of the dynamic nature of verse form, as it responds to changing conceptions of the place of poetry, its functions, and the situation of poet and reader. If the modern poem's form suggests a greater independence of art as object, it also demands a greater effort from the audience to participate in its very composition. It is as if the challenge of relationship is become greater, with artist, art, and audience more isolated from each other; but also, therefore, that crossing the poem's distances requires a greater energy which, like the jump of an electric charge from pole to pole, sparks a more dramatic accomplishment.

Personification 8

Poetic figures can be small or large, brief moments in a text or general organizing principles. Personification, like poetic conventions (topoi) or simile, can take either form and size. Yet even when appearing as a single or discrete image in a text, personification has wide implications for poetic language generally; and its historical course marks important developments in the history of poetry.

Personification is basically a type of comparison and in this sense is a subset of simile and metaphor. But it is a comparison of a particular kind, in that it always likens something that is not human to the human realm. The comparison may be implicit, as in metaphor, or explicit, as in simile. Or, as in the earliest personifications, an animate figure may represent an abstraction or idea, or may project as an acting person emotions or concerns that are internal to human experience. Edmund Spenser, for example, has characters in *The Faerie Queene* called "Despair" or "Sans Joy" (without joy) or "Una" (unity). In these cases, an emotion (despair, joy) or an abstract idea (unity) is represented as a human character, that is, personified. Personification here is closely linked to allegory. (There is another closely related figure, *prosopopoeia*, where an inanimate object or absent, imaginary, or dead person or thing speaks, acts, or moves.) In personification, then, something not itself a human person acts, speaks, or otherwise exhibits human traits, creating a comparison between the human and non-human realms. The category can, however, be subdivided in turn, depending on whether the non-human term is animate or inanimate, alive or dead, abstract or concrete, and so on; and in accordance with the mode of representation employed.

Although personification is just one kind of comparison, it is in practice a very pervasive and overarching poetic category. After all, poets are humans; and the tendency to compare just about anything to the human world is a powerful one. Indeed, it is almost irresistible and in some sense is implicit in every comparison. The very fact that it is we humans who construct comparisons gives to them inevitably some human aspect, some reference to human experience and human orders of organization. Nevertheless, the construction of personification varies from historical period to period.

There are periods in which personification was more common than in others, and more obviously central to poetic imagery and structure. The Renaissance still often personified abstractions, as had been the norm in the Medieval period; Spenser does this with "Despair" and the many other characters in the *Fairie Queene*. In nineteenth-century Romanticism, personification shifted more toward original images blurring the lines between the human and natural worlds and became the overriding poetic figure. The power to see ourselves in nature, as Wordsworth puts it, becomes a defining power, and project, of Romantic poetry: to describe nature as alive and sensible and feeling as humans are. A poem that introduces personification may be more or less self-conscious about it: may simply use it, or may make the use of personification itself an important issue in the text, in a self-reflective way. Such self-conscious reflection on personification is characteristic of Romantic and, even more urgently, of post-Romantic verse.

We have seen a Romantic use of personification in the Wordsworth poem, "I wandered lonely as a cloud." There the various images of the poem—the cloud, daffodils, and stars—all finally referred to the poet's own self. Each of these therefore gained human features; that is, each was personified. In another Romantic poem, Wordsworth's "The World Is Too Much with Us," personification is at once the central figure, the central organizing principle, and the self-reflective center. We might even say that the poem is about personification, its sources and purposes:

> The world is too much with us; late and soon,
> Getting and spending, we lay waste our powers:
> Little we see in Nature that is ours;
> We have given our hearts away, a sordid boon!
> The sea that bares her bosom to the moon;
> The winds that will be howling at all hours,
> And are up-gathered now like sleeping flowers;
> For this, for everything, we are out of tune;

It moves us not.—Great God! I'd rather be
A pagan suckled in a creed outworn;
So might I, standing on this pleasant lea,
Have glimpses that would make me less forlorn;
Have sight of Proteus rising from the sea;
Or hear old Triton blow his wreathèd horn.

This poem is a sonnet—an Italian sonnet, but one in which the octave falls distinctly into two quatrains, and the sonnet's "turn" is slightly delayed to the middle of the ninth line, at the exclamation "Great God!" Within these distributions, each section centers in a particular kind of imagery. The first quatrain uses an imagery of measure. "Too much," "late," "soon," "little," all involve apportionment—the parceling out of parts and the placing or weighing of one against the other. This impulse of division and measure is crystallized and assigned in the second line. "Getting and spending, we lay waste our powers." The diction is expressly economic. We treat "the world" like a great bank account, clocking in our work time and thinking only in terms of what we can earn in order to buy. Such material measure is almost the opposite of personification. Instead of seeing the world in terms of our inner lives, we make our inner lives into an image of material, commercial exchanges. But, in a twist on this commercial language, the poet at once suggests that all of this "getting" of the world is really only "spending." To treat the world as an acquisition, something to be measured and materially possessed, is not a true gain, not a true use of our powers, but their misuse and depletion. It is to "lay waste our powers." It is, then, this material world that is "too much with us," that lays waste "our powers" as poets and as feeling, thinking beings. The poet, already in the first quatrain, begins to move toward what he will urge as a more proper, indeed more truly rich, relation to "Nature." He does so, however, first by lamenting our failure to achieve this proper relation—or perhaps by accusation. "Little we see in Nature that is ours; / We have given our hearts away, a sordid boon!" This fourth line continues the economic imagery: giving away, boon, all imply material exchange, material loss and gain. But it is not a material thing being subjected to this commerce. It is "our hearts" that we have given away—like a material thing, to its, and our betrayal. What ought we to do instead? This is hinted in the third line. Now, "little we see in Nature that is ours." We should instead see in Nature what is ours—should see nature in terms of ourselves—that is, we should personify.

The poem thus contrasts two ways of seeing the world. According to the first, the world is only material. It is something to use and measure. According to the second, the world is seen as meaningful to us as human beings in our emotional and spiritual lives, which is to say, within humanized, personified terms of reference. This second way of seeing, the second quatrain proceeds to explore. The shift from the first quatrain to the second is marked exactly by a shift into personification. "The sea that bares her bosom to the moon" makes the sea feminine, comparing it to a lady baring her bosom (a topos is also suggested here, of mercy, or charity, often figured by bared breasts). Similarly, "the winds" are described as, if not quite human, then at least potentially animate and alive, when they "will be howling at all hours." Even now, when they are quiet, they are personified. "Up-gathered now like sleeping flowers" compares the winds to flowers, and both are personified as "sleeping."

There is a further element in each of these personifications, with further implications regarding personification itself. The action of the sea-lady who bares her bosom is one of opening, of giving, even of exposure. In personifying, the poem implies, we are opening ourselves up to the world, giving ourselves to it—and therefore also to ourselves. The winds that howl "at all hours" contrasts with the measured "late and soon" of the first quatrain's economy. Now we are not tied to a mechanical time clock. We enter freely into the processes of nature. And finally, if the wind is "up-gathered now like sleeping flowers," then we, again, are directly involved, for it is we who gather flowers, who embrace them in pleasure and appreciation; and also it is we who need to be awakened.

The eighth line, which spills over into the sestet, again laments and accuses, declaring not our success in seeing in nature what is ours, but our failure to do so. Yet again, the negative statement of our lack of success implies a positive one as to what we should be doing—even as it also raises questions about how far, in the end, we can succeed. "For this, for everything, we are out of tune; it moves us not. . . ." We should be in some harmony with nature, rather than imposing on it a mechanical measure. We should be moved by it, entering into it and allowing it to enter into us— crossing the very boundaries between ourselves and nature, as occurs in personification. But we do not.

At this point, the sonnet turns, breaking out into invocation and desire.

> . . .—Great God! I'd rather be
> A pagan suckled in a creed outworn;
> So might I, standing on this pleasant lea,
> Have glimpses that would make me less forlorn;
> Have sight of Proteus rising from the sea;
> Or hear old Triton blow his wreathèd horn.

The imagery of this last section is now mythological. The outworn creed of the pagan is the old Greco-Roman mythology, to which Proteus and Triton as sea gods belong. Earlier images are carried forward. The "sleeping" winds now arise as Proteus, and their "howling" becomes shaped as Triton's music. This mythological imagery is no longer the kind of personification we found in the second quatrain. Yet, as we understand from this poem, mythology itself is in some sense personifying. It animates nature, giving it active and intentional life, as expressed in these god-figures. Yet this last section of the sonnet contains, as before, lament. The poet declares that he would like to see nature as mythology once did: to see it as alive and full of purpose, and therefore as close to him, with himself as part of it. But he also admits that this creed is outworn. We are no longer able to see nature in this way. The syntax of the sestet is conditional, based in an unrealized "if." If I were a pagan, then, "So might I, standing on this pleasant lea, / Have glimpses that would make me less forlorn." But the condition is not realized: I am not a pagan. Nor is the vision stable. It comes only in "glimpses." The poem in this sense admits the impossibility of fully leaving the dominant world of getting and spending, the world in which the poet finds himself, which is material and commercial.

Nevertheless, we have had, in this poem at least, "glimpses" that would leave us less forlorn. At least in some conditional, imaginary state, we have seen Proteus and Triton. For all its gainsaying, the poem has conjured these potent, visionary figures. And we have seen the sea and wind come to human life, come toward us in their activity, and become full of meaning for us. That is, the poem's accusations finally goad us toward exactly what it is lamenting we have lost. It achieves the impossible. At least within the space of the poem, it awakens us beyond getting and spending, to a relation with nature that is more intimate, and to a self that is more open, more expressive, more attuned to a Nature that we here see to exist beyond our measure.

This kind of description of inanimate nature in terms of human sensibility has been called *pathetic fallacy*—the false, which is to say imaginary, projection of pathos, feelings, onto nature. The possibilities and implications of a personified nature, of how far, or how convincing, assertions of community between the human and the natural can be, is a consistent Romantic concern. The degree of self-conscious concern, and anxiety, about the limits of personification are the subject of a poem written later in the nineteenth century, "Spring and Fall" by Gerard Manley Hopkins (1844–1889):

> Márgarét, áre you gríeving
> Over Goldengrove unleaving?
> Leáves, líke the things of man, you
> With your fresh thoughts care for, can you?
> Ah! ás the heart grows older
> It will come to such sights colder
> By and by, nor spare a sigh
> Though worlds of wanwood leafmeal lie;
> And yet you will weep and know why.
> Now no matter, child, the name:
> Sórrow's spríngs áre the same.
> Nor mouth had, no nor mind, expressed
> What heart heard of, ghost guessed:
> It is the blight man was born for,
> It is Margaret you mourn for.

Hopkins addresses his poem to a young girl who is grieving over the falling leaves in autumn. He sees her grief as her childish sense of relation to objects in nature as though they were alive, which is to say as though they had human feelings: "Leaves, like the things of man, you / With your fresh thoughts care for, can you?" The child personifies nature, sees in it her own feelings and her own fate. Therefore she is sad when the leaves die. Hopkins, in the next step of the poem, then questions this personification, this sense of identification between the girl and nature. It will, he says, pass with age: "Ah! as the heart grows older / it will come to such sights colder." The personification is here seen as limited. There is no real

identification between the human and natural worlds. Such iden-
tification is due only to the child's own imagination, one which has
not yet come to an adult sense of boundaries between the self and
world. The identification doesn't exist in nature, but only in the
child's "fresh" mind.

This recognition was always part of Romanticism too. It is one
reason that Romantic poets often refer to the figure of the child, or
the peasant, living unself-consciously in nature. And yet, the sense
of the limits of personification, perhaps always recognized by the
Romantics, by no means forces them to renounce it, or makes it
illegitimate. In the Hopkins poem, there is in the end a reassertion
of personification despite its genuine limits. For, after dismissing the
identification with nature as only childish, Hopkins goes on to re-
affirm it, if on somewhat different grounds. "You will weep," he says,
even when you are older and outgrow childhood's sense of nature
as alive. There is a genuine sorrow that the death of the leaves does
make us feel. This sorrow Hopkins presents (although he also says:
"no matter, child, the name") in terms of original sin: "the blight
man was born for." Hopkins was, by the time of writing this, a con-
vert to Catholicism and a Jesuit priest. To him, the grief and sor-
row that sooner or later falls to everyone has a particular name and
nature—the falling into sin and mortality of all human beings since
the first Fall of man and woman in the Garden of Eden. This Fall,
we recall, brought death into the world, not only for humankind
but also for nature. The "Fall" of the poem's title is shown also to
mean the Fall into death and division that is the poem's fuller con-
cern. How the two—the fall of nature's leaves and the Fall of man—
come together has to do with kinds of personification. On the one
hand, the poem undercuts the child's direct identification with na-
ture. This will be outgrown. Moreover, the true source of sorrow
proves not to be in nature, but in man. It is not the leaves, but
"Margaret you mourn for." The poem strongly recognizes that the
move of personification is a move of projection—not a simple unity
between self and nature, but a seeing of oneself in nature, which
finally is a mode of seeing oneself.

The poem thus in one sense dismisses personification, or treats it
critically. But the poem also validates personification. Margaret *has*
recognized her own plight in the scene of the falling leaves. They
have been an important part of her recognizing the truth about
herself—that she is mortal, that her life will in the end, like the

leaves, be blighted to decay. Within Hopkins's religious faith, this recognition of sin and mortality finally points to a "Spring" beyond nature, in redemption—a "Spring" named in the title but not included within the poem's natural setting. The identification with nature which personification implies becomes in the poem so complex as to be almost paradoxical. In contemplating nature, Margaret can come to a true recognition of her own fate. This fate, though, finally points her beyond her natural self, to a spiritual life that is specifically and uniquely human. She is left finally with a sense not of nature, but of herself: "It is Margaret you mourn for." Yet it is only by way of nature that she is able to come to this self-recognition. And to the extent that in her self-contemplation in nature she comes to realize her unique spiritual selfhood, personification remains a powerful and valid mode.

In poetry written subsequent to Romanticism—call it Modernism or post-Romanticism—there is an increasingly critical sense of personification as limited in what it can claim, but also of its importance to understanding and asserting the human position. Because of this, personification in modern verse is strangely balanced between a sense of its inevitable importance, alongside a resistance to it, a skepticism about how far it can take us. Poem after poem seems to be asking: in what ways, and to what extent can we compare ourselves to nature? Indeed, on what basis do we make comparisons at all? Can we know whether, and how, these likenesses exist, or are they in the end products of our own imaginations and our own language patterns? And yet, can we ever do without them?

Personification is placed in this somewhat tense and precarious position in "The Snow Man," a poem by the twentieth-century poet Wallace Stevens (1879–1955):

One must have a mind of winter
To regard the frost and the boughs
Of the pine-trees crusted with snow;

And have been cold a long time
To behold the junipers shagged with ice,
The spruces rough in the distant glitter

Of the January sun and not to think
Of any misery in the sound of the wind,
In the sound of a few leaves,

Which is the sound of the land
Full of the same wind
That is blowing in the same bare place

For the listener, who listens in the snow,
And, nothing himself, beholds
Nothing that is not there and the nothing that is.

The very figure of a snow man is particularly interesting when approached through the problem of personification. In some sense, it is the ultimate personification—the shaping of the actual material of nature into a human figure. Yet it is also the opposite of personification, since it seems also to make man into natural substance: a kind of *reification*—making living beings into *res*, things. The poem seems to be caught between these two possibilities. This is especially so in that the snow man is also a figure for the poet himself, as he tries to position himself in some plausible, but still poetic relation to the natural world.

Thus, the poem on the one hand urges the human to cease its impositions, to try to thin itself out further and further until it approaches some kind of transparency. Only then can it become the scene it witnesses, entering into that scene by erasing its difference from it. That would be to "have a mind of winter," to be oneself "cold a long time." As a man of snow oneself, one could then "regard the frost" and "behold the junipers shagged with ice" not as apart from them, but as part of them. And then one would be able "not to think / Of any misery in the sound of the wind, / In the sound of a few leaves." That is, one would resist personification. One would not hear in the wind any human emotion, any misery (or joy). One would not see in nature one's own condition reflected (or projected). One would defeat exactly what Wordsworth insists poets should do.

This extreme is one to which Wallace Stevens in his verse repeatedly returns. And yet, even as he does so, he also admits it to be hypothetical. He calls, on the one hand, for a kind of factual encounter with the world that would not be mediated by poetic figures such as personification. But he also shows how difficult, how impossible it is to achieve this—and also, how undesirable. Even when trying to assert a world without human features, he can do so only by negation, by resistance. To describe the sound of the wind and leaves in themselves, without human reference, he still requires human reference, personification, even if by way of denial: "not to think / Of any misery." The factual world as something beyond the human can only be encountered by emptying it of the human. The human is in this way still projected, if only in order again to be retracted.

The poem, then, traces not a simple absence of personification, but the attempt specifically to erase it. The fourth stanza goes far in this direction. "The sound of the land / Full of the same wind / That is blowing in the same bare place" almost eliminates the human altogether. The poem here gauges how far this elimination can be taken. But the poem then also comes to consider the consequences of the experiment. Without the human, what is left is a kind of relentless repetition—the sound, the same, blowing in the same. The listener has become, let us grant, "nothing himself," nothing but the snow he witnesses and listens to. This accomplishes an absolute reduction: it succeeds in beholding "Nothing that is not there," which seems to be a way of saying: only what is there. It is the dream of science, of pure fact.

But Stevens has phrased this absolute in the negatives we saw him use earlier. He goes on to complicate it by a further use of the negative—"and the nothing that is." This is a very difficult line, and can sustain many interpretations. To me, it tends to retract, or at least strongly question, the very dream that seemed to motivate the poem. To succeed in eliminating the self from the scene is, it turns out, not to achieve an absolute world of fact, but a world that is empty. Without the presence of the human, there is, for humans, very little left to the world. And yet this final negation in the poem is, with some gesture toward paradox, made as an affirmation: "the nothing that is." The idea of such a nothing—a world without the human—is, for a human, a great act of imagination. It is indeed an idea, a human notion, and one very difficult to attain and construct. The poem ends, then, with an almost paradoxical re-affirmation of the human presence it sets out to eliminate. For eliminating the self is shown to be a tremendous act of human invention.

This is one reading of a poem that can be interpreted in many ways. The burden on the reader to construct his or her understanding of a text is characteristic of Modernism. Within the specific perspective of this poem's treatment of personification, we see a supreme self-consciousness that makes the text as much a consideration of the possibilities, or justifications, of personification as an application or use of it. Personification within modernity thus

has taken a particular turn, becoming almost a form of its own theo-
rization. The poem doesn't just employ but also investigates the
possibility of personification. This self-questioning has been the
mode of personification in post-Romantic poetry. But each period
has had its own mode. Personification provides a vivid example of
how the figures of poetry are themselves historicized, changing
through time and acquiring different functions and effects at differ-
ent historical moments. This becomes more clear by contrasting
Stevens's hesitant and self-conscious use of personification, with its
use in an earlier, pre-Romantic poem, such as "Love (3)" by George
Herbert (1593–1633):

> Love bade me welcome; yet my soul drew back,
>   Guilty of dust and sin.
> But quick-eyed Love, observing me grow slack
>   From my first entrance in,
> Drew nearer to me, sweetly questioning,
>   If I lacked anything.
>
> 'A guest,' I answered, 'worthy to be here.'
>   Love said, 'You shall be he.'
> 'I, the unkind, the ungrateful? Ah, my dear,
>   I cannot look on thee.'
> Love took my hand, and smiling did reply,
>   'Who made the eyes but I?'
>
> 'Truth, Lord, but I have marred them; let my shame
>   Go where it doth deserve.'
> 'And know you not,' says Love, 'who bore the blame?'
>   'My dear, then I will serve.'
> 'You must sit down,' says Love, 'and taste my meat.'
>   So I did sit and eat.

The extraordinary beauty of this poem unfolds on many levels. It
has to do with the poem's metrical shape, with the way Herbert uses
the natural language of speech in a poetic scheme of highly wrought
order and control. This in turn intensifies the homeliness of the fig-
ure of Love, who is portrayed very concretely as a gracious host at
a banquet; but is also the image of love as an emotion; and is finally
an image of Christ as divine host, divine lover, and divine grace. That
is to say, Love here is a personification. It is not a personification of

nature as landscape, but of an emotion or experience, made here into a human figure. It is also a personification of the divine nature; but this only reconfirms and realizes who and what Christ is to the Christian—that is, the human incarnation of divine love and grace.

Personification here differs significantly from the Romantic and post-Romantic examples we have been examining. Not only the objects of personification, but the source or ground of the personification is different, as is the resulting figure. Here, it is not a private vision, constructed as a humanized comparison, which is at work. Rather, an interior emotion—Love—is cast as a human figure, projected into an acting, speaking person. But even as an emotion, Love here is not merely private and personal. The poem's personification grounds the emotion of love in a higher metaphysical principle, indeed as a Divine Person, who exists before and beyond this figure, which represents, but does not invent it as a poetic act of imagination. The result approaches *allegory*, which traditionally used personification in this way: as acting figures representing interior states, often grounding them in metaphysical or moral realities.

In this poem, what is represented through personification is the dogma of Christian communion—the way Christ redeems the sinner, who is in himself undeserving; graciously welcoming him to the communion banquet of divine Love and Mercy. The "meat" at the end is Christ's own body, the eucharist through which each of the redeemed becomes one in Christ. But Love in the poem is also love in a more emotional sense, a love that confronts someone who, out of his own history and guilt, has come to feel that he will never be able to experience such welcome and acceptance from another. This is the focus of the second stanza. These allegorical levels extend, but do not displace, the concrete action of the poem, initiated in the first stanza, which depicts the greeting of a guest by the welcoming, gracious host. Here, then, an abstract, or emotional, or spiritual value or power is personified as an acting person. This kind of personification is very prevalent in Medieval and Renaissance literature. In this poem, it becomes a way for investing human activity with spiritual value as human and social love take on divine reference. Nor is the human imagination the ultimate source of personification here, as it is in Romanticism. Rather, it is God's own incarnation as man, his own willingness to subject himself to personification, that is the source, for this poem, of poetic power.

Poetic voice is often assumed, in the lyric, to mean the voice of the poet. A generalized speaker, called a "lyric I," allows the poet to speak in some pure language, perhaps as the spirit of poetry itself. This notion, however, applies to only one kind of poetic voice. Even in cases where the poem does seem to present the poet as speaking in general, there always remains the individual person as well. Conversely, when the poet seems to speak in his or her own voice, she or he still is speaking as a poet, in poetic language, and not merely privately or casually. To the extent that the poet's audience is implicated in poetic utterance (as we saw it to be in the very structure of verse forms), there is always a further point of reference in the poem as well. Besides the speaking person, there is also the person spoken to, whose responses or expectations may be felt as a point of view, or an implicit voice, which is more or less acknowledged within a given text. There are lyrics that make this doubling of voice quite explicit and central to their discourse. Such texts build into the poem the fact of an audience, or of someone being addressed (addressee), making the poem not a pure lyric voice, but more like a dialogue—perhaps a philosophical debate or argument; perhaps a seduction; or perhaps some other kind of persuasion or explanation. Even a "lyric I" that does seem to be speaking as a single poetic voice may in fact represent or inscribe a multiplicity of voices, a number of different points of view or ways of seeing and speaking.

Poetic voice, that is, rather than being a pure, single, or personal voice, can be complex and orchestrated, with a range of different representations, different stances and points of view, for a variety of purposes. It certainly also involves diction, which can help define a poem's speaker, whether in the role of author or of characters who may be quoted or introduced as other speakers in the text, almost in the mode of reported or represented speech. The complexity of poetic voice is most obvious in poems that are quite explicitly structured through a speaker who is not the poet. In such a poem, the speaker is specifically defined or presented as an invented character and is often presented as if speaking to an invented addressee. This form is called a *dramatic monologue*, a poem which seems to be a speech taken from some dramatic encounter between an imagined character and someone he or she addresses. It was perfected by Robert Browning (1812–1889), whose "My Last Duchess" can serve as an example:

> That's my last Duchess painted on the wall,
> Looking as if she were alive. I call
> That piece a wonder, now: Frà Pandolf's hands
> Worked busily a day, and there she stands.
> Will't please you sit and look at her? I said
> 'Frà Pandolf' by design, for never read
> Strangers like you that pictured countenance,
> The depth and passion of its earnest glance,
> But to myself they turned (since none puts by
> The curtain I have drawn for you, but I)
> And seemed as they would ask me, if they durst,
> How such a glance came there; so, not the first
> Are you to turn and ask thus. Sir, 'twas not
> Her husband's presence only, called that spot
> Of joy into the Duchess' cheek: perhaps
> Frà Pandolf chanced to say 'Her mantle laps
> Over the lady's wrist too much,' or 'Paint
> Must never hope to reproduce the faint
> Half-flush that dies along her throat:' such stuff
> Was courtesy, she thought, and cause enough
> For calling up that spot of joy. She had
> A heart—how shall I say?—too soon made glad,
> Too easily impressed; she liked whate'er
> She looked on, and her looks went everywhere.
> Sir, 'twas all one! My favour at her breast,
> The dropping of the daylight in the West,
> The bough of cherries some officious fool
> Broke in the orchard for her, the white mule
> She rode with round the terrace—all and each
> Would draw from her alike the approving speech,

Or blush, at least. She thanked men,—good! but thanked
Somehow—I know not how—as if she ranked
My gift of a nine-hundred-years-old name
With anybody's gift. Who'd stoop to blame
This sort of trifling? Even had you skill
In speech—(which I have not)—to make your will
Quite clear to such an one, and say, 'Just this
Or that in you disgusts me; here you miss,
Or there exceed the mark'—and if she let
Herself be lessoned so, nor plainly set
Her wits to yours, forsooth, and made excuse,
—E'en then would be some stooping; and I choose
Never to stoop. Oh sir, she smiled, no doubt,
Whene'er I passed her; but who passed without
Much the same smile? This grew; I gave commands;
Then all smiles stopped together. There she stands
As if alive. Will't please you rise? We'll meet
The company below, then. I repeat,
The Count your master's known munificence
Is ample warrant that no just pretence
Of mine for dowry will be disallowed;
Though his fair daughter's self, as I avowed
At starting, is my object. Nay, we'll go
Together down, sir. Notice Neptune, though,
Taming a sea-horse, thought a rarity,
Which Claus of Innsbruck cast in bronze for me!

Although this poem is spoken by one person, and is hence a monologue, it is very specifically addressed to someone else. This means that, from the outset, there are at least two points of view inscribed into the poem: the speaker's and the addressee's. These are discovered in the course of reading the poem, with specifically orchestrated moments of recognition, confrontation, and disclosure. Here, the Duke of Ferrara (the setting is Renaissance Italy) is speaking. As we learn later, he is speaking to the envoy of a count from a neighboring court, giving him a tour of the castle and its art treasures. And, as we learn at last, the envoy has come to negotiate a dowry for the count's daughter, who is slated to become the duke's next duchess. Just why the duke is in need of a new duchess, we learn in the course of the monologue.

Thus, in this text, all we hear are the duke's own words. Nevertheless, we hear them directed to an addressee who has come on particular business. We hear in them this addressee's response, sometimes as specifically marked by the duke, who seems to be answering a question, or a look or gesture, of this envoy. These two points of view or attitudes of speaker and addressee make up the first structural tier of the poem. Although the poem is made entirely of the duke's speech, we hear through it the answering voice of the addressee to whom it is addressed.

We also hear much more than that. Indeed, we as readers are no less central to this poem's structure than is the count's envoy. We too are its audience. And the poem is addressed to us in ways no less calculated and intricate than it is addressed to the envoy. That is, our position or attitude, our answering voice or response, is also taken into account and registered through the poem. We as readers then function as another point of view or attitude. That makes three. But if we say the poem is addressed to us in calculated ways, we must go on to ask by whom. Not by the duke certainly, but rather by the poet. The poet is finally directing the poem's utterance, using it in ways that make the duke say more than he knows, and not only to the envoy, but to the reader, each of whom hears him somewhat differently. A dramatic monologue in Browning's sense thus involves not one but four positions, four participants in its discourse: the speaker, the addressee, the poet, and the reader.

What a dramatic monologue of this kind does is exploit these differences of position in a complex interplay of multiple understandings and responses, ironies and implications. The first and most pointed irony is of course against the duke, who certainly intends to present himself, but has little idea of how much he has, in this speech, given himself away. What exactly has he disclosed? Let us begin with his point of view. He is conducting his guest on a tour of his palace, with special emphasis on his cherished art collection. He is partly himself enjoying his own treasures, about which he cares a great deal, and partly impressing on this envoy the wealth and taste he believes his art collection to display. This he feels will strengthen his position in negotiating a dowry. The envoy will report to the count the great wealth and prestige of the duke, showing him to be a most desirable suitor.

It is to the duke incidental that among these art treasures is a portrait of his last duchess, his previous wife whom he is now in the business of replacing. To him, that is, what he is showing is one among other artworks, acquired by him in one among other ways, with a history that adds to its appreciation much as other artworks are appreciated through their histories. This seems, at least, to be what he consciously admits to himself. For him, the subject of his discourse is the work of art. But for the envoy, and even more for us, the subject of his discourse is himself. Notice how often he refers to himself: "my" last duchess; "I call" that piece a wonder; "I said 'Frà Pandolf by design." Here we catch him carrying on both ends of the conversation. It is not clear whether he has allowed the envoy to speak; whether the envoy has signaled some question by a look; or whether the duke assumes a question he happens to want to answer (as with others visitors who, he says, "seemed as they would ask me, if they durst"). What we learn about him in any case is how much he likes to speak for others, how much he likes to control what he and they say ("by design") and see ("none puts by the curtain I have drawn for you but I").

And yet we also see how partial this control is, how deeply undermined it is by the duke's incredible self-ignorance. His description of his last duchess, from which we learn why she is his "last" duchess, that he had her killed (after the portrait was painted), shows him to be arrogant and cruel, self-centered, and, above all, possessive. Some of this he may himself feel. As he explains, he could perhaps have told her how much he disliked her generosity and sweetness of temper, when he and only he should have been her object of attention: "She had a heart . . . too soon made glad." Yet telling her directly would involve "some stooping; and I choose / Never to stoop." The duke seems to feel this arrogance is his due, entitled to him with his "nine-hundred-years-old name." Still, however much he knows about himself, we who listen to him know more, and the dramatic irony—the discrepancy between the character's and the audience's knowledge—runs against him and in our favor. It is we who see how wrongful is his arrogance and cruelty. He does not see this himself.

How much of this irony is caught by the count's envoy is less clear. We assume he has been at least somewhat unnerved by the ruthless egotism of his master's future son-in-law. Perhaps we see some sign of shock during the display of the portrait, which the duke however takes as a question about the artist. Perhaps there is some flinch or recoil or gesture of escape hinted in the duke's: "Nay, we'll go together down, sir." But we have no indication that the envoy intends to advise his master against the match. We feel he may sufficiently share the duke's world to be impressed by the duke's power. Nor does he object in any way to negotiating marriage as a matter of dowry and object transfer. The envoy is in any case only partially revealed to us, since we can only guess at his reactions by the way the duke reacts to him.

But surely we have better access to ourselves, to our own reactions and attitudes. How do we hear the duke? Our most comfortable role is to judge the duke, who of course earns our dislike. But our own position is not exhausted by harsh judgment of the speaker. Nor is our superiority to him entirely assured. We have, it is true, caught the terrifying drive to possession which motivates the duke, causing us to shudder when he assures the envoy that, despite his insistence on the dowry that is due to him, the "fair daughter's self" is the duke's true, as he puts it, "object." What he wants is to own the other's self, as he wanted to own the self of the last duchess in a way that she somehow denied to him. But while we may be remote from the kind of ownership that involves dowries and titles, we are not entirely removed from what this poem suggests to be another kind of ownership, that of art. In the portrait, the duke has finally achieved the control and possession over the last duchess he desired. There is in the poem a peculiar series of substitutions in which the last duchess's living person becomes a matter of pigment and color, line and design. Her "depth and passion" and "earnest glance" have been transferred from her to the portrait, as part of its aesthetic achievement. Her living blush has become "that spot" of color on canvas. "Paint," the duke goes on to say, "Must never hope to reproduce the faint / Half-flush that dies along her throat." This chilling remark rivets us in the knowledge that the flush on her throat is now nothing but paint, and that it did in fact die after she sat for this portrait. The duke is very pleased with this final possession of his duchess in art, where she remains, as he states twice, "as if alive." For the duke, art is another mode of possession, control, and ownership. But even without his malice, the poem—which is to say the poet—poses us with the question of our own possessive desires, even in so apparently innocent, indeed interesting a form as art. Perhaps art too can become a mere object of possession and status. When we hear the final clang at the poem's end, where the artist casts his subject "in bronze for me," we cannot but wonder at our own habits of appropriation as well.

In terms of poetic voice, what is outstanding about this, as in Robert Browning's other dramatic monologues, is the multiplication of points of view that the poem incorporates, distributes, and directs. Although this poem is structured as the duke's speech, it is also very much the poet's utterance, in a quite different way than any controlled by the duke. These two voices in the poem here work more or less against each other. What the duke asserts, the poet subverts. The two voices are also engaged in a number of different conversations at once. The duke's is directed both at the poem's addressee-envoy and at the reader, who responds to each of the poem's other three participants—speaker, author, and addressee. The four-part construction, which includes poet, speaker, auditor, and reader, each plays off, undercuts, supports, and crosses with the other. The result, for the reader, is a mixed experience of critical detachment and judgment, on the one hand, against the speaker; and yet also of being implicated in the speaker's presentation, if only because any use of a first-person voice initiates (even if in the end it is not fully sustained) an identification of the reader with the "I" who speaks. The first-person "I" is always, in some sense, a seduction. The reader's experience, then, can be described as representing one point of view on the text, but also as shifting between the others in varying degrees of identification and detachment.

The dramatic monologue is one case where the question of poetic voice becomes central and is specifically dramatized. The fact that the "speaker" is a dramatic character clearly distinguishes him or her from the poet, whose voice, however, is no less represented in some manner through the speech-act of the invented character. To speak of the reader or an implicit addressee as "voices" involves extending the term "voice" into more metaphorical, or theoretical, usages. But "voice" is a useful term for indicating the way in which in lyric (as in fiction) different points of view, and also different stances, positions, roles, and even references become drawn into a text.

The dramatic monologue may seem a special case, dramatic in ways that ordinary lyric is not. But this difference is far from complete. Consider, for example, the seduction poems we have analyzed: Edmund Waller's "Song" ("Go lovely rose . . ."); Spenser's

"My Love Is Like to Ice"; John Donne's "The Flea"; Andrew Marvell's "To His Coy Mistress." In each text, the poet is in some sense speaking. But he does so as a seducer. His speaking role in the poem is that of a lover attempting to persuade his lady to requite his desire. There may be, in each case, a historical lady who had been so beguiled by the poet as a historical person. But even if this were so (and it need not be), the poet's self-representation in the poem is more than auto-biographical. It incorporates all sorts of conventional imagery, modes of address, and poetic forms that make the speaker quite stylized. It is as (conventional) lover that the poet speaks in such texts. And he also retains an independent role as poet, to the extent that each text incorporates elements that distance it from mere seduction. In the case of John Donne, the self-representation as lover co-exists along-side a self-representation as courtier: witty, charming, and audacious, but in a constrained and controlled manner. In the case of Marvell, a reminder of death as a warning against seduction appears alongside the plea to make haste. Thus, in each case, the distinction between speaker and poet contributes to the texture and complex effect of the poem. The speaker has his desire, and the poet has his.

There is, in the seduction poem, a similar differentiation between the addressee and the reader. The poem, in each case, is addressed to a lady, whose response is not recounted but whose vulnerability to persuasion directs the poem's rhetoric. We as readers are distinguished from the lady. Only for her is the seduction immediately sexual, and we witness and assess her position from beyond it. Yet, the reader to some extent shares the lady's position, in that our time is also short, and mortality is a pressure under which we live and to which we must respond. We may not be seduced sexually, but we are vulnerable to the poem's argument and urgency. Thus, as in a dramatic monologue, four viewpoints, or voices, are projected. The speaker may be less explicitly dramatized than a dramatic monologue's fully invented character, but he is not merely identical with the poet. He is cast in a role, that of seducer, which the poet may regard quite critically. And the implicit audience of the poem, the lady, is distinguished in important ways from the reader who is affected by seduction, but not toward the same end.

In each of these texts, different figures in the poetic discourse create a complex statement of multiple voices, in complex relation to each other. In other poems as well, the speaker's voice crosses with, but is not fully absorbed into the poet's voice. In "A Poison

Tree," as we saw, the childlike voice of the speaker turned out not
to be Blake's, who in the end quite dramatically broke away from
identification with the speaker. In "Prayer Is a Little Implement,"
Dickinson similarly introduced a devotional voice which proved not
to be entirely hers.

But what of poems apparently written in a single voice, one not
overtly dramatized, but instead spoken by the "lyric I" of the poet?
I think that we can say that even in seemingly straightforward cases,
there will be some multiplication of poetic voice. The poet will al-
most inevitably have some audience in mind, if only the reader,
whom she or he will be addressing, and whose response she or he
will be taking into consideration as a participant in a dialogue felt
to a greater or lesser degree. And the poet will almost inevitably be
presenting himself or herself in some role, even if it be only the role
of the poet. If the speaking voice in a text assumes a role it is called
a *persona*. The term persona, derived from drama, means mask. It
denotes a speaking voice that is stylized, or fashioned, or slanted in
ways that distinguish it from the actor, or, in poetry, from the poet.
The term's application is clear when there is an obviously invented
dramatic character speaking in a text, such as in "My Last Duchess."
But one can also speak of a persona when the speaker is not an ex-
plicitly dramatized character. The poet can take on the voice, or
persona, of a child, as Blake does in "A Poison Tree." The poet can
take on the voice, or persona, of someone in prayer, as Emily
Dickinson does (and also resists) in "Prayer Is the Little Implement."
The poet can speak as a seductor, as he does through many poems
in the English tradition. The sonnet tradition as a whole is founded
in, or deploys, a number of poetic personae: lover, courtier, and even
poet brooding over fame and immortality.

Each of these stances informs not only the speaking voice of the
text, but also its topics, imagery, strategies, and purposes. In Sir
Philip Sidney's (1554–1586) sonnet sequence *Astrophel and Stella*, for
example, Sidney's biographical role as courtier repeatedly informs
the verse. Sonnet 41 is about a tournament in which Sidney partici-
pated that was staged by Elizabeth as court-pageantry:

Having this day my horse, my hand, my lance
Guided so well that I obtained the prize,
Both by the judgement of the English eyes,
And of some sent from that sweet enemy France.

In describing the courtly action of the tournament, Sidney as speaker attests his prowess with the lance in the pageant. But this serves also as an image for his prowess as a poet. And both in turn serve (and are served by) his role as lover, since the ultimate judge of the contest is his beloved, Stella, whom he courts in this display and who is the ultimate "prize":

> Stella looked on, and from her heavenly face
> Sent forth the beams, which made so fair my race.

Thus, Sidney's persona here combines several roles—courtier, lover, poet—which all are mutually defining. Sidney, moreover, is fully aware of this complex and artful construction. As he writes in sonnet 45, where he represents himself as a servant pleading for his mistress's grace: "I am not I, pity the tale of me."

The notion of poetic voice can be used in still broader ways. In the course of a text, a poet may refer to some body of material; some set of conventions; some topical interest or political situation or concern; a theological or philosophical, commitment or dispute; or some aesthetic conception. This particular issue then connects the work with what might be called a conversation going on around it; and its introduction into the text may be described as an additional voice, which the poet engages, either to support or to dispute it. George Herbert writes out of a body of faith that his work supports and realizes; just as Dickinson's writing contests orthodox positions. Shakespeare's sonnets tend self-consciously to address conventions of sonnet-writing, which he ironizes or uses in original ways, thus also complicating and redefining his own voice as speaker. Sonnet 130 is a famous example:

> My mistress' eyes are nothing like the sun;
> Coral is far more red than her lips' red;
> If snow be white, why then her breasts are dun;
> If hairs be wires, black wires grow on her head.
> I have seen roses damask'd, red and white,
> But no such roses see I in her cheeks;
> And in some perfumes is there more delight
> Than in the breath that from my mistress reeks.
> I love to hear her speak, yet well I know
> That music hath a far more pleasing sound:

I grant I never saw a goddess go;
My mistress when she walks treads on the ground.
   And yet, by heaven, I think my love as rare
   As any she belied with false compare.

This "anti-Petrarchan" sonnet invokes conventions in praise of the idealized lady in order to complicate them. The *hyperbole*, or exaggeration, of the lady's eyes, lips, breasts, hair, and cheeks in a blason-like list, here subverts itself, by exposing such praise to be hyperbolic and finally untrue: a "false compare." Diction plays its part. The elevated language of sonnet-love, like the image of the mistress herself, is brought down to earthly "ground" by such low-diction words as "wires" and "reeks." The poem's power, however, is felt only when this address to the Petrarchan conventions is recognized. It is a voice answering back another, conventional sonnet voice that the poem implicitly engages.

There is, as well, a different kind of lady in this sonnet, a "dark lady" of uncertain character and reputation instead of the adored, high personage of the sonnet tradition. It is one of Shakespeare's remarkable departures from the traditional sonnet that in place of the elevated lady, his are addressed first to a young man and then to a dark lady, neither of whom has ever been identified with certainty. This shift in address means not only that the sonnet's addressee has changed but with and through it many of the energies that make up the sonnet as a verse form, including the sonnet's speaker. The dark lady's implicit presence introduces her as a kind of new voice in the poem, as the sonnet itself suggests: "I love to hear her speak." But the poet's own persona, and voice, is also altered. It engages, contentiously, the traditional sonnet speaker's acts of praise. And it takes on the role of a different lover, addressing his lady not in hyperbolic supplication, but in terms that are more human, although, as the concluding couplet implies, not less powerful.

To speak of the conventions of the sonnet as a kind of "voice" which this sonnet addresses and answers back, is to use the notion of poetic voice in a rather broad, figurative sense. Like notions of multiple voices in fiction, a poem's relationship to literary tradition, or to political, philosophical, and religious issues can be thought of as the conversation between different voices. But even within a narrower use of the term, poetic voice can take on different roles in the poem and can exhibit a range of balances and mixtures. On the one hand, even the most apparently personal "I" of a poem, in which the poet seems to be speaking through no voice except his or her own, has in it some act of self-representation, some enactment of a role; and to this extent the poem never offers a simply unself-conscious voice. On the other hand, even when a persona is constructed as a dramatized figure through whom the poem is speaking, the 'mask' always retains some reference to the poet. The boundaries between a lyric I and other represented voices are therefore very varied and flexible.

The importance of poetic voice in a text can also vary: that is, poetic voice may be a central, or a more secondary aspect of the text. In the case of Percy Bysshe Shelley (1792–1822), poetic voice becomes particularly central, thrusting the poet into prominence so that the whole text becomes a kind of figure for him, and claiming special powers for the poet that endow him with almost preternatural sources of authority. Shelley's mastery of poetic voice can be glimpsed in his sonnet "Ozymandias of Egypt," where he succeeds in inscribing in small compass three, even four voices:

I met a traveller from an antique land
Who said: Two vast and trunkless legs of stone
Stand in the desert . . . Near them, on the sand,
Half sunk, a shattered visage lies, whose frown,
And wrinkled lip, and sneer of cold command,
Tell that its sculptor well those passions read
Which yet survive, stamped on these lifeless things,
The hand that mocked them, and the heart that fed:
And on the pedestal these words appear:
'My name is Ozymandias, king of kings:
Look on my works, ye Mighty, and despair!'
Nothing beside remains. Round the decay
Of that colossal wreck, boundless and bare
The lone and level sands stretch far away.

The sonnet opens in the voice of the poet as "I," who recounts what "a traveller" tells him (the second voice), including the inscription on the monument representing Ozymandias's voice (also hinted at in his "sneer of cold command"). The statue itself expresses the vision, or viewpoint, or voice of the "sculptor" who "well those passions read." A kind of reflection on the sonnet as pledged conventionally to a monumental fame that defies death, this poem instead records the decay of monuments, gradually but inexorably worn away by the desert sands. From among the poem's echo-chamber of voices, the poet's emerges in oracular warning against the arrogance of human power, especially when imposed through tyrannical assault. The very embedding of this Ozymandias voice in a series of reports and representations by others chastises its claim to speak above and dictate to others, asserting against the disdain of this "king of kings" the potency of counter-voices.

Oracular, prophetic, and urgent: in Shelley poetic voice acquires mythological dimensions and powers, while however retaining strong political and historical commitments. The political passion of Shelley's voice sounds clear and sharp in these stanzas from his poem "The Masque of Anarchy":

II
I met Murder on the way—
He had a mask like Castlereagh—
Very smooth he looked, yet grim;
Seven blood-hounds followed him:

III
All were fat; and well they might
Be in admirable plight,
For one by one, and two by two,
He tossed them human hearts to chew
Which from his wide cloak he drew.

This is as ferocious a poetic voice as ever was. Here, Shelley gives archetypal shape to his political assault, through the mask, and the seven bloodhounds.

Poetic voice as mythological impulse and historical force becomes both topic and structure in Shelley's powerful "Ode to the West Wind." Throughout this poem, a strong pattern of apostrophe and personification blurs the line between the human voice and the forces of nature, both of which turn out to be deeply implicated in the forces of history. The poem's opening (vocative) lines, "O wild West Wind, thou breath of Autumn's being," unleash the power of apostrophe to give human shape to what it addresses, a personified power reinforced by the images of "breath" and "being." But these images then reverberate back onto the poet figure who is speaking, and who the "West Wind" itself mirrors through a rich invocation of biblical tradition (by way, not least, of Milton) where the wind is the divine voice of prophecy (*ruach elohim*). This circular gesture in which the poet invokes the wind which represents the poet, comes to realization in the poem's final section:

> Make me thy lyre, even as the forest is:
> What if my leaves are falling like its own!
> The tumult of thy mighty harmonies
>
> Will take from both a deep, autumnal tone,
> Sweet though in sadness. Be thou, Spirit fierce,
> My spirit! Be thou me, impetuous one!
>
> Drive my dead thoughts over the universe
> Like withered leaves to quicken a new birth!
> And, by the incantation of this verse,
>
> Scatter, as from an unextinguished hearth
> Ashes and sparks, my words among mankind!
> Be through my lips to unawakened earth
>
> The trumpet of a prophecy! O, Wind,
> If Winter comes, can Spring be far behind?

The poet, having granted the wind agency, pleads to become the wind's agent, its "lyre." Poetry and world become images of each other, together a "tumult" of "mighty harmonies" that burst forth in "the incantation of this verse." As a "trumpet of prophecy" the poetic wind marks a path of destruction through old nature, which is no less a figure here for old history, toward a new creation which for Shelley is fundamentally political. This revolutionary vision, however, takes shape above all as an impetuous poetic voice, a "Spirit fierce" at once invoked and driven, conjured and commanding. The wind emerges as the poet's word; the poet's word drives the wind. Poetry here becomes almost pure voice, the central figure of the text as it calls nature and history to a new birth.

The question of poetic voice offers a special invitation to consider gender and its poetic roles: in what ways do women speak, in poetry, as women? To what extent do they project a feminine viewpoint? But gender may potentially affect almost every element of poetry. Are there particular kinds of imagery that women, or men, might introduce? Is a male stance implicit in (some) traditional verse forms? Would a woman writing in these forms then alter them? If poetic conventions make up a literary tradition, what access do women have to it? Is there a women's tradition of poetry? Are there specific figures, or self-representations, especially associated with women (or with men)? May there even be some sort of gendering embedded in language, in its grammatical orders or usages or constructions?

The very posing of these questions reflects a shift in critical consciousness and discussion. They are relatively new, and are part of an effort to recover and assess the writings of women that have been traditionally pushed to the side, if not altogether omitted, from literary history. Answering them requires investigating the history of literary production and reception; of education; and of gender roles in political, social, and literary spheres. Women's access to an education that could serve as the foundation for literary creativity remained limited up until the nineteenth century. This lack of education obviously constrained women's writing. Poetry presumes, first, literacy, but also a command of the conventions and forms out of which new literature can be created.

The procedures of preservation and transmission also worked against any sense of a women's literary tradition. When women did write poems, they were not incorporated into a curriculum or corpus of works that was passed down. Each woman writer therefore often found herself inventing anew not only her materials, but even more, her role as poet. This question of poetic role is crucial and far-reaching. Claiming the mantle of poetic authority, of self-confident creativity, and of command of an audience, is deeply problematic within the history of feminine roles in culture and society.

The course of women's writing through history has therefore been highly discontinuous. Rather than building on earlier efforts and examples, each woman poet has had, until recently, to make a new beginning. Just this recognition of a history lost and needing to be recovered is a concern only of twentieth-century women's poetry, as is the sense of writing in the name of a woman's tradition that can build on prior works. In twentieth-century writings, the questions of gender in poetry have become increasingly self-conscious and have entered into the composition of the poems themselves. Such self-conscious reflection on issues such as the role of a female poet, or the way a female poet may assume and perhaps redefine the poet's role; on female experience, as registered in point of view, or imagery, or formal expression, or even language; has become the very material for poetry. These topics, and this self-consciousness concerning them, in themselves mark a gendered element in poetic creation.

A list of characteristically feminine figures in poetry might include female speaking voices; female actors; domestic imagery and spaces, traditionally the domain of women; traditional female roles, such as daughter, wife, sister, and mother; female experiences, such as pregnancy and birth; responsibilities such as childcare and sickcare that have typically been delegated to women; traditional female occupations, such as sewing, cloth-making, and cooking; and gendered sexuality. These might extend more broadly into compositional questions. A female voice may be overtly or covertly dissident, projecting a muted and marginal stance against a dominant, official one. Such contest, overlap, merging and distinguishing between dominant and subordinate voices is important in the writing not only of women, but of other groups that are marginal ethnically or socially. Women may introduce different, dissenting, or critical viewpoints into traditional philosophical or religious positions, as in a greater emphasis on everyday and concrete life that has been noticed in women's writings. Literary roles may change dramatically as women shift from the position of silent listener or implicit reader to assertive speaker and authoritative creator. It has even been claimed that language is itself gendered. This, however, seems to me questionable and reductive, closing women off from a full range of possible expression.

Historically, women's writings have been logical as well as associative, experimental as well as traditional, and cannot be characterized in one stylistic way. Yet, female experience in a historical sense may itself comprise a stratum from which arise common representations and new perspectives on culture. Pursuing common threads through women's social experience can serve descriptive as well as theoretical purposes, exploring how women's place in society has been defined in the past. The fundamental definition of woman's social place—as relegated to a private realm and excluded from the public one—has far-reaching implications (if also obfuscations). This gendered division of social space is both ancient and widespread, although in historical fact far from consistent in practice. It is reflected, in literary terms, not only in the kinds of settings women writers have often introduced into their work, but in the very possibility of their writing at all. To write, and certainly to publish, is to go forward into a public realm.

The exterior difficulty and internal ambivalence of such a venture deeply penetrate women's verse: in the history of its publication, including the need for anonymity or pseudonymity when publishing at all; in the kinds of topics women may feel authorized to address; in the genres they feel they can work in; and, perhaps above all, in the modes of women's self-conception and self-representation. On the one hand, to write and publish become acts bordering on rebellion, and may channel or express a sense of anger or outrage at the norms which prevent women from doing so. On the other, women often have hedged their literary enterprises with apologies, defenses, and assurances that their goals, and selves, remain modest. Modesty is not an exclusively female virtue or mode of self-representation; religious writings by men also often project it (though men tend to prostrate themselves before God, whereas women are apologetic in mundane and literary senses, before human audiences). Yet it has through the ages been asserted as a specific, and defining, female norm. Again and again in poetry by women, modesty serves as a central mode of self-representation. It may even be called a specific (and specifically feminized) topos, the modesty topos. As such, it provides a complex frame, at once constraining and reassuring, complicitous and subversive, disarming even as it enables the woman to write and perhaps even to define a female vantage point.

There were some early English women poets. Mary Sidney Herbert (1561–1621), Countess of Pembroke and Sir Philip Sidney's sister, for example, wrote poetry, as did her brother. Yet even she, privileged, educated, and aristocratic, was constrained in the kinds of writing she felt she could undertake. Rather than devoting herself to clearly original works, the Countess of Pembroke, along with other women of her time, engaged mainly in translation (although arguably in highly original ways); not to mention editing, circulating, and in some sense recreating her dead brother's opus. Her family connections at once protected and positioned her, in a familial definition of self that may itself be gendered; yet they also compromised her autonomous position. Lady Mary Wroth (1587?–1651?), her niece, went farther in asserting herself as writer with a distinctive woman's voice. She daringly wrote in genres beyond those, such as letter-writing and diaries, that were comfortably associated with women's (private) spheres; she often replaced heroes with heroines and otherwise challenged women's subsidiary positions, asserting their interests and values. Her *Pamphilia to Amphilanthus* is a sonnet-sequence that makes clear reference to her uncle Sir Philip Sidney's *Astrophel and Stella* but is spoken from a female position (Pamphilia means "all loving," while the name of the unfaithful Amphilanthus means "lover of two"). Wroth in this sequence explores the conventions of sonnet-writing as shaped through address to a lady, by adopting the reverse position of a lady sonnet-writer, thereby incorporating and representing female subjectivity and experience. "False Hope Which Feeds but to Destroy," for example, opens with imagery based in conception, gestation, and miscarriage:

> False hope which feeds but to destroy, and spill
> What it first breeds; unnatural to the birth
> Of thine own womb; conceiving but to kill,
> And plenty gives to make the greater dearth.
> So tyrants do who falsely ruling earth
> Outwardly grace them, and with profits fill
> Advance those who appointed are to death
> To make their greater fall to please their will.
> Thus shadow they their wicked vile intent
> Coloring evil with a show of good
> While in fair shows their malice so is spent;
> Hope kills the heart, and tyrants shed the blood.

For hope deluding brings us to the pride
Of our desires the farther down to slide.

Uncle Sir Philip had begun his grand sonnet-sequence with a
metaphor of childbirth as labor into poetic birth ("Thus great with
child to speak, and helpless in my throes," Sonnet 1). It is striking
that in Wroth's sonnet, motherhood is a trope of defeated pro-
creativity, an image of betrayed hope, violently figured in the agony
of abortion. Femininity and productivity seem excruciatingly at
odds. The second and third quatrains interestingly turn to public
imagery, a realm banned to women. It is figured with no less twist-
ing terror. Tyrants misrule and misleadingly raise up those they
intend from the start to bring down. The sonnet's conclusion could
belong to any homiletic literature condemning pride. Yet, it is still
an unusual end for a Renaissance sonnet, running counter to the
more typical reaffirmation of the sonnet itself as an enduring monu-
ment of poetic fame. Its contrast to, say, Shakespeare's "When in
disgrace with fortune and men's eyes" is instructive. While Shake-
speare's sonnet opens in discouragement, it turns at the end to love
(what Wroth offers as the very emblem of disappointment) as tran-
scending any public favor or achievement: "For thy sweet love re-
membered such wealth brings / That then I scorn to change my
state with kings." Mary Wroth concludes neither with uplifting love
nor public acclaim, but with their bitter renunciation. Her couplet's
final warning against vanity takes its place within an enduring and
recognizable female retraction, a specific call to women to retreat
from pride, accomplishment, and desire.

Perhaps the first woman poet to (re-)gain a broader currency in lit-
erary discussion is Anne Bradstreet (1612–1672), who was also the first
published poet of America. Her work almost uncannily projects
modes and issues that will remain central through the subsequent
history of women's poetry and poetics. Daughter and wife to two
governors of the Massachusetts Bay Colony, and the mother of eight
children, Bradstreet remained within the norms of early Puritan
American society. Nevertheless, she produced a body of poetic work
on both personal and public topics. Her "The Author to Her Book"
was written after an edition of her verse (The Tenth Muse) had been
published without, as she claimed, her prior permission or knowledge.
The poem takes the problem of female publication as its subject, in a
complex of strategies and images that are striking and enduring:

Thou ill-formed offspring of my feeble brain,
Who after birth didst by my side remain,
Till snatched from thence by friends, less wise than true,
Who thee abroad, exposed to public view,
Made thee in rags, halting to th' press to trudge,
Where errors were not lessened (all may judge).
At thy return my blushing was not small,
My rambling brat (in print) should mother call,
I cast thee by as one unfit for light,
Thy visage was so irksome in my sight;
Yet being mine own, at length affection would
Thy blemishes amend, if so I could:
I washed thy face, but more defects I saw,
And rubbing off a spot still made a flaw.
I stretched thy joints to make thee even feet,
Yet still thou run'st more hobbling than is meet;
In better dress to trim thee was my mind,
But nought save homespun cloth i' th' house I find.
In this array 'mongst vulgars may'st thou roam.
In critic's hands beware thou dost not come,
And take thy way where yet thou art not known;
If for thy father asked, say thou hadst none;
And for thy mother, she alas is poor,
Which caused her thus to send thee out of door.

This poem pursues an elaborate analogy: author is to mother as poem is to child. Authoring itself becomes feminized, and creative power gestational. The poem's scenes are largely domestic. The literary work of revision is figured as care-giving: face-washing, cleaning, training, and clothing a child, with a particular reminder ("homespun cloth") that cloth-making was the task of women at home. Gender is also particularly marked in the poetic voice the poem constructs, which is pointedly humble, woven of concession, apology, and self-deprecation. The child-poem is an "ill-formed offspring of a feeble brain," a domestic product whose exposure to public view displaces it, leaving the faulty result open to censure from (male) critics, while leaving the mother-author embarassedly "blushing."

The poem in its overt rhetoric, established through poetic voice, thus announces itself as unequal to its task. This is a modesty of apparently immense restriction. And yet, the text offers at the same time a counterrhetoric in its figural command. The very accomplishment of its elegant and highly controlled analogy belies the denial of ability which it proclaims. Apparently observing female restrictions, the poem converts them into prodigiously crafted poetic figures. Especially prominent are puns on poetic construction itself: the "halting" metrical feet whose "joints" are stretched; the "rubbing off" of printer's spots; the "rags" which go into paper-making. The command implicit in the poem's texture's peeks through in the odd line: "If for thy father asked, say thou hadst none." Is the poem illegitimate, or autochthonous? Not least, the poem, for all its disclaimers, is written as a dedication to further publication of her work. The concluding lines telescope the poem's double stances. Even while the author declares herself apologetically "poor," she does, in this text, send her poem "out of door" into the public realm.

The modesty exhibited by a Puritan woman may seem quite alien to later norms. Yet its rhetorical markers are perhaps surprisingly enduring. They form a central poetic mode for women poets throughout the nineteenth century. Even such twentieth-century women poets as Marianne Moore (1887–1972) and Elizabeth Bishop (1911–1979) construct their voices with a restraint noted by Bishop herself. In a memoir on Moore, Bishop comments: "I have a sort of subliminal glimpse of the capital letter M multiplying . . . Marianne's monogram; mother; manners; morals; and I catch myself murmuring, "Manners and morals; manners *as* morals? or is it morals *as* manners?"

Bishop herself denied any specifically feminist commitment in her work. Many feel her writing projects a quite neutral, descriptive surface, with little inflection in terms of voice. In Bishop's poetry, however, an apparently unitary or indifferent poetic voice may indeed register various stances and positions. One must distinguish between unitary style and multiplications of voice. A poet might construct a variety of personae and styles and yet still represent through them his own point of view, his own voice, as is often the case with Ezra Pound. Bishop's work points in the contrary direction. Her style may be consistent, but she nevertheless may represent a range of perspectives and viewpoints. The very indifference or muting of her voice may be a gendered mode of restraint in Bishop's self-projection. And specifically female voices often do figure in her verse, as in her "Songs for a Colored Singer."

I
A washing hangs upon the line,
    but it's not mine.
None of the things that I can see
    belong to me.
The neighbors got a radio with an aerial;
    we got a little portable.
They got a lot of closet space;
    we got a suitcase.

I say, "Le Roy, just how much are we owing?
Something I can't comprehend,
The more we got the more we spend. . . ."
He only answers, "Let's get going."
Le Roy, you're earning too much money now.

I sit and look at our backyard
    and find it very hard.
What have we got for all his dollars and cents?
    —A pile of bottles by the fence.
He's faithful and he's kind
    but he sure has an inquiring mind.
He's seen a lot; he's bound to see the rest,
    and if I protest

Le Roy answers with a frown,
"Darling, when I earns I spends.
The world is wide; it still extends. . . .
I'm going to get a job in the next town."
Le Roy, you're earning too much money now.

This first song is a kind of dramatic monologue. A character, who is clearly not the author, is speaking. And yet, the poet remains in complex relationship to this "persona," as also to the second speaking voice in the text, the reported remarks of the speaker's husband. The poem in some ways falls rigorously into gendered alignments. The woman's domestic surroundings—washing, closets, the backyard—stands in contrast to the man's urge to move—"Let's get going." The woman seems quite narrowly defined by this domestic world, anxiously striving to keep up with the neighbors. The man's horizons open beyond not only the narrow space of home but also beyond bourgeois values. But in these senses, Bishop herself seems rather more like the man. Particularly her love of travel, a major part of both her life and her work, is ascribed to him. The poem also represents the woman's plight as not simply of her own making. Her involuntary dependence on the husband, her domestic references, and also responsibilities, imply restrictive roles (but also commitments?) which strongly contrast with the man's freedom to go out into the world.

In this poem, there are a number of distinct patterns of intercrossing voices. There is the woman's stance toward the man, and the poet's toward the woman and the man, within the frame of society's views of gender structures and their requirements, assumptions, and geographies. In general, some multiplicity of voices inevitably enters into any poem, with the poet in dialogue with, and therefore addressing and representing, readers, figures from her own and from general history, and various positions held by her society. The perspective of gender offers another grid on which such poetic constructions of voice, as well as imagery, setting, scale, character, etc. can be mapped.

It is the claim of a feminist poetics that gender should be noted and that it carries with it a history and a politics of literary usages and social expections. Such a critical perspective of course equally extends to poems written by men. From a gendered point of view, for example, the female speaking voice in "Songs for a Colored Singer 1" is no less striking than, say, the total absence of any female reference in Dylan Thomas's "Do Not Go Gentle into That Good Night," which pursues its resolute way through a list of archetypal men: wise men, good men, wild men, grave men, concluding with an agony of son/father.

In a period where both men and women are writing—which is to say, increasingly through the nineteenth and twentieth centuries—questions arise concerning how gender may refract common aesthetic impulses and assumptions into distinctive expressions. The ascribed voice of dramatic monologue, for example, is a Modernist technique Pound and Eliot self-consciously developed in their efforts to attain a less subjective, more impersonal and more sharply defined poetic frame. It has been argued, however, that H.D. (1886–1961), who was closely associated with Pound in the Imagist movement, not only was herself decisive in this cultivation of dramatic monologue but also applied it in ways that specifically derived from and represented her womanhood. Certainly the uses to which

H.D. put her dramatizations are quite different from T. S. Eliot's rather abstract projection of solipsism in "The Love Song of J. Alfred Prufrock," or of character as the Mind of Europe in "Gerontion." In Modernism in general, some crisis of discontinuity with past traditions is at work, generating various strategies of relationship and recovery. In H.D.'s poetry, the projection of a character is often in the service not only of historical recovery but also of redress. H.D. sets out to reclaim lost voices of women, particularly of female figures who have been represented within male mythologies but whose viewpoints have been neglected if not suppressed. One early exemplary text is "Eurydice," which opens:

I
So you have swept me back,
I who could have walked with the live souls
above the earth,
I who could have slept among the live flowers
at last;

so for your arrogance
and your ruthlessness
I am swept back
where dead lichens drip
dead cinders upon moss of ash

This text inaugurates a series of stunning inversions, whose implications widen. The story of Orpheus and Eurydice is one of tragic love, in which the defeat of love is caused by its very intensity, and of male regret, after Orpheus's involuntary look back banishes Eurydice again to the hell from which he has been trying to rescue her. H.D. presents the myth instead through the anger, disappointment, and resentment of Eurydice, who sees Orpheus's gesture as a destructive carelessness if not a dominating arrogance. The poem traces Eurydice's progressive efforts to come to terms with her now irreversible fate. The poem concludes:

VII
At least I have the flowers of myself,
and my thoughts, no god
can take that;

I have the fervour of myself for a presence
and my own spirit for light;

and my spirit with its loss
knows this;
though small against the black,
small against the formless rocks
hell must break before I am lost;

before I am lost,
hell must open like a red rose
for the dead to pass.

Just how convincing this declaration of independence may be remains unclear. The move to self-reliance may seem more defiant than desirable. Certainly it is attained at great cost. But the poem acts to reverse many accepted orders: the (male) gesture of love is unmasked as hostile; hell (and the unconscious) is asserted over the higher world; fated acquiescence becomes apocalyptic vengefulness. Not least, the female viewpoint finds expression against the male's, and in this attempts to reverse the directions of history itself.

H.D. asserts feminized positions against traditions of male ones in her work in a number of ways besides dramatized personae. The poem "At Baia," for example, seems to be a recasting of the *carpe diem* tradition to the extent that the woman, who speaks in the poem, rejects the dream of flowers sent in courtship as perilous (although this rejection also has its costs). And yet, H.D.'s efforts to recover lost feminized traditions equally register the discontinuities it seeks to amend. Her experiments in feminized characters speaking their suppressed experiences were anticipated by many nineteenth- century women poets whose work, however, almost immediately vanished from view after their deaths. Particularly, nineteenth-century poems written about or as if spoken by female biblical figures abound. There is, for example, a sequence of poems written around the figure of Vashti from the Book of Esther. Vashti's defiance of the king—undertaken in the name of modesty— had, apparently, tremendous appeal to these women living in a culture of domestic restriction. Frances Harper (1825–1911), a free black who was one of the most politically radical women of nineteenth-century America, makes clear what is at stake in her treatment of the Vashti story:

"I'll take the crown from off my head
   And tread it 'neath my feet,
Before their rude and careless gaze
   My shrinking eyes shall meet.

. . . .

Strong in her earnest womandhood,
She calmly met her fate

And left the palace of the King,
   Proud of her spotless name—
A woman who could bend to grief,
   But would not bow to shame.

Harper offers a strange mix of fulfilled and contested gender roles. Vashti, bidden to come before the court unveiled, defies the king in the very name of modesty. She refuses to be reduced to mere property or to be displayed as an object and asserts instead her independent personhood. Transmuting the extremely feminized imagery of veiling itself, she makes her "shrinking" a mode of self-assertion. She at the last throws off her queenly status as defined through relation to the king, claiming instead her own (still feminized) "spotless" virtue and, above all, her own identity and voice as "name."

In the late twentieth century, such rebellious expressions of female dissent and protest against inherited cultural norms became more overt and explosive. The restrained indirection of Marianne Moore and Elizabeth Bishop gave way to the direct ideologizing of Adrienne Rich and the disturbing wildness of Sylvia Plath (1932–1963). But gendered readings are not only a matter of unearthing feminized viewpoints. Rather, they explore how gender generally structures experience, not only for women, but also for men. Plath's work reflects across a wide range of Western assumptions and cultural organizations. A poem such as Plath's "The Applicant" is not centered (only) on the implications of a bureaucratic system for women, but rather, on the place of both women and men within denatured, routinized relationships:

First, are you our sort of person?
Do you wear
A glass eye, false teeth or a crutch,

A brace or a hook,
Rubber breasts or a rubber crotch,

Stitches to show something's missing? No, no? then
How can we give you a thing?
Stop crying.
Open your hand.
Empty? Empty. Here is a hand

To fill it and willing
To bring teacups and roll away headaches
And do whatever you tell it.
Will you marry it?
It is guaranteed

To thumb shut your eyes at the end
And dissolve of sorrow.
We make new stock from the salt.
I notice you are stark naked.
How about this suit—

Black and stiff, but not a bad fit.
Will you marry it?
It is waterproof, shatterproof, proof
Against fire and bombs through the roof.
Believe me, they'll bury you in it.

Now your head, excuse me, is empty.
I have the ticket for that.
Come here, sweetie, out of the closet.
Well, what do you think of *that*?
Naked as paper to start

But in twenty-five years she'll be silver,
In fifty, gold.
A living doll, everywhere you look.
It can sew, it can cook,
It can talk, talk, talk.

It works, there is nothing wrong with it.
You have a hole, it's a poultice.
You have an eye, it's an image.
My boy, it's your last resort.
Will you marry it, marry it, marry it.

Plath (like Eliot) has a genius for voices. Here, the rhetoric of bureaucracy, captured in the most appallingly ordinary diction, becomes the governing order through which men and women approach one another. The woman is reduced to a set of functions—bringing teacups and rolling away headaches as a secretary or a nurse. These are placed on the same level as companionship (if this term can be applied to "Come here, sweetie, out of the closet") and other domestic acts, including (again as if equally) to sew, to cook, and to talk, talk, talk. A "living doll" indeed, with the idiom unpacked and exposed.

The poem's sweep through gender roles is far-reaching, including the mourning rites in which the woman herself is to be dissolved, with perhaps a hint at suttee, the forced burning of the widow on her husband's funeral pyre: "To thumb shut your eyes at the end / And dissolve of sorrow." But the poem subtly and ferociously crosses gendered language with other kinds. The poem goes on to observe: "We make new stock from the salt." Here a kitchen-method for making soup (with an allusion to Lot's wife?) itself dissolves into terms of industrial recycling and commercial assurance. Just so, the count of anniversaries as silver and gold are at once and no less counted as stock-values (picking up the earlier image of "stock"). Like a bond that matures, the woman represents an investment over time. But the first promise is: "Naked as paper." Invested as paper money, the woman can also be written over in any way that suits.

The reduction of the woman to mere function is cruel and complete: "You have a hole, it's a poultice. You have an eye, it's an image." She will fill and be utterly defined by (sexualized) need. And yet, the woman is not the sole figure to suffer reduction in this text. The unpleasant opening projects the male as no less disjunctive, piecemeal, wanting, disturbed. He, as "The Applicant," is as compromised and flattened as is she who may be assigned to him. The commercial format of relationship consumes him as it does her. The role of suitor is remade as "this suit—Black and stiff." The whole poem recasts that romantically magic moment of the decisive question: will you marry me? One must ask: Who is asking? Whose language is this?

One feminist theory of voices posits that the dominant social group projects a dominant language, which subordinate groups then adopt and internalize. To unearth, or achieve direct expression of, the subordinate, female voice is one goal of feminist writing and

criticism. Plath's poem complicates this model. In her represen-
tation, a dominant language of commercial and bureaucratic pro-
cessing dominates all others. Its flattened and detached structures
incorporate female and male, with gender one distribution of func-
tion. The female is perhaps more effaced than the male. But the
reduction of the woman entails the reduction of the man, in a
poetic voice that is disturbed and accusatory.

Poetic Rhythm: Meter 11

With poetic rhythm, we have come to a topic that is in some sense the very heart of the matter of poetry. Yet, it can be a mistake to begin a discussion of poetry with meter. The full weight of the importance of the rhythm of the words in poetry can only be felt if you already have some experience with poetry. Otherwise, counting out the accents and the syllables seems at best mechanical, at worst meaningless. But to people immersed in poetry, the sounds of the words, in their rhythms and repetitions, are perhaps the fundamental poetic experience. This is why many of the important discussions of poetry by poets, including many revolutionary moments of transition and redefinition, are put in terms of metrical systems; why many poets say that their writing begins with a rhythmic phrase, even before any specific idea of the poem has come to them; why when you remember a poem, often what you remember is its distinctive rhythm; and why many poets seem unique and even defined through the rhythms characteristic of their writing.

This emphasis on rhythm is directly tied to one of the distinguishing aspects of poetry (although other writing can be poetic in this way): the fact that the particular words of a poem used in the particular order and way the poet uses them are irreplaceable. No other word will do, will fit. What you are experiencing when you experience the poem are those specific word patterns and rhythms, and no other. As the poet Stephane Mallarmé remarked, a poem is not made out of ideas, but of words.

To study the rhythms outside of a poetic context and the whole complex of patterns that make up the poem is to miss the experience that alone makes these rhythms accessible and significant. At the same time, explaining just how and why they are significant is one of the most delicate challenges. In this regard, the greatest temptation is to overemphasize what Alexander Pope called "representative meter." In his "Preface to the Iliad," he describes how Homer's "Measures, instead of being Fetters to his Sense," would "give a farther Representation to his Notions, in the Correspondence of their Sounds to what they Signified." Pope's *Essay on Criticism* offers much-quoted examples of just such mimetic or representative meter. After mocking-while-doing how "ten low Words oft creep in one dull line," or dragging out a "needless Alexandrine" "That like a wounded Snake, drags its slow length along," Pope shows how to do it right, imitating his subjects in his sounds: "But when loud Surges lash the sounding Shore, / The hoarse, rough Verse shou'd like the Torrent roar."

At issue here is the poetic effect of connecting a particular rhythm to a particular meaning. This can indeed heighten the pleasure of poetry, not to mention attest to the skill of the poetic craftsman. Nevertheless, imitative forms alone finally provide a very limited understanding of the functions and powers of poetic meter. It does occur that a rhythm speeds up, or slows down, just like what the poem is talking about. But this is not the central role of poetic rhythm, which works on many levels and does more than illustrate some point of content.

Metrical study can be very elaborate and technical. But meter is, fundamentally, a pattern of emphasis. A given line is defined as having a number and pattern of units. This may be based on accent, or on syllable count, or on some combination of the two, with each unit called a *measure*, or *foot*. The pattern of emphasis begins as a system of expected or established schemes of repeating beats or stresses across the line length: in English, most often five beats to a line of ten syllables. Every language has its own special rhythms, which poetry regulates, or patterns into a design, as it does other features of language. The metrical scheme builds a regular pattern of emphasis in the poetic lines. What it works with to build this rhythm (at least in English) is the way words are *stressed* or *accented*. One syllable receives the accent. Another is unaccented. This is true whenever we speak English. But when we speak, we don't necessarily follow a regular pattern, repeating the same order or sequence of accented and unaccented syllables. In poetry, such a regular pattern is established, although, as we shall see, it is *never* followed perfectly. The true art of meter involves not merely the fulfillment of an established distribution of stressed and unstressed syllables— what John Hollander has called the *metrical contract*. The expectation of a rhythmic pattern is one no (good) poem follows slavishly. Instead, metrical conduct within a poem plays off of variations from, or rather within, a basic framework (this is sometimes called counterpoint). The poetic artist works within, which is to say with and also against, the pattern of expectation, varying its applications and realizations for many different effects. Here, it is useful to recall the discussion of syntax. With syntax, there is a basic, expected set word order, which the poet respects. But the poet is also free to vary from the expected word order, especially when she or he wants to draw special attention to a word or phrase. This is a general rule: anything unexpected draws attention. The unexpected event is highlighted, or given special emphasis.

Meter works this way too. It at once presumes and defies the norms without which it could not even exist. The poem proposes a regular pattern of stressed and unstressed syllables, which it then, sooner or later, also breaks. This is not an error. What happens is, the regular pattern sets up an expectation, which the poet can then surprise. This brings added attention, or weight, to the words that deviate from the pattern. Every departure from the normative, which is to say hypothetical, pattern draws a kind of attention to itself. How that attention might then contribute to the poem varies greatly from text to text or line to line.

The distribution and order of accents in a poem is really the distribution and order of accents in ordinary speech (and the greater the poet, the more this is felt). And yet the poet has greater control, or gives greater premeditated care, to how these accents will be arranged and put together, to create a particular sound for his or her poem. Sometimes the poet works toward making a poem almost indistinguishable in its sound from ordinary speech. Sometimes the poet works toward something much more highly orchestrated, or melodic, or even harsher than ordinary speech would be. Poetry until the twentieth century was closely identified with and even classified by metrical patterns, so an enormous amount of attention has been devoted to their description and classification. In general, when a poem starts out, you expect it will be in some pretty closely specified metrical pattern, which will be the base against which it will play its orchestrated variations of emphasis.

Fortunately for readers of English, despite the many metrical possibilities, very few patterns are actually used in most English verse. The options for English versification were largely narrowed by the fourteenth century, mainly because of the triumph of Geoffrey Chaucer (1343–1400). It was Chaucer who regularized the English line into ten syllables with five beats, also introducing rhyme in the form of couplets as well as other rhyme schemes. Before Chaucer, neither syllables nor rhymes were specifically regulated. Instead, there had been a tradition of Old English verse which relied only on accent: that is, on how many strong beats there could be in a line. This is called *accentual* verse. Syllables are not counted. The lines vary in length, but are held together both rhythmically and through sound repetition. Four heavy stresses or beats are separated by a felt pause or break in the line somewhere near the middle (*caesura*). The lines are further bound together through *alliteration*, the heavy repetition of sounds, not by rhyming, but by grouping together words that begin with the same letter. (This poetic practice can also of course be used with many kinds of metrical form, as when Samuel Coleridge's Ancient Mariner tells how "The fair breeze blew, the white foam flew, / The furrow followed free"; or when Tennyson's Lady of Shalott watches where "The Shallop flitteth silken-sailed / Skimming down to Camelot.") We will not spend much time on this accentual-alliterative model, because it in fact was abandoned in the development of English verse (although some twentieth-century metrical experiments have led back to such accentual-alliterative patterns). *Sir Gawain and the Green Knight* is one of the few accentual works still read widely today (after being lost for several centuries). One brief example from a translation into modern English of the poem can give a sense of this pattern of two beats . . . pause . . . two beats (each half-line is called a *hemistich*), with alliterative repetition of the starting sounds through the word groupings:

> There hurtles in at the hall-door an unknown rider,
> One the greatest on ground in growth of his frame:
> From broad neck to buttocks so bulky and thick,
> And his loins and his legs so long and so great,
>
> .   .   .   .
>
> And in guise all of green, the gear and the man:
> A coat cut close, that clung to his sides,
>
> .   .   .   .
>
> With trim hose and tight, the same tint of green,
> His great calves were girt, and gold spurs under

He bore on silk bands that embellished his heels,
And footgear well-fashioned, for riding most fit.
And all his vesture verily was verdant green.
                    (Translated by Marie Borroff, li. 136 ff.)

The Green Knight "HURtles in at the HALL-door // an UNknown RIder,"in a series of *h* words. The ensuing pattern of *g*-words (greatest on ground in growth; guise all in green the gear; great calves were girt, and gold) pound out the extreme strangeness of this visitor's intrusion into the court.

We will return to the question of accentual meter when we discuss modern metrical experiments. For now, we will turn to the metrical pattern that proved to be the winner in the history of English verse. This pattern was based on Greek, Latin, and French usages. Its novel feature was syllable count. Instead of just counting the heavy beats, syllables are also counted, and they contain or hold the system of accents across the line. The basic English pattern to emerge (from Chaucer) is ten syllables, with five accents, in a scheme of unaccented, accented; unaccented, accented; or te-TA te-TA te-TA te-TA te-TA. The basic metrical unit, or foot (or measure), of two syllables, unaccented, accented, is called an *iamb*: te-TA. The five accented beats it provides in a line of ten syllables is called *pentameter*. The basic English line is therefore called *iambic pentameter*.

By far the greatest part of English verse is written in just this metrical format. But of course, this is only the basic pattern, out of which the poem makes its music through switches and changes:

The beat goes on without a stop or break;
With five each line, just like a metronome.
But if it never varies, no mistake,
You end up with a very boring poem.

There are, in English, really two variations to (or within) this iambic pattern. The first is to reverse the iambic foot. Instead of unaccented/accented (te-TA), there is accented/unaccented (TA-te). This is called a *trochee*. The difference can be heard between *Do NÓT*—an iamb—as in the villanelle by Dylan Thomas:

Do NÓT go GÉNtle ÍNto THÁT good NÍGHT

and *DÓnut*—a trochee (accented/unaccented): DÓnuts HÁVE a FÚNny HÓLE. The same difference can be heard between desSERT (iamb), the after-dinner treat, and DÉsert (trochee), the expanse of sand.

The second major variation on iambic te-TA is two strongly accented syllables in a row: TA-TA. This is called a *spondee*. The pattern becomes, neither Do NOT (iamb) nor DOnut (trochee), but DON'T DON'T (spondee). These changes can be seen in the Dylan Thomas poem. The lines after "Do NÓT go GÉNtle ÍNto THÁT good NÍGHT" go:

ÓLD ÁGE should BÚRN and RÁVE at CLÓSE of DÁY
RÁGE, RÁGE aGAÍNST the DÝing ÓF the LÍGHT.

Here there is room for discrimination. "Old age" might be read as iambic or spondaic. But "Ráge, ráge" is certainly a spondee. The problem remains how to identify whether a syllable is or is not accented. This is finally a matter of ear, and there are always cases that can go different ways. But some helpful suggestions are:

1. A single syllable word that carries weight, that is, that takes emphasis, usually has the accent. Single syllable nouns are such a case.
2. Words that do not carry weight or significant emphasis, such as articles and prepositions, usually are not accented.
3. Parts of words such as prefixes and suffixes usually do not take the accent.
4. The more accents there are, the slower the pace of the line.

The important thing to note is that the great majority of English verse can be *scanned*, or metrically interpreted, through these three measures or units or feet: an iambic base, with trochaic and spondaic variations put in to prevent the deadliness of mere repetition, give emphasis to certain points in the line, and work special effects.

To keep the line from droning on too much
The poet WILL STRIKE CHANGes (with spondee),
VARying METric ORder (through trochee);
He Even can CARry it (dactyl) to such
(enjambment) Lengths (pause), without losing the beat's touch.

This last longer line of twelve syllables is called an *alexandrine*, which was a French norm for what became the ten-syllable line in English. Line length in fact can vary, and is not restricted to the pentameter (five measure) five-beat, ten-syllable lines. There is also the *tetrameter* (four measure) four-beat, eight-syllable (octosyllabic) line, which William Blake uses in his poem "A Poison Tree." There is *common meter*, or hymnal meter, which mixes eights and/or sixes— tetrameter lines with *trimeter* (three measure) three-beat, six-syllable lines, or even *dimeter* (two measure) two-beat, four-syllable lines. Lines can go longer as well, on beyond the twelve-syllable alexandrine to the seven-beat *fourteener* line, used in some kinds of popular ballads and verse.

Besides the two-syllable iamb, spondee, and trochee, there is the *dactyl*, a three-syllable foot (TA-te-te), and its inverse, the *anapest* (te-te-TA). There are other metrical units as well, used less often, mainly in special circumstances. There is a foot, or accent group, of two unaccented syllables together, called a *pyrrhic*, which is usually caught between some sort of metrical switch. There are also metrical effects involved in line phrasing. Enjambment, as we saw, suspends a word at the end of a line, completing the phrase in the following one. This is a syntactic strategy; but it also involves a flowing over of accent pattern. Finally, there is the question of pauses. In ordinary syntax, you pause at predictable places: the end of a phrase, or a sentence. The poet, however, is free to decide where to place the pauses within a poem's lines. The natural place to pause is at the end of a line; and often the end of a phrase or sentence will coincide with the line ending. But the poet can choose to time these pauses inside the line too, really at any place s/he may wish. A very heavy pause in the middle is called a *medial caesura* (the pause, or caesura, can in fact occur almost anywhere on the line).

We all can agree that memorizing these terms in themselves is rather tedious and has little meaning unless set within an actual poem. Besides, conveniently, iamb, trochee, and spondee will cover most eventualities. In the sonnet tradition, for example, as we've seen, the base line is iambic pentameter. But this base-line meter inevitably and necessarily serves as the frame for significant departures from it. We can refer to Shakespeare, who, unsurprisingly, is as great a master of meter as of other elements in the poetic medium. His Sonnet 60 begins:

Líke as the wáves máke towards the pébbled shóre,
Só do our mínutes hásten tó their énd;
Eách changing pláce with that which góes befóre,
In séquent tóil all fórwards dó conténd.

The expectation is of ten syllables to a line, with five beats in an accented pattern of unstressed/stressed, te-TA. But this poem opens at once in variation, with trochees: LÍKE as / the WÁVES, MÁKE towards / the PÉB/bled SHÓRE: trochee, iamb; trochee, iamb, iamb. We are tempted to hear in this pattern the pounding of the tide. This is picked up in the next lines, each of which opens with a trochee and then follows iambic patterning: SÓ do / our MÍN/utes HÁS/ten TÓ / their ÉND; EÁCH chang/ing PLÁCE / with THÁT / which GÓES/ beFÓRE. The last line of the first quatrain switches back to an opening iamb; but then, at one of the sonnet's dramatic junctures, it moves into a spondee: In SÉ/quent TÓIL / ÁLL FÓR/ wards DÓ/ conTÉND. The drive forward is made in the rhythmic fabric of the verse, which turns to spondee (TÓIL ÁLL FÓRwards); with the added emphasis of syntactically creative deviation, as "ALL" and "FORwards" each hovers between a noun and an adjective.

The sonnet form is very rigorously framed in its meter, as in its other patterns. Songs can be much more flexible, each one establishing pretty much the pattern it pleases, then working within whatever base has been constructed. This song from a play by Ben Jonson (1572–1637) (*Cynthia's Revels*) is specifically devoted to metrical rhythm and its effects:

Slów, slów, frésh fóunt, keep tíme with mý salt téars;
Yet slower, yet, O, faintly, gentle springs:
List to the heavy part the music bears,
Woe weeps out her division, when she sings.
    Dróop hérbs, and flówers;
    Fáll gríef in shówers;
Our beauties are not ours:
O, I could still
Like melting snow upon some craggy hill,
    Dróp, dróp, dróp, dróp,
Since nature's pride is now a withered daffodil.

Jonson still plays through the iambic pentameter. He keeps a basic ten-syllable line, with some short four-syllable (dimeter) lines. ("Flowers" and "showers" each acts as one syllable through elision by *synaeresis*: the joining of two vowels in one sound. Other forms of elision, or the dropping of a vowel to fit a metrical unit, are *syncope*—dropping a vowel before a liquid or nasal, as in wand'ring—and *apocope*—dropping a final vowel before an initial vowel, as in th' for the or t' for to.) The poem then ends with an alexandrine, or twelve-syllable closing.

The outstanding feature of the poem, however, is its distributions of stresses. Jonson goes far toward giving each syllable a full accent. That is, he moves the meter as much as he can toward spondee. This has the obvious function of imitating the poem's subject, the drops of the fountain. But there is a more general control of time through pacing. The poem shows how heavy accenting slows the speed of the line down, while the regular iambic pattern speeds it up. "SLÓW, SLÓW, FRÉSH FÓUNT," four strong beats, two spondees; then iambic pentameter: "keep TÍME / with MÝ / salt TÉARS." While we expect the unaccented syllable to be a sort of filler word—the, an, with—it can also handle a word of stronger accent, like "keep" and "salt" (unless these are really more spondees). Then again, in the second line: "YÉT SLÓW/er, YÉT"—spondee/ iamb, but so slowed as to drag out even the "er"; and again, "Ó, FAÍNT/ly"—spondee—into iambs: "GÉN/tle SPRÍNGS." The third line is introduced by a trochee: "LÍST to / the HÉAV/y PÁRT / the MÚ/sic BÉARS." List indeed. HÉAVy is heavy, PÁRT takes on its full part, and the MÚsic BÉARS a very large burden. Then, spondee / trochee / iamb: "WÓE WEÉPS / ÓUT her / diVÍ/sion, [pause] WHÉN / she SINGS." Note, "division" is a pun on musical improvisation, meaning variation on a stated theme. The four-word lines barely drop below spondee: "DROÓP HÉRBS, / (AND) FLÓWERS; FÁLL GRÍEF / (IN) SHÓWERS." The four syllables are so slow paced they seem to demand full accenting, so that even the unaccented "and" and "in" have no space to be swallowed, but seem to carry full weight.

Lines seven and eight more or less return to a quicker iambic pace. But "DRÓP, DRÓP, DRÓP, DRÓP" leaves no choice but spondee. How would one distinguish accent among identical, repeated words? The last line offers steady iambs, as the song hurries to its conclusion about how time hurries to its conclusion. The meter here is certainly imitative, representing the fountain's own sounds. But beyond this, the poem projects how time itself is mediated through its measures, not least its linguistic ones. It is not merely "woe," but the passing of time that the poem describes.

The relationships between metrical and other poetic orders can be explored by looking back on poems already discussed in terms of other topics, this time marking the metrical patterns. Let us therefore return to Browning's "My Last Duchess."

> Thát's my lást Dúchess páinted ón the wáll,
> Lóoking as íf she wére alíve. Í cáll
> That píece a wónder, now: Frá Pándolf's hánds
> Wórked búsily a dáy, and thére she stánds.

Browning is renowned for his ability to reproduce the cadences of a speaking voice. He does so by his skillful variations within his basic metrical frame, which remains iambic pentameter—in this poem carried through rhymed couplets, or pairs of rhyming lines (a device that dates back to Chaucer, as we shall see in the next chapter). The poem opens with a spondee: "THÁT'S MÝ LÁST DÚCHess," underscoring from his very first words the pointing (*deictic*) possessive claim of the duke. The second line starts with a trochee—"LÓOKing"—and then abruptly reverses to iambic pattern for "as ÍF she WERÉ aLÍVE." What follows is an enjambment. "Í CÁLL" (spondee again, again the duke declaring his own activity) / "that PIÉCE a WÓNder, NÓW." The phrase is wrapped around from line to line. Then a stop midsentence (this is a *medial caesura*). The pause or break is followed by a spondee—"FRÀ PANdolf's HANDS/." Enjambment again wraps the syntax around to the next line, into a spondee: "WÓRKED BÚSiLY a DÁY." Break or pause on the comma. "And THÉRE she STÁNDS" brings the first sentence to a close with regular iambs. The end of the line finally coincides with the syntactic unit, and before the mystery of how she "stands" not alive, but as a portrait.

Browning is noted for a kind of choppiness or harshness that brings the poetic rhythm close to speech, an effect of these repeated spondees and enjambments. Gerard Manley Hopkins carries this even further. Hopkins was deeply committed to metrical experiment. Among other notions, he wanted to loosen things up from pure syllable count, recalling the accentual-alliterative verse, which was the road not taken by English poetry after the medieval period. Hopkins thus measures his verse in accent, with a margin of freedom from syllable count. He employs heavy stresses, often marked by strong alliteration (although he does not abandon rhyme). Let us look back on "Spring and Fall," now with an eye toward meter. Hopkins himself marks his accents in this text. Counting the syllables per line reveals that they vary from seven to eight to six syllables in a line. But most lines contain four heavily stressed beats, often distributed in an unexpected way—that is, a way unexpected by the norm of iambics.

Thus the opening line goes: "MÁRgaRÉT, [pause] ÁRE you GRÍEVing." You might call this a line of trochees rather than iambs, with a strongly alliterative G carried over and into the next line. Hopkins called his metrical experiment "sprung rhythm," but it might be described as writing in trochees (and spondees), substituting trochees for iambs as the base line norm. Thus, the second line is also trochaic: "Óver/GÓLDen/GRÓVES un/LEÁVing." But the third line resists regular scansion or metrical assessment. "LEÁVES, LIKE the THÍNGS of MÁN, [pause] YÓU." Spondee, iambs, and one strong accent—more important than the traditional names is the strong four beats. The fourth line is hard to place within an iambic scheme, again tending to trochee and spondee: "with your FRÉSH thoughts CÁRE for, CÁN YOU?" "ÁH! ÁS" is spondaic, followed by a few lines based in trochee:

ÁH! ÁS the HEÁRT grows ÓLDer
It will / CÓME to / SÚCH sights/CÓLDer
BÝ and / BÝ, nor / SPÁRE a / SÍGH
though / WÓRLDS of / WÁNwood LEÁFmeal LÍE"

Scanning Hopkins is a bit subjective. His peculiar stress patterns sometimes end up accenting words ordinarily left unaccented. But the "strong" words, even when in a "weak" spot in the line, continue to pull more than an unaccented word would do. For example, "And YÉT you WÍLL weep ÁND know WHÝ" is iambic; but "weep" seems to carry more than an unaccented beat, although perhaps less than a fully accented one. Even the four-beat system isn't absolutely kept. "Nor MÓUTH HÁD, no nor MÍND, exPRÉSSED" may be four beats. But both "nor"s again seem to carry more than an unaccented weight.

Hopkins's theory of meter is closely tied to his theory of poetry as a whole, which expressed his regard for each individual unit, in both world and language, as a manifestation of spiritual meaning. But many poets discuss their verse in metrical terms. John Milton, in commenting on *Paradise Lost*, makes his starting point his quite innovative use of blank verse—that is, iambic pentameter, but un-rhymed. Before him, it had been used mainly in verse drama, and the poem, while narrative, uses many dramatic techniques. Blank verse, particularly in Christopher Marlowe's hands, had become a highly nuanced instrument for registering speaking voices under dramatic pressure. What blank verse loses in terms of rhyme-structuring, it gains in flexibility (although, because of this lack of tight self-definition, blank verse is less often used in short lyrics). Poetic integration and design is attained through intricate patterns of repetitions and reversals across lines, and through word placement and enjambment in lineation. Milton in any case man-aged to write a narrative poem of thousands of lines with the sus-tained intensity of lyric verse. Here is a speech by Satan, who has just seen and overheard Adam and Eve in the garden of Eden:

> Sight hateful, sight tormenting! thus these two
> Imparadised in one another's arms,
> The happier Eden, shall enjoy their fill
> Of bliss on bliss, while I to Hell am thrust,
> Where neither joy nor love, but fierce desire,
> Among our other torments not the least,
> Still unfulfilled with pain of longing pines;
> Yet let me not forget what I have gained
> From their own mouths. All is not theirs, it seems;
> One fatal tree there stands, of Knowledge called,
> Forbidden them to taste. Knowledge forbidden?
> Suspicious, reasonless. Why should their Lord
> Envy them that? Can it be sin to know,
> Can it be death? and do they only stand
> By ignorance, is that their happy state,
> The proof of their obedience and their faith?
> O fair foundation laid whereon to build
> Their ruin.
>
> (Book IV)

This rehearsal for the arguments Satan will brandish to induce Eve to fall makes use of a network of rhetorical devices, which give the blank verse its strength and cohesive power. Parallel word repetitions, such as "SÍGHT HÁTEful, SÍGHT TORMÉNTing!" (in spondaic pattern), or "Of BLÍSS on BLÍSS," sinuate into antithesis ("bliss on bliss, while I to Hell") and ornately complex word orders: "One fatal tree there stands, of Knowledge called, / Forbidden them to taste. Knowledge forbidden?" *Parallel* repetitions of knowledge / forbidden / / knowledge / forbidden also take shape as a *chiasmus*, or reversed sound and word pattern in: *"Forbidden them to taste. Knowledge forbidden?"* (Chiasmus will be more fully discussed in chapter 12). Enjambment emphasizes key words placed, in Satan's mouth, in compromising contexts. "Why should their Lord / Envy them that?" stresses the word "Lord" even as Satan negates it with his dreadful measure of "envy." This yoking of Lord / envy in effect suggests an oxymoron, with which this passage also concludes, again made emphatic with heavy accenting and enjambment: "Ó FÁIR FOÚNDAtion LAÍD whereÓN to BUÍLD / THÉIR RUÍN."

John Hollander has written a self-enacting definition of blank verse in his book *Rhyme's Reason*:

Iambic five-beat lines are labeled *blank*
Verse (with sometimes a foot or two reversed,
Or one more syllable—"feminine ending").
Blank verse can be extremely flexible:
It ticks and tocks the time with even feet
(Or sometimes, cleverly, can end limping).

There is a sub-subgenre of poems such as this devoted to illustrating metrical effects. Samuel Taylor Coleridge wrote one called "Metrical Feet":

Trochee trips from long to short
From long to long in solemn sort
Slow Spondee stalks; strong foot! yet ill able
Ever to come up with Dactyl trisyllable.
Iambics march from short to long;—
With a leap and a bound the swift Anapaests throng . . .

Alexander Pope studs his *Essay on Criticism* with such self-illustrating verses, as with self-commenting poetics:

But most by numbers judge a poet's song,
And smooth or rough with them is right or wrong:
In the bright Muse though thousand charms conspire,
Her voice is all these tuneful fools admire;

. . . .

While they ring round the same unvaried chimes,
With sure returns of still expected rhymes;

. . . .

If crystal streams "with pleasing murmurs creep,"
The reader's threatened (not in vain) with "sleep";

Some poetic meters seem almost to be self-referring, in that they are so closely attached to some particular verse form as to immediately invoke it. The anapest's relation to limerick is such:

There once was a limerick school,
Which made anapestics its rule;
    All that stomp and pound-pounding
    Just never stops sounding
Like cymbals strapped on a lame mule.

On the other hand, genius can uncover in an eccentric metrical form new possibilities. T. S. Eliot did this with the dactyl. Eliot generally experimented with neglected meters, writing his *Four Quartets*, for example, in a new mode of accentual verse. *East Coker* recreates astonishingly the cadences of an earlier English, within a four-stress line:

On a súmmer mídnight, you can héar the músic
Of the wéak pípe and the líttle drúm
And sée them dáncing aróund the bónfire
The assóciátion of mán and wóman
ín dáusinge, sígnifying mátrimonie—

Each line varies in syllable count but contains two strong beats / pause / two strong beats, as in the earlier verse also recalled by the diction and stylization.

A great innovator in free verse, Eliot observed that no verse that is any good is ever merely free. To my mind, one of Eliot's most stunning achievements is his homology of dactyl with jazz rhythms. Somehow he saw in "TA-te-te" the BOOM-ch-ch of jazz. This is the case at a climactic moment in *Murder in the Cathedral*, where the assassins come in chanting, "Where is Becket, the traitor to the king; Where is Becket, the meddling priest?" in what is essentially jazz rhythm:

> Aré you washed in the blood of the lamb?
> Aré you marked with the mark of the beast?
> Cóme down Dániel to the líons' dén,
> Cóme down Dániel and jóin in the feast.

BOOM-ch-ch, BOOM-ch-ch. Eliot's great play, *Sweeney Agonistes*, is written largely in dactyl-jazz:

> Whén you're alóne in the míddle of the níght and you
>   wáke in a swéat and a héll of a fríght
> Whén you're alóne in the míddle of the béd and you
>   wáke like sómeone hít you in the héad
> Yóu've had a créam of a níghtmare dréam and you've
>   gót the hóo-ha's cóming to yóu
> Hóo hóo hóo

In an early essay, Eliot had written that poetry begins with the beating of a drum. Here he recovers the rhythmic, underlying base of poetic experience, which is also the most powerful (and most pleasurable). He reminds us that within and through metrical technique, poetry is our living language.

Poetic Rhythm: Sound and Rhyme

12

Like metrical rhythms, sound rhythms of poetry are at once the most natural and the most technical of poetic features; mechanical to study and yet a compelling and even defining element of poetry. As with meter, sound patterns can be identified, but in a different sense their effects resist discussion. And, as with meter, the sound structures and patterns that make a poem can't be appreciated outside the many overlaying patterns of language in a text. Yet they do not merely correspond some other feature, such as a "meaning" (which may be in any case only part of what the poem is about) which they in some way illustrate or imitate. Sounds exist first at a level of pure sense enjoyment, of appreciation of words for their own sake, as rhythmic play that may also include multiple relationships through etymology and pun (*paranomasia*). Language in poetry is, to an exceptional degree, material. Poetry celebrates the materiality of language: the shape, sound, body of words, as they embody, and structure, linguistic experience.

Let us take a poem, to start, by Wallace Stevens. Stevens is a gorgeous poet, whose poetic strength particularly displays itself in word play and word sound. Some of his poems almost approach nonsense—poetry organized around the pure sounds of its words.

Bantams in Pine-Woods

Chieftan Iffucan of Azcan in caftan
Of tan with henna hackles, halt!

Damned universal cock, as if the sun
Was blackamoor to bear your blazing tail.

Fat! Fat! Fat! Fat! I am the personal.
Your world is you. I am my world.

> You ten-foot poet among inchlings. Fat!
> Begone! An inchling bristles in these pines,
>
> Bristles, and points their Appalachian tangs,
> And fears not portly Azcan nor his hoos.

Obviously, the most important thing this poem is about is its sounds: its exuberant organization of Ch and Ke and Te and He (not to mention Fat! Fat! Fat!). If you are to enjoy the poem, this is the first and last thing you must enjoy. It is poetry close to music, that is, to pure sound pattern. But the poem is nevertheless more than the nonsense—that is, sound released from semantic meaning—that it also always remains. "Iffucan of Azcan," for example, are pun words for the poetic figures of comparison (as-can) and supposition (if-you-can), with "Chieftan" a grand personification of poetic imagination itself. As such, he is treated with fun, as the big boss, the "damned universal cock," trying to make everything over in his own image, even the sun. Against this imposing Person, the bantams (small but aggressive domestic roosters from West Java—although here first and always a word-sound) insist on their own "I": "I am the personal. Your world is you. I am my world." This line is a kind of chiasmus— a pattern of reversal in word and sound order. The framing words here are repeated in reverse order: world-you-my-world. It also asserts a fundamental Romantic subjectivity. Each of us sees the world through his or her own viewpoint and vision. Yet the poem makes this the basis for a celebration, not of one commanding visionary, but of multiple views, as each bantam asserts his own world. Thus, the "inchling" bantams, despite the Chief "ten-foot poet," are also poets who bid him begone, fearing not "portly Azcan and his hoos"—his Who, or his poetic whose.

Stevens's celebration of multiplicity, while also thematic, makes its loudest assertion through the sounds of the verse, of which Stevens offers a wide variety. There is *alliteration*, the repetition of first sounds in succeeding words (henna hackle halt), and *consonance*, the repetition of consonantal sounds at the end of (or even inside) successive words (the n in caftan, tan, henna). There is *assonance*, the repetition of vowel sounds at the end of (or even inside) successive words (a in tain, can, can, caf/tan, tan). The poem's second line is another kind of chiasmus, that is, a *sound chiasmus*, in which specific sounds, even if not whole words, are repeated inversively: tan/henna/ hackles/ halt. The melodic richness in

Stevens's work often derives from this sort of sound inversion. But sound patterns interweave with other figures: the personification of "Chieftan"; the simile of "as if the sun was blackamoor"; the *apostrophe* (direct address) of "Fat! Fat! Fat!" The poem then is full of sense, but not least the sound sense of its bristling ps, ts, bs, hs.

One sound repetition Stevens here avoids is rhyme; at least formal rhyme, in a scheme with full sound reproduction (he does include caftan / sun, tail / personal). Rhyming has generated a whole terminological vocabulary of its own, depending on the order of repeated sounds (*rhyme scheme*) within varying stanza lengths: there are rhymes that occur within line units of two (*couplet*), three (*tercet*; terza rima), four (*quatrain*; ballad stanza) five (*quintet*; limerick), six (*sestet*; sestina), seven (*septet*; rhyme royal), eight (*octave*), and nine (*Spenserian stanza*). (Of course, poets are free to set up their own metrical and rhyme schemes within their own chosen stanza lengths.) There are different degrees of rhyme, from *full* (such as "Azcan / Caftan" in Wallace Stevens's poem on Bantams quoted above) through various kinds of *off-*, *part-*, or *slant*-rhymes (as in Stevens's "tail / personal" or Sylvia Plath's "The Applicant" quoted in chapter 10 where "crutch" part rhymes with "crotch," "person" with "then," and "salt" with "suit," "fit," "that," and "start"). There are also different rhyme placements: *end* rhymes occur at the end of the line, and *internal* rhymes fall somewhere inside the lines. *Rime-riche* is the use of two words that are pronounced the same way without having the same meaning (*homonyms* and *homographs*). Broken rhyme breaks a word anywhere (beginning, middle, or end) to create a sound repetition. Another issue is the extent to which a verse proceeds line by line (*stichic*) or is organized as stanzas (*strophic*).

But the point of these sundry rhymings can be generalized. (1) Rhyme, like meter, is a system of emphasis. Rhyme words are granted an extra weight, a highlighting, a demand for attention, especially if they take the naturally emphatic position of the last word on a line, as end-rhyme. (2) Rhymes assert some further relationship between the rhymed words. The fact that words rhyme links them together. Are they opposites? synonyms? the same, or different parts of speech? Are they on the same level of diction? Is the relation between them one of deflation? elevation? irony? contradiction? reiteration? In sum, rhymes join with other relationships between words in the intricate network of patterning which together creates the poem's sense.

The sonnet, because of its highly formal nature, provides an intensive stage for examining rhyme (and sound) relations and functions. This, in any case, is the position taken by John Keats. While writing in the subgenre of sonnets on the sonnet, he examines in sonnet form the sonnet's formal patterns of figuration, rhythm, meter, sound, and rhyme:

> If by dull rhymes our English must be chain'd,
> And, like Andromeda, the Sonnet sweet
> Fetter'd, in spite of pained loveliness,
> Let us find out, if we must be constrain'd,
> Sandals more interwoven and complete
> To fit the naked foot of Poesy:
> Let us inspect the Lyre, and weigh the stress
> Of every chord, and see what may be gain'd
> By ear industrious, and attention meet;
> Misers of sound and syllable, no less
> Than Midas of his coinage, let us be
> Jealous of dead leaves in the bay wreath crown;
> So, if we may not let the Muse be free,
> She will be bound with garlands of her own.

This sonnet is, as it itself announces, an elaborately interwoven structure. Its general figure is one of personification. Poetry in the sonnet is a lady (hardly a new idea: that is, a muse). The poem develops complex chains (its own figure) of similes and metaphors: the sonnet as "chain'd" by "dull rhymes" is compared to a prisoner who is "Fetter'd." The sonnet-as-prisoner is like "Andromeda," giving this 'lady Poesy' a mythical narrative frame, which is picked up later with Midas, who however acts as a figure for the poet. The metal of the chains also may look forward to the metal of Midas's gold coinage, and even to the interlacing of the bay wreath crown, the laurel wreath traditionally awarded to poets. The chains again recur at the end, with the Muse still "bound," but this time by "garlands of her own."

Chains and mythology are, however, only two of this poem's interweaving image structures. There is also music—the lyre's chords and stresses—in reference to the sonnet's metrical patternings. And there is clothing—sandals and finally garlands. All of these images beautifully intercross, so that the sounds and syllables are also compared to coinage, which are in turn like the leaves of garlands that finally bind the Muse in an ennabling and celebratory sense. And of course the "naked foot of poesy" refers both to a personified foot and to a metrical one. The interrelationships between these several images create an intricate figural web.

But it is not only this sonnet's images that are interwoven but also its rhymes and sounds and metrics. The sonnet fulfills almost exactly the ten-syllable requirement (one line, "By ear industrious and attention meet," may spill over into eleven syllables, or may involve elision). It is also basically in iambic pentameter: "If BÝ dull RHÝMES our ÉNGlish MÚST be CHÁIN'D." But from the start the poem distributes its pauses oddly, a metrical complication it sustains throughout. "And, [pause] like Andromeda, [pause] the Sonnet sweet" (end stop? or enjambment?) "FÉTTer'd"—a trochee, and pause, then "in SPÍTE of PÁINed LÓVEliNÉSS": here it is the syntax, among all these pauses, that is elaborate. We are still in the middle of the comparison with Andromeda, but with the compared term "the Sonnet sweet" sandwiched in. Then again a trochee, with a pause: "LÉT us find OÚT," and then a switch in the image, midstream, from chains to trochaic "SÁNDals," and from pained constraint to clothed nakedness.

Pure sound should not be neglected, especially not the "rhymes" which the poem starts by calling dull, an accusation it then disproves. Rhyme is a feature of verse that first looks very important; then unimportant and merely mechanical; and finally very important again. There is the challenge, especially in English, of finding rhyme words that appear completely natural and necessary, and not just contrived to fit the rhyme scheme (one of the marks of a minor poem). Accomplishing this often involves the whole syntax of the line, which needs to be constructed so as to prepare for the rhyme it must then offer with apparent effortlessness. Moreover, the relation between rhyming words involves more than sound. The fact of the rhyme brings the two words into special, emphatic contact. It is a contact that will often exploit some relation of semantic meaning and may also raise interesting questions involving the syntax of the rhymed words. In this sonnet (which resists being broken into standard sonnet units of quatrains, octaves, or sestets, since the first pause comes after six lines, perhaps suggesting a reversal of the standard Italian octave/sestet grouping), we have: chain'd/constrain'd (with an internal rhyme "pained," and the part-rhyme "find"). These words seem to rhyme in meaning as in sound, in mutual confirmation. "Fetter'd" and "Let us" also suggest an internal rhyme, although pointing in opposite directions, later picked up by "jealous." "Sweet" goes nicely with "complete," but the first six lines as a complete syntactic unit do not complete their rhyming pattern. We have still to wait to match "loveliness," which rhymes with "stress." "Stress," at once a word of music and of metric, is particularly stressful, spilling over through enjambment into "/ Of every chord," followed by one of the poem's many orchestrated pauses. As to "Poesy," we don't get to its rhyme until much later, first as applied to the poet: "Let us be," and then, near the end, in the thirteenth line, by which point we may have a better sense of how the Muse, for all these constraints, may be "free." The end-rhyme pattern as a whole is indeed most free for a sonnet, running: *abcabdcabcdede*.

There is still more to the rhymes, as they intercross with word-play. In "attention meet" (which itself names the effects of rhyme: gaining attention), "meet" is not a verb, but an adjective meaning deserved, fitting. This picks up on the earlier image of the sandal, "to fit the naked foot of Poesy," and applies generally to metric. There are many other word-plays in sound: misers/Midas; less/jealous; in spite/inspect. There are full internal rhymes such as weigh/may/bay/may. The poem opens with a series of assonances: by/rhymes/like/spite/find. We notice a sustained pattern of L sounds throughout: dull, like, loveliness, lyre, less, leaves, garlands. There is the repeated "let" of "Let us find out," "let us be," "let the Muse." This balances semantically against "must be chain'd, must be constrain'd" and moves the poem in its progress from constraint to controlled freedoms.

The sonnet is this sonnet's main subject, but the poet also figures large. In weaving the poem, the poet also constructs and assembles the materials of his craft, as well as himself as craftsman. His activity is telescoped in the line, "By ear industrious, and attention meet," which is satisfying partly through its sound chiasm: ea—us (ous), tion—ee. There is, indeed, an astonishing range of carefully poised sound repetitions in the poem. Generally, the poem shows how the poetry of the sonnet resides in, rather than being hemmed in by, such an elaborately woven fabric of sound.

Rhyme sequence can be a highly orchestrated art, in which rhymed words are linked in many senses other than sound. George

Herbert is a master of rhyme in this way, as in, for example, his emblem poem, "Easter Wings":

> Lord, who createdst man in wealth and store,
> Though foolishly he lost the same,
> Decaying more and more,
> Till he became
> Most poor:
> With thee
> O let me rise
> As larks, harmoniously,
> And sing this day thy victories:
> Then shall the fall further the flight in me.
> My tender age in sorrow did begin:
> And still with sicknesses and shame
> Thou didst so punish sin,
> That I became
> Most thin.
> With thee
> Let me combine,
> And feel this day thy victory:
> For, if I imp my wing on thine,
> Affliction shall advance the flight in me.

This is a shape-poem, adding visual design to its linguistic ones. It is devoted to Easter, intensely focusing the mystery that the moment of the greatest suffering is also the moment of the greatest redemption. This is a mystery in which every Christian participates, as the avenue of his own redemption in Christ—so that, in the words of this poem, "Affliction shall advance the flight in me." But our interest here is rhyme rather than doctrine. The poem proceeds in *ababa; cdcdc* fashion. But the rhymes are joined together in much more than sound sequence. Wealth and "store" rhymes with a "more" that is really less, since it measures advancing decay, and then arrives at the diminished "poor." This is the poem's motion of descent, obviously realized as well in its metric of progressively constricted lines. Similarly, in the second stanza, "sorrow did begin" finds a syntactic and logical as well as aural completion in "sin" and "thin," while "shame" is all that man, without grace, "became." Then, at each center, there is the turn from descent to ascent, mim-

icking the conversion from death to resurrection that Easter cele-
brates. Again, the rhymes above all mediate this turn. "With thee,"
"harmoniously," "in me," and again, "with thee," "victory," "in me,"
encapsulates the movement of faith Herbert is recounting, of how
man becomes one in Christ. "Rise" and "victories," "combine" and
"thine," are linked as the sequence of grace itself.

Herbert's consciousness of rhyme as a powerful way to bind
words together in meaningful sequence is dramatized in another
poem, "Denial," which examines this binding power by suspend-
ing it. The power of association is emphasized by its absence through
dissociation, by playing on changes or departures from the expected
sound repetition of rhyme. The poem begins:

> When my devotions could not pierce
> > Thy silent ears;
> Then was my heart broken, as was my verse:
> > My breast was full of fears
> > > and disorder:

The sequence of rhyme mimes the verse's broken utterance. Here,
the very possibility of harmonious verse is made dependent upon a
sense of an answering divine audience. This being lacking, the stanza
registers disordered rhyme, most notably in the final line's failure
to rhyme: what is called a *thorn* line. This is a pattern the poem fol-
lows until its last stanza restores a full rhyme pattern, as a sign of its
hope in the divine auditor:

> O cheer and tune my heartless breast
> > Defer no time;
> That so thy favours granting my request,
> > They and my mind may chime,
> > > And mend my rhyme.

We see here, as so often in poetry, that "time" at once refers to the
personal time of experience and the metrical time of the poem, as
does "rhyme," which stands as both a poetic and a spiritual restoral.

Emily Dickinson, whose entire work may be said to inhabit the
disturbed spaces which Herbert resolves at the end of "Denial,"
particularly developed the art of partial rhyming. Dickinson's is a
very calculated art of incompletion. Her syntax requires that her

word groups be painstakingly pieced together. And her sound repe-
titions are purposefully kept off—and slant:

> I reason, Earth is short—
> And Anguish—absolute—
> And many hurt,
> But, what of that?
> I reason, we could die—
> The best Vitality
> Cannot excel Decay,
> But, what of that?

> I reason, that in Heaven—
> Somehow, it will be even—
> Some new Equation, given—
> But, what of that?

This poem pursues a quite rigorous rhyme sequence, but one of
steady deviation from any fully realized rhyme. Short/absolute/
hurt; die/vitality/decay; heaven/even/given: these sequences of
end words only half-echo each other. This insistence on partial re-
alization accords with the syntax of the poem, which is abruptly
truncated into discrete phrases, leading, however, not to any re-
sumed conclusion, but rather to the lack of one. There is a refrain,
or repeated line from stanza to stanza, but it is an unrhyming thorn
line of intense internal repetitions: "But, what of that?" If theodicy
is the justification of God's goodness despite the existence of evil
(an enduring poetic topic and structure), then this poem is a model
un-theodicy or antitheodicy, where even the fulfillment of divine
promise would not be enough to justify suffering. What it confronts
is the absolute lack of correlation: between earthly experience and
heavenly promise, the very concordance Herbert names as the
ground for accomplishing his own beautifully melodic resolution.
In the first two stanzas, the middle half-rhyme contrasts with its
framing words, in a failure of redemptive meanings: "absolute"
between "short" and "hurt"; "Vitality" between "die" and "decay."
The final stanza intensifies the off-rhyming, adding "reason" and
"equation" to "heaven/even/given" before all fail to account, or
to redeem, the disjunctions of this world or this text.

In the history of English verse, there have been swings back and
forth between greater and lesser flexibility, stricter and looser for-

mal requirements. Chaucer, for example, in many ways established the iambic pentameter line and its arrangement into rhymed couplets (later called *heroic couplets*). But Chaucer used the pentameter couplet in very open ways, with rather loose rhymes and rhythms. And he generally wove his couplets into an ongoing narrative or descriptive fabric which kept one line moving into the next. His pentameter couplets are therefore much more malleable and porous than the heroic couplet developed in the eighteenth century by Dryden and Pope. The use of the couplet in eighteenth-century poetry is much more closed. Each two-line unit is a polished frame in which words are carefully set. The syntax tends to be precise and intensive. Diction is made to count, with specified meanings that pull against other, expected ones. Tight rhetorical patterns configure into diverse designs. Alexander Pope is the master at this sort of lapidary couplet.

> Had ancient Times conspir'd to dis-allow
> What then was new, what had been ancient now?

This couplet from Pope's imitation of the *First Epistle of the Second Book of Horace* intricately intercrosses the rhetorical devices of antithesis, balance, and chiasmus (see chapter 13). "Ancient" contrasts with "new"; "new" matches "now." "What then was"/"what had been" balance and repeat (with a caesura between) as a central chiasmic pivot between "ancient" and "ancient." The whole is a rhetorical question, and the rhyme is exact.

Pope here, as surprisingly often, is offering a self-commentary on poetics, writing poems on poetry. The closure of his couplet-units makes it tempting to lift them out of context, but Pope develops his images through a series of couplets:

> Here she beholds the Chaos dark and deep,
> Where nameless Somethings in their causes sleep,
> 'Till genial Jacob, or a warm Third day,
> Call forth each mass, a Poem, or a Play:
> How hints, like spawn, scarce quick in embryo lie,
> How new-born nonsense first is taught to cry,
> Maggots half-form'd in rhyme exactly meet,
> And learn to crawl upon poetic feet.
>
> (*Dunciad* I)

Pope conjures the creation of the world, but as an un-creation. This inversion, or negation, of the impulses to creative order occurs within each couplet, and almost each line, but is also developed through the whole passage. "Dulness" as the presiding Goddess looks down on a Chaos she will only deepen, and a sleeping matter which may awaken, but not into true namings. The teeming waters of primitive life spawn embryos, which will give infant cry. But the cry will be nonsense, the spawn will be "Maggots half-form'd." "Scarce quick in embryo lie," even as it seems to assert life-sources ("quick"), instead makes them "scarce" and gives them the "lie." The whole passage is a figure also for the internal world of poetic production, but of the Dunces, and elaborately correlates each of these malformed unbirths with styles of language (poems, plays, hints, rhyme, poetic feet) that, however, fail (the "poetic feet" only "crawl"). And yet, all this disorder is etched into the meticulous orders of these pentameter couplets, with each rhyme not only complete, but based on a single monosyllabic word to ward away any possible slack (Pope eschews disyllabic or *feminine* rhymes, with their unaccented final syllables, or feminine endings.

After Pope, the pentameter couplet again became almost irregular or invisible, as poets pulled rhymed words across syntactic and metrical enjambment rather than enclosing them in tight phrasing. Browning's "My Last Duchess" marks the difference: "That's my last Duchess painted on the wall, / Looking as if she were alive. I call / That piece a wonder" can only be recognized as couplet-rhyme with ear industrious and attention meet. In the twentieth century—or really, already in the nineteenth, with the radical experimentation of Walt Whitman and, in different ways, of Gerard Manley Hopkins and Emily Dickinson—the norms of formal versification begin to become undone. Ezra Pound speaks of breaking the pentameter and of "Form" in terms of "a 'fluid as well as a 'solid' content." And yet he, like Eliot, warns against merely free verse, where "vers libre has become . . . placid and verbose. . . . The actual language and phrasing is often as bad as that of our elders without even the excuse that the words are shovelled in to fill a metric pattern or to complete the noise of a rhyme-sound" ("A Retrospect").

Free verse does not rely on pre-established formal patternings of meter and rhyme, but gives prominence to other figures to organize the poem. In many ways free experiments have involved a return to earlier verse measures, before English made its metrical decision for iambic pentameter. Gerard Manley Hopkins's rhythms refer back to the accentual-alliterative patterns of Old English verse, before Chaucer instituted the more French form of syllable count with steady-paced accenting in iambs. And both W. H. Auden and Marianne Moore experiment with *syllabic verse* based on counting syllables regardless of accenting. This recalls both the metrical patterns of French, which rely on the number of syllables in the line, and the meters used in classical Greek, which counted lengths of syllables rather than accents and stress-beats (called *quantitative* verse). Such a system of arranging long and short vowels does not readily transfer into a heavily accented language such as English.

Marianne Moore institutes syllable count rather than accents to establish the lengths of her lines. This, however, does not mean that she dispenses with all familiar forms of verse rhythms. She uses rhyme, for example, both at line ends and internally. Her verse also retains a kind of steady, elegant measure. But this is partly due to her insistence that even unaccented, neglected syllables receive a kind of respectful attention. Rhyme in Moore's poetry works in a similar fashion. One thinks of rhyme as the most aural of all of poetry's arts—the clear repetition of sound signaling something significant, such as a line end, or some word deserving special underscoring. In Moore, the expectation of rhyme is used with very particular premeditation. Rhyme is not her master. Moore rhymes when it suits her, mixing rhymed and thorn or unrhymed lines as she sees fit. Rhyme, with metric, become less a pattern to be heard than to be seen, with each verse form a design on the printed page, recalling in some ways the visual emphasis of the shape-poem.

What Moore does is introduce lines of some particular syllable count she has chosen, in some order also of her choosing. She then repeats the particular pattern established in the first stanza through succeeding ones.

> For authorities whose hopes
> are shaped by mercenaries?
>> Writers entrapped by
>> teatime fame and by
> commuters' comforts? Not for these
>> the paper nautilus
>> constructs her thin glass shell.

Giving her perishable
Souvenir of hope, a dull
white outside and smooth-
edged inner surface
glossy as the sea, the watchful
maker of it guards it
day and night; she scarcely

eats until the eggs are hatched.
Buried eight-fold in her eight
arms, for she is in
a sense a devil-
fish, her glass ram'shorn-cradled freight
is hid but is not crushed;
as Hercules, bitten

by a crab loyal to the hydra,
was hindered to succeed,
the intensively
watched eggs coming from
the shell free it when they are freed,—
leaving its wasp-nest flaws
of white on white, and close-

laid Ionic chiton-folds
like the lines in the mane of
a Parthenon horse,
round which the arms had
wound themselves as if they knew love
is the only fortress
strong enough to trust to.

In this poem, "The Paper Nautilus," the form of the opening stanza is in some sense arbitrary. The lines do not follow any fixed, traditional pattern of syllable count, and there is no guiding pattern of accented beat. But its format is then carried through the poem. Here there are five stanzas of seven lines each. Each first and second line has seven syllables; each third and fourth line has five syllables; each fifth line has eight syllables; each sixth and seventh line, six syllables.

There are some minor departures from this pattern, but it is on the whole steady. The same is true, in a regular-irregular way, of the poem's rhymes. Every second and fifth line rhymes, while other lines join in now and again, with internal rhymes contributing. Thus in the first stanza, Moore rhymes "mercenaries" (2) with "these" (5) (and with "authorities" [1]). She also repeats "by" (3) and "by" (4). In the second stanza, "perishable" (1) joins with the main rhyme of "dull" (2) and "watchful" (5) (recalled in the third stanza by "devil" [4]). "Scarcely" (7) perhaps picks up the "by" from the first stanza, but not as a regular pattern (the rhyme makes an appearance in the fourth stanza with "intensively"). "Surface" (4) perhaps goes with "nautilus" (1:6) which perhaps again is echoed in "flaws" (6) and "close" (7) of the fourth stanza, and "horse" (3) and "fortress" (6) in the last. I say "perhaps," because one of the things Moore does is leave the question of rhyme somewhat open. You find yourself asking of rhyme: does it or doesn't it? There is the same possibility and uncertainty with "hatched" (3:1) and "crushed" (3:6); "in" (3:3) and "bitten" (3:7) as well as with patterns of internal "rhyme," where "watched" in the fourth stanza seems to match "hatched" in the third, or "wound" follows "round" in the last stanza.

This uncertainty or openness is a second important feature of Moore's rhymes, after the irregularity of her rhyme schemes, and it leads to a third one. Rhymes, like most special effects in verse, usually serve a function of emphasis. Usually, rhymed words have some special significance, earning them their added weight. But Moore allows any syllable, however insignificant, the dignity of rhyme. She will often choose unimportant, unaccented words or syllables as her rhyme base. Here we see "by" and "——ly" elevated to rhyme. Even the main rhymes involve suffixes, as "ies" of "mercenaries" with "these." This is also the case with "(watch)ful" (2:5) and "dull" (2:2). Actually, Moore's meter and rhyme work in harmony. Her method of syllable-count suppresses the difference between unaccented and accented word units, making all equal. Just so, no word is too unimportant for her to notice it with rhyme.

But here we already have entered the realm of Moore's general aesthetic commitments, which "The Paper Nautilus," like many of her poems, is also about. Moore's poetic makes you attend to every apparent insignificance; makes you appreciate subtle relationships (as in the alliteration of L and the long I and A assonances of the last stanza: "laid Ionic chiton-folds / like the lines in the mane"). This is Moore's very idea of devotion and dignity: quite like the devotion and dignity of the paper nautilus itself, who is a kind of artist too (as well as mother). Her production is only a "thin glass shell," one that is above all "perishable," that shows outwardly only its "dull" surface but creates on an inner surface that is hidden a texture "glossy as the sea." Yet for all this fragility, not to mention the tedious patience of construction, the "glass ram's horn-cradled freight" resists being crushed. It is durable to its purpose, which is to protect the eggs hatched there until they abandon the shell that has given them haven. Here, what joins together is impermanence with dedicated purpose—the willingness to accept a particular task and see it through, within a fragile temporality.

Yet, as the poem shows us, this is a devotion worthy of respect. Note the heroic imagery that creeps in: the comparison to Hercules (albeit in a rather unheroic moment, bitten by a crab) and, above all, the comparison to the great works of ancient Greece, to Ionic columns and a horse on the Parthenon. Moore constructs here in her own similarly restrained and understated fashion a monument to the devil-fish that accomplishes its modest, but as we see essential and admirable task. The implication for poetry is announced in the first stanza, when Moore contrasts her crustacean with "writers entrapped by teatime fame and by commuter's comforts." The art of shell-making reflects Moore's own art of writing—with its quiet construction out of unassuming word units. Each is a figure for the other, a painstaking representation of process and discrimination. Rhyme, meter, word sounds, images come together through a delicate attention to what only seems insignificant, but to which Moore pays homage in a poetic that is as profoundly creative as it is strongly devotional: where "love is the only fortress strong enough to trust to."

Rhetoric: More Tropes

13

When we think of poetic imagery, what we often think of are images of comparison: simile and metaphor and personification. But there is a wide range of poetic tropes, or figures, which have to do with the shape of material within the poem but may not involve the kind of comparison we most associate with poetic imagination. These are rhetorical figures that organize what may be called the poem's linguistic body, the elements of sound and rhythm, of word order and relationship. This does not mean, however, that their power is superficial. While they may rely on word order or positioning, or relationships of contiguity, these tropes are fundamental to poetry. In poetry, we never merely look through, but always also look at, the words that comprise the text. It is poetry's claim that this ordered materiality of language, this poetic body, is profoundly significant and integral to poetic meaning.

What is a trope? A trope is a unit of rhetoric. But what is rhetoric? Rhetoric is the artful and calculated organization of words in writing or speaking so that they can have the greatest impact. This has to do with the ordering of words and components of words, the ordering of phrases, and finally the ordering of sentences into an argument. If the text were a playing field of, say, football, then the words are the players and the tropes are the plays. Unless you organize the players into formations, positions, and patterns, you will never score a goal. The rhetorician (or poet) organizes words into formations, positions, exchanges, and patterns, so as to achieve the greatest impact, emphasis, in short, power.

We have already identified one shape-trope, so to speak, when discussing the material of poetic sound. A chiasmus, as we noted, is a pattern in which a sequence is repeated in reverse: sound A, sound B, sound B, sound A, or word A, word B, word B, word A. In such a case, the design of the poem is strengthened, even if the sequence does not propose some startling likeness that makes you see or think about something in a new light, from a new angle. Chiasmus, as a mere ordering of words or sounds, has a distinguished place in nonsense writing. T. S. Eliot's *Old Possum's Book of Practical Cats*, for example, makes use of it:

> The Rum Tum Tugger is a Curious Cat:
> If you offer him pheasant he would rather have grouse.
> If you put him in a house he would much prefer a flat,
> If you put him in a flat then he'd rather have a house.

House/flat : flat/house. The words wind and unwind. But there is a continuity between Eliot's nonsense and his sense. If we return to his "Love Song of J. Alfred Prufrock," we find there: "there will be time / to prepare a face to meet the faces that you meet;/ there will be time." Here whole phrases are chiasmic: there will be time / a face to meet : the faces that you meet / there will be time. The effect is incantatory. There are many such ordering patterns in language, which contribute to the design of the poem as a highly wrought, intensively self-conscious piece of language. These rhetorical tropes can have a very powerful effect, can make a very strong impression, and are certainly an integral part of the poem's expression.

There are as well tropes that do not rely only on word order, but offer additional specific relationships between the elements in the poem. Among these are *parallelism*, which balances or matches like with like. *Antithesis* brings opposite conditions together, in a contrast that can intensify into paradox, producing an *oxymoron*. *Puns* (paranomasia) play on words' multiple meanings, as do plays on *etymological* histories. There are still other tropes that are basically grammatical: *anaphora* is the repetition of the same word at the beginning of successive clauses or verses; *zeugma* is the use of one word to govern several phrases without being repeated. The following stanza from Spenser's *Faerie Queene* I.iv, describing Avarice, the fourth figure in the pageant of Deadly Sins, provides many examples:

> Most wretched wight [creature], whom nothing might
>   suffise,
> Whose greedy lust did lacke in greatest store,
> Whose need had end, but no end covetise [covetousness]

Whose wealth was want, whose plenty made him poor,
Who had enough, yet wishéd ever more;
A vile disease, and eke in foote and hand
A grievous gout tormented him full sore,
That well he could not touch, nor go, nor stand:
Such one was Avarice, the fourth of this faire band.

Spenser's rhetorical skill not only constructs but intensely overlays trope on trope, providing at once almost a demonstration by example and also a sense of how tropes intensify in their effect when used in specific contexts and in mutual relationship. Among the figures incorporated into this stanza are:

ANAPHORA   Whose greedy lust / Whose need / whose wealth / Whose plenty

PARALLELLISM   Whose wealth was want, [//] whose plenty made him poor

CHIASMUS   greedy lust / lacke greatest

OXYMORON   "lacke in greatest store" (where store and lack are opposites); "wealth was want" (wealth and want are opposites); "plenty made him poor" (plenty and poor are opposites; plenty paradoxically makes him poor)

ZEUGMA   That well he could not touch / nor go / nor stand (well he could not touch, well he could not go, well he could not stand)

PUN / ETYMOLOGICAL PLAY (PARANOMASIA)   "Whose need had end [aim], but no end [termination] covetise"; "whom nothing might suffice" (nothing would be enough for him; or, he would be satisfied only if everything were reduced to nothingness); "the fourth of this faire band," where "band" means group but also bond, the bondage that binds Avarice to the other deadly sins and to his own sinful nature (in this case, the band/bond is "faire" in the sense of just) (Avarice is himself of course an allegorical personification).

Of perhaps special importance are *metonymy*, where one word is associated with another not through similarity but through some spatial association, and *synecdoche*, in which a whole object is represented through some specific part of it. These figures represent by being next to or near to, attached to, worn by, carried by, or part of what they represent. This Spensarian stanza introduces both metonymy and synecdoche in the line "A vile disease, and eke in foote and hand." "Foote and hand" as parts of the monster Avarice's body are synecdoches, representing his state of restless grasping. Similarly, "A vile disease" is something associated with his person metonymically, but it also stands for him, for who he is. Other examples can be found in Alfred, Lord Tennyson's (1809–1892) "The Lady of Shallot," in which the lady, when "in her web she still delights / To weave the mirror's magic sights," is represented by the "web" she weaves on her loom and the "mirror" that reflects it—objects she handles and uses but that also (or thereby) metonymically stand for her. Conversely, Sir Lancelot is represented metonymically by "his blazon'd baldric," "mighty silver bugle," and other details of armor that show his heroic prowess and knightly status. Or again, an example of synecdoche is evident in the image of the bird's wing in "Sympathy," a poem by Paul Laurence Dunbar (1872–1906: "I know why the caged bird beats his wing / Till its blood is red on the cruel bars." The wing synecdochically stands for the bird's longing for the freedom that the cage of history and of race denies him, painfully and indeed violently. It has been argued that such associations by contiguity or spatial relation are as fundamental as simile and metaphor in constructing image-systems, perhaps especially in fiction, and even more especially realist fiction. But these tropes play their significant role in poetry as well. And they never simply function in neutrally descriptive ways. They always also carry with them a representative element, a significant image of what they portray.

Tropes, then, are the names given to the different kinds of rhetorical word formations that writers and speakers have recognized to be particularly effective. Repetition, for example, gives shape and structure to a poem. It can serve, as we saw, to help organize a sonnet; recall how the opening lines of each quatrain may echo each other, repeating syntactic patterns in ways that strengthen the structure and bind the sonnet together. Or, repetition can give an effect of chanting or incantation, or a musical effect. Or it can serve to emphasize a main point. Contrast (antithesis) similarly can be used to structure a sequence—in a logic of opposition rather than repetition. But contrast also can be used to add a sense of strangeness, conflict, or dramatic clash. With oxymoron, contrast becomes self-contradiction, resulting in dramatic and intense images or clashes of ideas. The highly structured sequences and reversals of chiasmus give a tightness and neatness to the poetic sounds or lines. Each of these, then, are word-formations, that is, tropes. They arrange the sounds and the logical workings of the poem, even if the mere fact of, say, repetition, may not seem to contribute new imagery or content to the poem.

There are many other tropes that have literary and poetic functions. Here, I will only be able to review a few examples of tropes that establish some figural relation between the parts of a poem other than likeness, as simile and metaphor do. There is, for example, William Butler Yeats's poem "An Irish Airman Foresees His Death." This is a beautiful, melodic, rich poem. And yet it does not contain a single metaphor or simile. Instead, it makes use of other poetic tropes for its imagery and design:

> I know that I shall meet my fate
> Somewhere among the clouds above;
> Those that I fight I do not hate,
> Those that I guard I do not love;
> My country is Kiltartan Cross,
> My countrymen Kiltartan's poor,
> No likely end could bring them loss
> Or leave them happier than before.
> Nor law, nor duty bade me fight,
> Nor public men, nor cheering crowds,
> A lonely impulse of delight
> Drove to this tumult in the clouds;
> I balanced all, brought all to mind,
> The years to come seemed waste of breath,
> A waste of breath the years behind
> In balance with this life, this death.

This highly wrought poem is constructed through a series of parallel repetitions and contrasting antitheses; through grammatical repetitions and anaphora; through references to place or location, as these metonymically relate to each other; and through chiasmus. The whole poem can even be said to be about placement. It explores how sharing a country may or may not obligate one to one's fellow countrymen. Mere conjunction within a territory need not impel a sense of likeness which could lead to love or loyalty.

Metonymy, or spatial contiguity, is thus the base image for the poem, with a related synecdoche that represents part for whole:

telescoping the entire territorial relation into the single place-name "Kiltartan Cross." Parallelism and antithesis, however, largely govern the poem's rhetorical development. The poem is made up of a series of oppositions. The third and fourth lines oppose: those that I fight / those that I guard; I do not hate / I do not love. The opening and closing of each line aligns against each other. "No likely end could bring them loss" similarly contrasts with "or leave them happier than before." The public, cheering crowd opposes the lonely impulse.

These antithetical or opposing pairs are often set into structures of rhetorical repetition, such as anaphora (Those that I / those that I), or parallelism (My country is / my countrymen; balanced all / brought all). The poem's final phrases form a beautiful chiasmus: "The years to come seemed waste of breath, A waste of breath the years behind." In this sequence, the antithetical "years to come / years behind" form the outside frame around the pivot of the chiasmus, "waste of breath / waste of breath." (This may be called a full chiasmus. There are also *part-chiasma*, where either only the outer frame, or only the inner pivot, repeat and reverse: *axya* or *xbby*). The poem's rhymes tend to posit relationships as well, of intensification or opposition: fate / hate; above / love; fight / delight; crowds / clouds; breath / death. In these ways, the poem achieves in its rhetoric the balanced deadlock which is also its subject. It is as though all of its opposing forces, both in imagery and language, come together to define what is finally a very specific moment or place, exactly at some center between skepticism and obligation, between past and future, "In balance with this life, this death."

Such tropes other than figures of comparison have been used to great effect in poems we have already looked at from other points of view. For example, if we recall "Naming of Parts," we can now see that the whole poem is built around synecdoches and metonymies. The poem follows the exercise of identifying the parts of a gun, against which it contrasts the natural world represented by specific parts of a garden. In each case, synecdoche—part / whole relationship—is at work. And yet there is a great difference between the way the parts of a gun form a whole and the way parts of a garden do. This is one of the underlying issues the poem is examining. The whole relation between the army camp and the garden is metonymic, a relation of place, as is the poet's placement between them—or perhaps his sense of displacement, as the two spaces seem to negate each other, with him caught between them. In this case, we may talk about whether the synecdoches ever come to completion, whether the parts ever make wholes; or whether the metonymic relation between places isn't invoked only to suggest unresolvable disjunctions.

In the case of Spenser's "My Love Is Like to Ice," we may now appreciate, besides the similes we first examined, its structure in terms of parallelism, antithesis, oxymoron, and chiasmus. "Ice" opposes "fire"; "cold so great," "hot desire." The poem's conflicting forces are artfully conducted through its end-rhymes: fire / desire / great / entreat; heat / cold / sweat / manifold. The third quatrain takes shape as a large chiasmus of paradoxical opposition. *Fire* which all things melt / should harden *ice* / *ice* which is congeal'd / should kindle *fire*. Yet these oppositions come together in love, itself the greatest paradox, yet the one most transfiguring, in which all things are possible.

Sonnets, as songs of love, are often devoted to paradox, a trope no less essential to the sonnet's structures and concerns than are simile and metaphor. However, any number of tropes may introduce witty and intricate relationships between word-elements, such as puns. Here is a sonnet by Shakespeare in which he plays with multiple senses of words in witty puns and paradoxes:

Why is my verse so barren of new pride?
So far from variation or quick change?
Why, with the time, do I not glance aside
To new-found methods and to compounds strange?
Why write I still all one, ever the same,
And keep invention in a noted weed,
That every word doth almost tell my name,
Showing their birth, and where they did proceed?
O, know, sweet love, I always write of you,
And you and love are still my argument;
So all my best is dressing old words new,
Spending again what is already spent:
For as the sun is daily new and old,
So is my love still telling what is told.

This poem offers a dazzling display of poverty. Indeed, its main claim is to be boring. And it does seem remarkably lacking in the rich imagery we expect from Shakespeare. This is felt in the way its words repeat. The poem reuses the same words again and again. "So" appears four times; "still" appears three times, as do "love" and "new." "All" appears twice, with the added echo of "almost," "always," and "already." Then there are the different forms of "spending" and "spent," and of "tell," "telling," and "told." But the repetition of specific words is only part of the more general sense of repetition one has reading this poem, which is after all its subject. It seems to be saying the same thing over and over again, full of repetitions such as "still all one, ever the same" or parallellisms such as "my verse so barren / so far from variation or quick change." These indeed seem not to offer anything new or different from what has already been said. Is the poem then poverty-stricken, a mere demonstration of its own inadequacy, as it seems to claim? Not at all. The poem implies and offers multiple senses of the individual words that appear repeatedly through the succeeding lines. There is, for example, in the first line one whole level of punning introduced through the sexual connotations of "barren" (infertile) and "pride," in the sense of sexual desire in females (*OED*). This is picked up later when the poet speaks of his words as "showing their birth," so that he becomes their father (or mother) ("pride" also can connote swelling, as in pregnancy). There is a second level of punning arising from the connotations of dress: "barren" can mean bare or naked, and "pride," the adornment of fine dress. This punning on dress is picked up when the poet claims to "keep invention in a noted weed," that is, in a familiar garment; and also when he talks of "dressing old words new, spending again what is already spent." Here both the expense and effort of dressing fashionably is invoked. But the image of fashion is implicit throughout the first stanza's references to changing with the times, through "new-found methods" and "compounds strange."

But these figures obviously also refer to more than dress. Methods and compounds, following the sexual meaning of "barren," point in a medical direction, as the mixtures for its cure. There is, however, another punning sense, which happens to evoke the poem's central topic. This is the question of poetry itself, "my verse," which is grammatically the poem's subject. Then "new-found methods and compounds strange" refer to compound words and newfound methods of writing that would, presumably unlike this sonnet, be more inventive, daring, and original. "Invention" in the next quatrain has this mainly literary meaning too. It connotes the original creation of something startlingly new and different, here however, in a pun combining writing with dressing, "kept in a *noted weed.*" "Variation or quick change" obviously in this context implicates not only fashion, but also verse writing, and specifically versification, that is, meter.

The metrical variation of this poem within the rather fixed and formalized rule of sonnet iambic pentameter displays great artistry. Thus, it begins with a trochee: WHÝ is my VÉRSE. The second line ends with a spondee: QUÍCK CHÁNGE. The next line again begins with a trochee: WHÝ with/ the TÍME, followed by spondee: to NÉW/FÓUND MÉTH/ods, and (pyrrhic)/ to CÓM/PÓUNDS STRÁNGE.

Back to the puns. The second quatrain repeats how repetitious the sonnet is, as was already said in the first quatrain. In doing so, it brings forward both the sexual implications and the dress imagery from the opening puns. The word "still," which will be repeated, is prominently placed within a spondaic system (WHÝ write I STÍLL ÁLL ÓNE) and can mean either (or both) all the time; and this minute, as though in constant stasis. The quatrain also introduces the word "tell," which comes back at the end in telling ways. It may be worth noting that the image of the "birth" of words suggests more than mere mechanical reproduction. The child after all does not simply replicate its mother or father.

The third quatrain begins the sonnet's "turn," which in the Shakespearean sonnet often doesn't occur until the concluding couplet. Ó KNÓW (spondee) SWÉET LÓVE (spondee) introduces the very high diction of the vocative address, here in the somewhat deflating context of the sonnet's insistent modesty. The next line seems again merest repetition, which is emphasized in the insistence on "and," a conjunction for pure addition: "I always write of you, / And you and love are still my argument." Here "still" has the sense of "continuing to be" or "remaining." "Argument" here mainly means the topic of the poem, as love is often the argument of the sonnet. Yet a specific argument about love also seems to be offered. On the one hand, the poet considers whether this subject of love isn't repetitive, monotonous, and thin (the vocative "sweet love" may be addressed to both the beloved and the topic). But the poem may finally argue for love's, and its own, rich variety. There is a variation (within constancy), exemplified in the following "so" of "So all my best is dressing old words new." "So," as we already noted, is used four times in the sonnet. Yet it is not used each time in the same sense. "So barren" and "So far from variation" uses "so" as an adverb of measure. But in "so all my best" "so" means therefore; while in the concluding couplet "so" acts as a comparative, meaning: just so is my love.

The four last lines almost form a kind of quatrain-unit, against the set convention of sonnet distribution. "So all my best is dressing old words new, / Spending again what is already spent" joins together the multiple figures we have identified of dress, poetics, and sexuality, with an added sense of finances (as part of the problem of sustaining fashion). The words of poetry are here, in a metaphoric construction, compared to clothes. But instead of any real change of garment, the poet makes "new" only what he already has. "New" here in fact means something like "again." But this is a rather new use of an old word, and the pull of poetic uses of words against their ordinary usage is part of the subtlety of a poem which examines the meanings of "invention." Even as the poem declares its own tedious repetition, it shows how repetition can open toward ever new and various senses. "Again" comes up again in the next line, this time in terms of "spending," with its connotation, common in Shakespeare, of the man "spending" himself in sexual activity, but also with regard to affording new clothes. "Spending" can mean spending time as well, which links up with the repeated uses of "still."

Most striking is the paradoxical claim involved in "spending again what is already spent." It asserts a kind of bankruptcy, which in the poem is first a bankruptcy of poetic imagination or energy. Yet it also, in its paradox, reminds us that love is a fund that can never be exhausted. One of love's defining features is just this paradox of plenitude, that however much is given, there is always more. The paradox therefore may look dismissive, as an exposure of bad practices; but it is instead high praise, even a boast. And this is reaffirmed in the couplet. To compare one's repetitions to the sun as ever new and old is to claim something great indeed. Here is the supreme strength and power of fertile energy. And to test this claim to its fullest, the concluding line is almost entirely made up of words already used: so, love, still, telling / told (this using of a single word in different cases, as before with spending / spent, is called *polyptoton*). But "so" is now given the new sense of comparison. "Love" here is neither the beloved nor merely the topic, but an emotion actively moving the speaker. "Still" has moved from the ongoing repetition of continuation to its nearly opposite meaning of holding still, of stopped eternity; while "telling" echoes back to "tell my name," and also the tallying of spending, since to tell also means to count. In the end what these puns add up to is a rich sense of language that, like love, can never be depleted; and that, like the sun, is ever old and new.

The paradoxical figure of oxymoron rivals the tropes of comparison—simile and metaphor—as fundamental to many poems, not only the sonnet. This is the case in the poem "Desert Places" by Robert Frost, a poem often discussed in terms of its themes, its existential predicament, and so forth. On a rhetorical level, the poem works through a pattern of oxymoron, which can form the basis for a textual analysis of it:

> Snow falling and night falling fast, oh, fast
> In a field I looked into going past
> And the ground almost covered smooth in snow,
> But a few weeds and stubble showing last.
>
> The woods around it have it—it is theirs.
> All animals are smothered in their lairs.
> I am too absent-spirited to count;
> The loneliness includes me unawares.
>
> And lonely as it is, that loneliness
> Will be more lonely ere it will be less—
> A blanker whiteness of benighted snow
> With no expression, nothing to express.
>
> They cannot scare me with their empty spaces
> Between stars—on stars where no human race is.
> I have it in me so much nearer home
> To scare myself with my own desert places.

Note how the poem almost does without the comparisons of simile and metaphor; although personification is an important force within it, as a kind of border possibility the poem is exploring. When I look into a field, the poem partly asks, to what extent do I see myself? Here, as so often, Frost is at a limit of Romanticism, of confident or excited or dramatic discovery of reflection between the self and nature. Instead, he seems to be examining and testing the very possibility of identifying with nature, of using it as a form of self-reflection.

The poem seems mostly to be descriptive. And yet, when we look more closely at it, we see that it is very hard to tell what is being described. "Snow falling" and "night falling" are hardly vivid visual objects. On the contrary, they almost define a condition of unseeing, of blocked vision. The field, too, is seen only while "going past," in a hurried and blurred fashion. Its ground is, moreover, hidden—"covered smooth in snow"—so that what is revealed is only some barely visible stubble.

The poem's opening thus already borders on a paradox of describing what cannot be described. The second stanza is similarly paradoxical, this time with regard to the question of belonging or not. The poet first declares that he does not belong to this scene. He is not part of it. "The woods around it have it—it is theirs." The field belongs to the woods, and not to the human passer-by. And yet even this effort to omit or bypass the human still relies on human categories. "It is theirs" grants to the woods a possessive right that only exists within the human world. "All animals are smothered in their lairs" also peculiarly crosses the human into this declaration of the remoteness from animals; for only to the poet do the animals seem smothered. This inability to achieve absence, or betrayal of it in the very attempt to declare it, becomes the center of the next lines. "I am too absent-spirited to count" at once tries to remove the poet from the scene and yet paradoxically declares his presence (note there is an open question as to who will count him: certainly not the animals?). "The loneliness includes me" is itself an oxymoron, since loneliness is a state of exclusion (and also a personification, since "loneliness includes," treats an abstraction as if it were performing an action). "Unawares," finally, contests its own claim, since true unawareness would also be unaware of itself.

The next stanza continues the personification, where the landscape seems to represent the poet himself—yet, again, paradoxically, through its exclusion of him. "And lonely as it is, that loneliness / Will be more lonely ere it will be less." Whose loneliness is this? It can only be the poet's, reflecting his own condition as he contemplates the field. Something oddly at cross purposes is felt here, accomplished in a chiasmic structure (lonely / loneliness / lonely): the poet is relating to the field through a lack of relation. This contradictory rhetoric emerges as direct oxymoron in "blanker whiteness" and "benighted snow." Whiteness is intensified to invisibility, a kind of darkness (be-nighted). As to "no expression, nothing to express," the line paradoxi-cally expresses that there is nothing to express; although paradox moves here toward a rhetoric of negation.

The last stanza brings a sudden shift in perspective. Having thus far looked at the snowy ground, the poet now turns to look into the night sky. This is a scene even more invisible than the others. It represents the most complete absence of the human—the "stars where no human race is." And yet, the stanza opens with clear personification: "They cannot scare me," as though the empty spaces could have any such intent. What we see happening is a kind of convergence between personification, oxymoron, and negation. The poem sets out to deny human presence; and yet, as we see re-peatedly, it cannot possibly succeed in eliminating the human, since the poem is itself a human utterance. But here it also achieves its triumph, paradoxically based in its defeat. In the end, the poet openly declares that through it all, he is indeed the center of his medita-tion. The desert places are within him, and these other, outer ones represent for him figures for his self-discovery and self-contempla-tion. At the same time, he has gone as far as he can toward imagin-ing a world without, or beyond, the human.

His relation to his surroundings is in one sense essentially met-onymic. To stand in a field, or under the sky, is a physical position-ing. But as poet, as human being, physical juxtaposition almost in-evitably occasions meanings personal to him, to his inner world and also to his place in the universe. He discovers that, even while he resists any identity with the universe, it is impossible for him not to personify, not to relate his surroundings in some meaningful way to himself and therefore to see himself in them. In the end, then, he gains the paradoxical insight that even his distance, or difference, from the world is profoundly self-revealing.

Incomplete Figures and the Art of Reading

14

Rhetorical tropes involving word orders and juxtapositions, and also images of comparison such as simile and metaphor, are figures whose various terms are in some sense contained, or designated, within the language of the text. The word order of chiasmus is read out through the line. The comparative terms of simile or metaphor are each proposed within the image's structure. X is like y in some way that names both, and indicates their connection. There are, however, structures of figuration or of representation in which the terms of the figural structure exceed the text, falling outside it in various ways. Such structures include what are often referred to as symbols, although they also implicate allegory, allusions, verse forms, voices, and other contextual and intertextual (i.e., inter-literary and interlinguistic) relationships, as well as certain kinds of ambiguity. I propose calling structures that point beyond the terms immediately given in a text (as in the case of symbols) incomplete figures.

In this sort of poetic structure, a term offered by the text is meant to "stand for" or represent something further, outside the text, which remains unnamed. The term is presented as a figure for some further term. But the text itself does not explicitly define what that further term is. The text withholds what its figure is a figure for, keeping open what the image is meant to represent. X stands for, is a figure for, y. But y is not named or identified within the text itself. In modern parlance, we can refer to the textual term as a *signifier*. But what it signifies is not explicitly specified within the text. This lack of specification may be essential to it, and may in fact never be completely resolvable.

Such an incomplete or open poetic structure puts a special burden on the reader, or rather, puts the reader in a position that in turn has implications for reading poetry in general. The second, undisclosed term may be indicated with greater or lesser precision. Some definite figural correlation may seem to be at work. Or, the figural intention may remain quite undefined, suggesting multiple representational possibilities (which may or may not cohere). What I would like to warn against is the reader's immediately leaping across the figural space to determine the suspended term that completes the figure. In general, if there is some intriguing textual challenge, attention should first be given to examining rather than resolving it. The function of the challenge is itself significant and should be explored before rushing to provide some answer in a conclusive and closed way. In the case of incomplete figures, deciding some particular and definitive corresponding term for the text's suggestive invitation can be reductive, betraying the poet's purposes and simplifying aspects integral to the poem's effects. It also obscures the importance of the inventive effort of the reader, the reader's central role in constructing the text as he or she reads. This is a role that many other poetic features also invite, such as lineation, syntactic suspension and ambiguity, diction choice, formal configuration, and, generally, the figural chains which compose a poem.

One striking example of an incomplete figure that is central and pivotal in the construction of a text is "The Sick Rose" in William Blake's *Songs of Experience*:

> O Rose, thou art sick!
> The invisible worm
> That flies in the night
> In the howling storm,
>
> Has found out thy bed
> Of crimson joy:
> And his dark secret love
> Does thy life destroy.

A rose may be a rose may be a rose; but not this one. Clearly it stands for something more. What is this more? As much emphasis must fall on the question as on the answer. The rose itself has a long history of association and figural suggestion. Here, as often elsewhere, it seems allied with love. But here, there is a sick, a "dark, secret love" (with sick/secret linked through sound). "The invisible worm" must represent some sort of corruption, which turns love's life-giving "joy" paradoxically or tragically or grotesquely into a death-giving destruction. But what is the "secret"?

The whole poem's figural structure turns on this "secret." The "crimson joy" of the "bed" suggests something sexual; and Blake, with his interest in prostitution and its ills, might certainly have a sexual disease in mind. But sex itself might be the disease, at least as it is treated by religious, socioeconomic, and (perhaps) gendered institutions that Blake often attacks, in secrecy and shame (there is an odd manuscript variant which reads "her" dark secret love). Perhaps Blake intends some admonitory echo of the seduction poems that liken virgins to roses. The poem also includes language conventionally associated with religious typologies: the "worm" has long been linked with the snake in the Garden of Eden, who in turn has been made an image of Satan, of evil, and finally of the apocalyptic dragon. The poem does seem to connect some interior corruption with some ultimate, even apocalyptic risk to the world as a whole, stricken by a "howling storm." This being Blake, perhaps it is the suppression of sexual desire which is here apocalyptic and sinful.

The point, however, is not to choose among these possibilities to finalize "what" the rose or the sickness is a "symbol" of. The term symbol is derived from the Greek word *symbolon*, designating the two halves of a coin, each of which is a token of a pledge to be confirmed on their being pieced together again. But it is significant that the symbol implies their separation. There remains a gap, a missing part, which the reader must contemplate, and which is purposely withheld. If the symbol is a sign, what it signifies remains suspended or kept back. This suspension must not be erased. In the case of the sick rose, a variety of possible signified implications come to mind: sexual disease, sexuality, sin, corruption, repression, shame. It is the very openness of structure, however, and lack of specification, that leads the reader to contemplate all of them—not to decide among them, but to consider the accumulation of associations between these various possibilities. The vocative opening, "O Rose," has the effect of direct address, projecting an audience. Blake seems to wish to awaken us to a web of mutually implicating alternatives. We also bring to the poem some sense of a theological and a social history of attitudes and values toward the body and sexuality generally, which we are called on to assess and even to judge.

These ambiguities or multiple meanings for the "Rose" figure do not make the poem incoherent, nor its interpretation arbitrary, subject to any reader's preferences. The poem directs its suggestiveness. Our effort at interpretation is not only goaded, but governed. It is governed through the relationships between the terms or signifiers that are proposed, in further relation to terms that are suggested but withheld, and within the contexts of culture, history, and discourses that situate us. The various implications of the poem's figures need not, and indeed may never be resolved into one unity. Yet this does not make the poem indeterminate in the sense of defying or collapsing meaning (although in liminal, mainly post-Modern instances, poems may do this). The model for approaching this mystery of meaning may be a Wittgensteinian investigation, which suggests that words take their places within a network of usages, as they are employed within the language of a community of speakers. The poem makes use of and reaches into this broad linguistic usage. But it also sets up its own frame within which its words (including both ordinary and extraordinary or highly specified meanings of words) take on specific resonances. The result is to heighten a sense of the very procedures through which words mean. The poem thus becomes a mode of self-reflection on language generally, making us conscious of how we use words and what we claim through them.

There can be specific guidelines as well. "The Sick Rose," for example, seems clear in its value judgments. The valence of sickness is more or less negative. Some corruption, whether it be the shamefulness of sin or the sinfulness of shame, is invoked in its destructive, concealed work. In other poems, however, whether the figure is positive or negative may remain unclear, in a different sense of incompletion. Robert Frost's "Stopping by Woods on a Snowy Evening" offers such a case of calculated ambivalence:

Whose woods these are I think I know.
His house is in the village though;
He will not see me stopping here
To watch his woods fill up with snow.

My little horse must think it queer
To stop without a farmhouse near
Between the woods and frozen lake
The darkest evening of the year.

He gives his harness bells a shake
To ask if there is some mistake.
The only other sound's the sweep
Of easy wind and downy flake.

The woods are lovely, dark and deep,
But I have promises to keep,
And miles to go before I sleep,
And miles to go before I sleep.

There is in this poem a fundamental ambivalence regarding just what the "woods" represent. The woods are lovely. Is their beauty deadly? Is death beautiful? What is the status of sleep here? The poem seems to be about the attractions, and fatal dangers, of identifications with nature. It is as if it exposes the other side of personification to be reification, reduction to a thing, warning that these crossings between human and inhuman worlds may be seductively destabilizing. The boundary between ourselves and our world is difficult, and yet necessary, to sustain. The odd figure of the horse (is this too a figure for some far-reaching symbolic meaning?) seems pivotal. The horse's personification is so obvious, even clumsy— and yet so fanciful, even comic—as to draw attention to itself and make its presence unmistakable. "He gives his harness bells a shake / To ask if there is some mistake." The company of another creature calls the speaker back from nature's inanimate pressure. But, again, some imposition, some transgression of boundary has occurred, re-making the horse according to some human image.

A reading of the poem cannot eliminate either the seduction of the wood, or its danger. As to what the wood "stands for," within the course of the poem it seems to focus on just this ambivalence, as a kind of comment on Romantic uses of nature and on the rhetoric of personification. In Frost, we can not escape the claims of our own figural impulses, our compulsion to compare, represent, personify. And yet we also must resist them.

This self-conscious use of personification is often felt, as we have seen, in Modernist or post-Romantic verse, and highlights the question of the historical element in poetry. Poetry takes place in history, and changes through history. We saw, in our earlier discussion of personification, how in the Renaissance (continuing traditions of the Middle Ages) personification could be almost a form of allegory. Some emotion or natural force or religious truth would be represented as an acting person, such as "Love" in the poem by George Herbert. Allegory in that poem is a figural representation of an abstraction, one that also has, for Herbert, an independent existence in metaphysical reality. In the Romantic period, we saw that personification tended instead to involve the poet's own act of vision—how he or she would interpret a landscape, say, as though it had human emotion or response which, however, finally reflected his or her own. In our own period of post-Romanticism or Modernism or post-Modernism even this personification as personal projection has tended, as we saw in Wallace Stevens and in Frost, to become a self-conscious affair. Our right to make such projections becomes a question we ask rather than a power we exercise. We might say that personification has become more and more expressly fictional: from representing a force considered objective and powerful in its own right, as in allegory, to a sort of half- claim about our own human powers and patterns of understanding. As Coleridge cries out in "Dejection: An Ode":

> O Lady! We receive but what we give,
> And in our life alone does Nature live:
> Ours is her wedding garment, ours her shroud!

This different handling of personification (and allegory) marks one of the shifts we find from Romantic to post-Romantic verse. Such a shift no doubt registers many factors. Changes in religious belief, philosophical paradigms, technology, relations to tradition and the past all frame and penetrate this and other imaginative norms and possibilities. One way of describing these changes is in terms of the audience of poetry, which no less has changed through history. Theories of reading have tended to emphasize psychological and cognitive experience, as these are mediated or conducted through a text's structural features. Lineation, for example, suspends attention at the end of the poetic line. It plays on a reader's expectation of how the line will continue, an expectation which may be surprised. Puns, and ambiguities generally, direct the reader to multiple meanings of a given word, which she or he will then try to negotiate within her or his interpretations.

But besides psychological, cognitive, and structural approaches, the art of reading can be historicized. Not only do tastes change, so that what one audience likes in one historical period another audience may dislike—and this can happen not only with particular works, but with whole genres, whole kinds of verse forms. But also readerships change. The groups of people who may be reading poetry in a given period vary. This is partly due to the technology of reading. The earliest poetry was oral, recited publicly, at gatherings such as festivals or religious rituals. Writing opened new possibilities. Instead of relying on formulaic repetition, such as is found in Homer's epics and Old English poetry, which is more easily remembered, a greater exactness of language becomes possible. But manuscripts were still limited mainly to a wealthy, privileged class in courts, castles, and universities, or to religious communities in churches, monasteries, or convents. Also the transmission of poetry would have been deeply affected by the preservation of manuscripts through copying, which of course also means errors (not to mention lost materials). With the invention of printing, the availability of texts becomes something entirely different: widespread and accessible (although this accessibility was resisted for some time through exclusive coterie circulation) and with more or less exact and easy reproduction. And of course we are now in the midst of further, almost unimaginable changes in the technology of reading and reproduction. Reprinting is a mere matter of xeroxing and faxing and microfilming and digitalizing and satellite-beaming via telephones and computers. The reproduction of all sorts of material is possible, including visual and audio effects.

In the earliest periods, such as in ancient Greece, access to literature would have been more or less public. Poetry was be recited before what we would now call a live audience (what, one wonders, would be a dead audience?). Through much of European history, the number of people who could even read was quite limited, mainly to the Church or the court. With the invention of printing, more people could have access to written material, while more people eventually could read it. This meant a shift from the small group of the learned and the privileged wealthy or religious (who often shared cultural norms), to a more general and diversified audience, including women. Reading also requires leisure, which until recent centuries few had other than the nobility and the clergy. But with a much broader audience, quite different tastes in literature also develop. Nor will the audience necessarily be educated in, or interested in, a whole history of literature which, as we have seen, framed individual works to a lesser or greater degree.

The difference in technology and the difference in audience correlate with differences in the place, or function, or importance of poetry from period to period. In the Medieval period, for example, poetry often had a religious function, with even private religious devotions structured through the communal forms of hymns and psalms. It has also had a political function, celebrating the deeds of national heroes or kings. As poetry has become more available, it has acquired more personal and private functions. This may seem at first glance a great widening in its function and interest; but in fact this is not the case. Poetry today sometimes seems almost entirely personal and private, with little function or place in a public world. One exception to this may be popular songs, whose texts are still called lyrics, and which can achieve, as in the very densely figured poetics of Bob Dylan, the intensity of expression which is poetry. And religious songs and hymns still hold their place within their communities, as do works with a political-social history, such as the slave spirituals.

Poetry as an elite art form, however, registered throughout the twentieth century an increasingly difficult relationship with its audiences. This is partly due to a twentieth-century commitment to formal experiment, which undermines a familiarity with prior forms that could help situate the reader. In the history of literature, poetic conventions, images, verse forms, even metrical patterns, reappear from text to text and period to period in new and creative ways. Sometimes these conventions are put under great stress. There are, in literary history, moments of rebellion and denunciation, when poets feel called to redress some failure, to respond creatively to a sense of exhaustion or depletion in poetic practice and possibility, or to represent some significant shift in outlook. When these changes occur, new language (diction) is introduced, which is to say also, new spheres of experience; new metrical patterns or variations or applications emerge; new kinds of imagery are investigated, or new twists are given to older kinds. Or, the importance of a specific poetic feature changes, so that something that was once central now comes to be marginal, and something incidental now becomes central.

In contemporary life, changes in the very status of the written word, as opposed to other kinds of media, surely have had their impact. New poetry responds to these, as to other cultural changes. But the more experimental the form, the more it must create or educate its audiences rather than rely on shared expectations and assumptions. Modernity's very pluralism and multiplicity makes it difficult to assume a common cultural norm to which poetry can refer or on which it can rely. There are as well particular challenges within the experimental forms of modern poetry. The fracturing of syntax such as occurs in, for example, the Imagist and Symbolist poem, and which substitutes radical juxtapositions of elements in place of clear and articulate syntax, makes poetry more difficult to decipher. That relationships among words or figures have to be pieced together seems to represent a more problematic effort, for poet and reader, of piecing together experience generally. More and more, each individual—writer and reader—must construct his or her own sense of order. Conceptual structures that might once have seemed given by, say, religious and metaphysical orders, now must be projected, constructed, adapted, or embraced by the individual.

The consequences of these shifts are as integral to the analysis of poetry as are formal and stylistic considerations. Walt Whitman, a great initiator of poetic experiment, makes them the topic, as well as the procedure, in one short text:

A noiseless patient spider,
I mark'd, where on a little promontory it stood, isolated,
Mark'd how, to explore the vacant, vast surrounding,
It launch'd forth filament, filament, filament out of itself;
Ever unreeling them—ever tirelessly speeding them.

And you, O my soul, where you stand,
Surrounded, surrounded, in measureless oceans of space,
Ceaselessly musing, venturing, throwing,—seeking the
    spheres to connect them;
Till the bridge you will need be form'd, till the ductile anchor
    hold;
Till the gossamer thread you fling catch somewhere, O my
    soul.

This poem turns on a specific figural correlation between the "noiseless patient spider" and "O my soul." Each of these terms of the figure is given one stanza, which is each made up of one sentence, with no regular line-length, no set metric, and no rhyme. The form is invented for the occasion, as an expression for this particular utterance (although Whitman does not break apart ordinary grammar). The first point of comparison between the spider and the soul is the creative invention, the marvelous energy of each. Each projects threads out of itself, through which it builds bridges to its world and indeed builds its world. There is a further implied comparison between this creative, energetic activity and the poet himself. The repetition of "mark'd" that describes what the poet does allies his seeing to his writing. The "filament, filament, filament" of the spider, which becomes a metaphorical "gossamer thread" of the soul, are also the lines of the poem. What the spider does is what the soul does is what the poet does.

As a metaphor, the correlation between the spider and the soul (and the poet) is given in the poem. These figures are to this extent contained in the text. And yet, there is an incomplete element in the figuration. The poem celebrates creative individuality, emphasizing how one's place in the world, and indeed the world itself, is produced out of the self. But the poem also registers disorientation, perhaps desperation. The power of the individual is enormous, but so are its burdens. He creates his world; but it surrounds him with an immense and vast nothingness, a "vacant, vast surrounding"; and without his exertions, it threatens to collapse. Situated in this measureless and empty expanse, the soul's actions are almost frenetic: "musing, venturing, throwing—seeking the spheres to connect them." Without this effort, there is no connection. Indeed, the poem does not definitely assert that any connection has been achieved. Its assertion is grammatically suspended as conditional: "Till the gossamer thread you fling catch somewhere." The "fling" is itself a rather desperate gesture. And there is no guarantee that the thread has, or will, attach itself, thereby attaching the self to the world or the world itself into some configuration.

Whitman's poem reveals a core ambivalence in Romanticism, where creative possibility of the self teeters between everything and nothing, utter (self-)assertion and total collapse. The poem's figures have, as in the Frost poem, an ambivalent valence. The web-spinning is marvelous, and it is perilous. Thus, although the poem's metaphorical construction is specified, its figures remain incomplete in several senses. In its own way, this poem represents a moment of the Romantic sublime. The confrontation with measureless expanse at once elevates and threatens to erase the poetic self. Moreover, no figure—no signifier—can ever fully or truly represent this infinite vastness. There is a fundamental and irrecuperable split, or discontinuity, or disproportion between the figure and what it invokes, the signifier and what it reaches to signify. In another sense, the ambiguous valence of the spider/soul/poet's activity points to the reader for decision, implicating the reader in the very burden of creating order that the poem projects. The reader, like the poet, must cast his/her interpretive threads through the text; and the burden of making sense out of it remains great.

Periodization is a highly fictional enterprise. Boundaries dividing Whitman's experimentation from later radicalizations (and earlier antecedents) are at best blurry, and have been subject to much controversy. We may say that Whitman's poem makes visible procedures of construction and interpretation that have always been at work in literature to varying degrees. In light of this poem, we see how even figures contained within a text extend beyond it for further reference: into the literary history of verse; and also into the contexts of readers' understandings, as enmeshed in the large and complex assumptions and practices that make up culture. It may be that in earlier periods, a clearer specification or determination of incomplete figures such as symbol or allegory was made possible by a more specified set of cultural systems and references, as shared by a smaller, more closely identified community of readers (the clearer specification of the symbol is a rather paradoxical feature, since within this era the symbol was also intended to represent something transcendent and beyond expression). The multiplication of cultural assumptions and the dispersion of reading communities now may make the incompleteness of a figure more evident, and more insistent.

The open structure of incomplete figures has become, I would argue, an increasingly central and self-conscious element in poetry. Yet this can work in different ways, with different intentions and effects. In the Symbolist poetry of the late Romantic and/or early Modernist periods, the whole text of a poem often composed a kind of incomplete figure, one representing a space of interiority—the workings of the mind—or the process of poetry itself in a self-referential manner. The opening of T. S. Eliot's "The Love Song of J. Alfred Prufrock" presents an invitation to wander:

Let us go then, you and I,
When the evening is spread out against the sky
Like a patient etherised upon a table;

Let us go, through certain half-deserted streets,
The muttering retreats
Of restless nights in one-night cheap hotels
And sawdust restaurants with oyster-shells:
Streets that follow like a tedious argument
Of insidious intent
To lead you to an overwhelming question . . .
Oh, do not ask, "What is it?"
Let us go and make our visit.

In the room the women come and go
Talking of Michaelangelo.

(This opening verse-paragraph takes shape as an almost-sonnet, with fourteen lines, in [almost] rhymed couplets.) But where in it exactly is Prufrock (if it is Prufrock speaking)? Well, he is on some street in the less reputable section of some city (St. Louis?). And yet he is also very much inside his own mind. The mind is deadened, like an etherized patient; his description of the sky reflects his own consciousness. The avenues in which he is lost are not (only) streets, but corridors of the mind, which he wanders hopelessly—streets that represent the "overwhelming question" which can only be located within him. Of course, in some sense our existence does take place within our own minds, where we experience it. This poem dramatizes that phenomenological insight. In terms of its figures, what it constructs is a cityscape; but this is an (incomplete) image for the interior mind. The figures in the poem point back to, implicitly represent, a state of consciousness.

But such a Symbolist figure of the mind is only one kind of modernist incomplete figure. Another type, prefigured in the writings of Edgar Allan Poe, may try to block the process of signification altogether. The poems then would offer signifiers but would attempt to defeat their power to signify. They act to block rather than to point to any reference or representation. This occurs in Poe's "Ulalume," where the title pretends to name his lost beloved but, like the supposed place names of "lake of Auber" or the "region of Weir," in fact names or signifies nothing but its own sounds. In "Dream-Land," Poe constructs a landscape that doesn't exist but is instead marked by a series of negations—"Bottomless vales and boundless floods . . . with forms that no man can discover"—pointing to its own non-existence "Out of Space—out of Time," a no-place of no reference. Such poems (and Poe altogether) remain, however, rather extreme cases, although they are wildly influential in France. There is another kind of poetry which makes incompletion an impelling principle and method, but not in ways that block all reference or collapse into a self-defeating, self-contradictory meaninglessness. Wallace Stevens implies the unfinished or open nature of figuration in "Notes toward a Supreme Fiction," with wide implications for poetry generally:

Two things of opposite natures seem to depend
On one another, as a man depends
On a woman, day on night, the imagined

On the real. This is the origin of change.
Winter and spring, cold copulars, embrace
And forth the particulars of rapture come.

Music falls on the silence like a sense,
A passion that we feel, not understand.
Morning and afternoon are clasped together

And North and South are an intrinsic couple
And sun and rain a plural, like two lovers
That walk away as one in the greenest body.

(*It Must Change*, IV)

Stevens, in this section of his "Notes toward a Supreme Fiction," proposes a series of figures, which are figures for each other: signifiers that signify each other in what is implicitly an endless series of further signifiers. Dual terms—man/woman, day/night, imagined/real, winter/spring, music/silence, morning/afternoon, North/South, sun/rain—form a processional in which each is distinct from, and yet intimately dependent upon, the other and on each other for their meaning. The list can never be finalized. The terms are in what may be called an open dialectical relationship, one that does not drive toward any synthesis. Instead, they take part in an ongoing process of mutual definition and implication, where terms never resolve into each other and instead continue to generate further terms.

Each figure, one might then say, is incomplete; as is the figural chain in which they take place. If we use the linguistic terms of signification, each figure is a signifier for further figures, which are in turn signifiers. The chain itself suggests the transformations of time, which is never still and always changes. As the poem declares, "This is the origin of change." In the poem, this temporal openness is celebrated as the very shape and impetus of creativity. From the embrace of differential terms "forth the particulars of rapture come."

This poetic passage is highly theoretical. It explicitly names among its creative poles the terms "the imagined" and "the real" that Stevens inherited from Romanticism. In Stevens, neither term has priority, nor complete independence from the other. The imagination without reality would be empty. Reality without imagination would be, well, unimaginable. Nor does the poem offer some emblem, or definition, of either. Neither term appears outside of the chains of its figures. Experience seems instead to unfold as "forth the particulars of rapture come," in the fertile creativity of figures generating figures in an ongoing and open chain. In one way each of the figures in the chain represents others through likeness, so that the images stand in metaphorical relationship to each other. But metaphor does not exhaust their relationships. Some of the oppositions seem related in spatial terms, suggesting metonymies or synecdoches, microcosms and macrocosms. Some are overt similes. Perhaps the yoking together of opposites recalls an oxymoron. And metaphor itself does not offer definitive and determinate likenesses, but suggests a much more fluid interrelationship between likenesses and differences. A man and a woman do not depend upon each other exactly in the way that day and night might do; and the poem does not specify just what the dependence involves, or state its nature. This is left entirely open.

The poem thus takes shape as words and figures that align and realign, form, depart, and re-form, pointing to and beyond each other. Stevens in this poem above all claims that such ongoing figural activity is productive, creative, imaging "the greenest body," our world, through words that are plural, changing, and celebratory.

Glossary

ACCENTUAL VERSE   Verse that works by counting only strong beats, regardless of syllable count. In its older forms, usually there were four strong beats to a line, separated into two rhymic units by a middle pause, called a *caesura*.

ADDRESSEE   An awkward term for the imagined person to whom a poem is addressed. The addressed person serves as more than a passive listener, but rather actively shapes the poem, as it is directed toward persuading or otherwise influencing or affecting him or her.

ALEXANDRINE   The longer, twelve-syllable line taken from French usage and Anglicized into the more usual ten-syllable English line. Sometimes an alexandrine will be introduced as the last line of a stanza done in ten-syllable lines, as in Spenser's *Faerie Queene*.

ALLEGORY   A figure that stands for some abstract idea or some internal state, as if that idea or state were an acting person or animated object.

ALLITERATION   The repetition of consonant sounds at the beginning of successive words.

ALLUSION   The reference in one literary text to another literary text.

ANAPEST   A metrical rhythm made up of three syllables to a measure, where the accent falls on the last of the three syllables. The meter of limerick.

ANAPHORA   A rhetorical arrangement in which a word or phrase is repeated to introduce successive clauses.

ANTITHESIS   A construction of phrases opposing elements or images; oppositional imagery.

APOCOPE   Dropping the last syllable or letter of a word (usually to make it fit metrically).

APOSTROPHE   Address to an absent or dead person or thing or to an absent idea as if it were a person.

ASSONANCE   The repetition of a vowel sound through successive words.

BLANK VERSE   Poetry that counts ten syllables with five beats (iambic pentameter) but doesn't rhyme. Its poetic strength comes in the flexibility and density of its syntax and imagery. Derived in theater, it is especially powerful in representing dramatized speech.

BLASON   A list of women's (or possibly men's) attributes, naming and praising each in turn.

BROKEN RHYME   A word broken at any place in order to create a sound repetition.

CAESURA   The pause or break in the metrical pattern of a line.

CARPE DIEM   A poetic convention declaring the urgent need to "seize the day," that is, to make haste to grasp life's opportunities while there is still time.

CHIASMUS   A pattern of reversals either of sounds or words, in the sequence of *xyyx*.

CONCEIT   An elaborate, complex, extended, and multitiered comparison.

CONCESSION   The rhetorical gesture of conceding the opponent's point, so as to better defeat it with one's own arguments.

CONSONANCE   The repetition of consonant sounds at the end (or even in the middle) of successive words.

COUPLET   Two successive lines linked together metrically and (usually) by rhyme.

DACTYL   A metrical unit of three syllables, the first accented and the second and third unaccented; jazz rhythm.

DEICTIC   A pointing word, such as "this" or "that."

DICTION   Selection of individual words according to their level of formality, ordinary context, and so on. Also called lexis.

DRAMATIC MONOLOGUE   A poem written as though spoken by a dramatic character, as his or her address to an implied but silent addressee.

ELISION   The dropping of syllables from words in a poetic line, usually to keep the meter.

ELLIPSE   The dropping of a word in a poetic line, either for metrical or grammatical purposes.

ENCOMIUM   A poem of praise.

ENJAMBMENT   The spilling over of grammar past the metrical line, so that the grammatical structure of a phrase is completed in the next line.

ETYMOLOGY   The history of a word's meaning and usage, often carried into a poem as an additional sense or echo of a word.

FEMININE RHYME / ENDING   A rhyme word that has two or more syllables, in which the second to last syllable is stressed but the last syllable is unstressed.

FREE VERSE   Verse that does not follow a regular metrical pattern.

FIGURE   A word or arrangement of words as they stand for, point to, or represent further senses and meanings.

FOOT   The basic metrical unit or measure, usually containing two or three syllables.

FOREGROUNDING   The art of emphasizing a particular word or poetic element by introducing it in a way that departs from expected usage.

HEMISTICH   A half of a metrical line.

HYPERBOLE   The rhetoric of exaggeration.

HYPOTACTIC   The more complicated grammar of subordinated clauses.

IAMBIC PENTAMETER   The major metrical line in English, made up of ten syllables with five beats, where an unaccented syllable is followed by an accented one, ta-TA, ta-TA, ta-TA, ta-TA, ta-TA. See also *meter*.

INTERTEXTUALITY   The interreferencing between texts through many possible methods such as direct quotation, sly echo, obvious omission, and so on.

IRONY   A disparity between viewpoints or understandings, whether due to a difference in knowledge (someone knows something someone else doesn't know), a difference in consciousness (someone knows that the artwork is an artwork), the difference between a word seeming to say one thing but meaning another, or the difference between what a word tries to say and the impossibility of saying it.

LIMERICK   A verse form of five lines written in anapestic meter, with a punch.

LINEATION   The art of line breaking, with the effect of giving the last word of a line special emphasis.

LITOTES   The rhetoric of understatement.

MATERIALITY   The material base of poetic construction, that is, the actual letters and sounds that make up the words and their designs and shapes.

MEMENTO MORI   A poetic convention of remembering death, usually through the vivid representation of some form of bodily decay.

METAPHOR   A comparison by applying or transfering a term associated with one thing to another.

METER   The organized rhythm of accented and unaccented syllables. The three basic metrical units (feet) in English verse are iamb (two syllables, one unaccented, one accented—do NOT); trochee (one accented, one unaccented—DOnut); and spondee (two accented syllables—DON'T, DON'T).

METONYMY   A figure in which one thing stands for another due to contiguity, spatial association, or positioning.

MICROCOSM/MACROCOSM   A poetic convention in which the human world is a representation in small (micro) of the cosmos as a whole (macro) and vice versa.

MODERNISM   A movement in poetry of the early twentieth century, with renewed emphasis on formal control and objectivity.

MODESTY   A poetic convention, usually employed by women, of disclaiming one's talents and abilities.

MUSE   A figure for poetic inspiration, usually feminized.

NONSENSE   Poetry that uses the sounds of words as its central organizing principle, with the semantic meanings of words secondary.

OCTAVE   A division of the Italian sonnet, grouping together the first eight lines, usually by rhyme scheme, but also in syntax, imagery, argument, and so on.

OFF-RHYME   Words that rhyme only partially.

OXYMORON   A tight, oppositional, self-contradictory, and hence paradoxical image.

PARALLELISM   Phrases in sequence that match grammatically and also in imagery or assertion.

PARATAXIS   A grammar of simple links and additions, without subordination.

PATHETIC FALLACY   The (false) ascription to nature of human feelings (pathos).

PERSONA   The "mask" the poet takes on in representing himself or herself in a poem.

PERSONIFICATION   The ascription of human qualities to non-human creatures or inanimate objects.

POLYPTOTON   A word repeated in various grammatical forms.

PROSOPOPOEIA   The speaking of something non-human, absent, or inanimate.

PUN (PARANOMASIA)   A word with more than one (unrelated) meaning.

PYRRHIC   A metrical unit of two unaccented syllables.

QUATRAIN   Four-line groupings, usually by rhyme, and also often in imagery and syntax. The component blocks of the first twelve lines of the English sonnet.

REFRAIN   Repeated phrases or lines in a poem, usually at intervals.

REIFICATION   The making of a person or animate creature into an inanimate thing.

RHETORIC   The art of word arrangements for increased impact or power of affect.

RHYME   Repetition of the end syllable sounds in successive words, either as full rhymes or as part rhymes in which the end consonants match but not the vowels; at the end of lines or internal to them.

RHYME SCHEME   Conventional or structured patterns of rhyme.

ROMANTICISM   A nineteenth-century movement in literature and culture emphasizing subjectivity.

SCANSION   The art of interpreting poetic meter.

SEDUCTION   The poetic convention in which someone (usually male) tries to persuade someone else (usually female) to sexual engagement.

SESTET   The last six lines of an Italian sonnet, grouped together by rhyme scheme, grammar, images, argument, and so on.

SHAPE POEM   A poem in which attention is paid to the visual shape of the text.

SIGNIFIER   A poetic unit that signifies some further reference, echo, meaning, representation, and so on.

SIMILE   A comparison that tells you it is a comparison, by using words such as "as," "like," or "resemble."

SONNET   A fourteen-line poem with tightly structured rhyme patterns, in iambic pentameter. The English sonnet divides into three units of four lines each (quatrains) and a rhymed couplet. The Italian sonnet divides into two units, the first of eight lines (octave) followed by six lines (sestet) with (usually) no rhymed couplet at the end, but rather structured through a variety of other rhyme patterns.

SPONDEE   A metrical unit of two stressed syllables. See *meter*.

STROPHIC   A poem organized by stanza groupings.

STICHIC   A poem organized by line groupings.

SYLLABIC VERSE   Verse whose meter is counted out by syllables, regardless of accent.

SYMBOL   An incomplete figure in which one term of representation is inside the text, but what it represents is outside the text.

SYNAERESIS   The converging of two contiguous vowels in a word, usually to keep a metrical pattern.

SYNCOPE   The suppression of a syllable in a metrical pattern.

SYNECDOCHE   A figure where a part is substituted for or stands for a whole, or vice versa.

THORN LINES   Unrhymed lines in a poem that also uses rhymed lines.

TOPOS   A poetic convention that is revisited by being reused through many literary works.

TROCHEE   A metrical unit of one stressed syllable followed by an unstressed one, in reverse of the iamb. See *meter*.

TROPE   A poetic or rhetorical figure that is an arrangement of words in a recognizable pattern which in many different ways represents, points to, or stands for further senses or meanings.

VOCATIVE   A lofty and formal address or invocation.

VOLTA   The "turn" in a sonnet, usually between sections, that points the poem in some new direction.

ZEUGMA   A grammatical arrangement in which one verb is used to govern a number of successive words or phrases.

Bibliographical Backgrounds

GENERAL BACKGROUNDS

There is a history of poetry, and there is a history of the interpretation of poetry. For the greater part of the twentieth century, the central mode of poetic interpretation, at least in America, was formalist, associated with a movement called New Criticism after a book of that name by John Crowe Ransom (Norfolk, Conn.: New Directions, 1941). Works important to establishing the New Critical method include Cleanth Brooks's *The Well-Wrought Urn* (New York: Harvest Books, 1945, 1975) and W. K. Wimsatt's *The Verbal Icon* (Lexington: University Press of Kentucky, 1954). This method of reading emphasizes the poem as a closed art object, to be studied in terms of the relationships between its formal parts, which come together in a final harmony. The artwork in this sense is seen to stand outside of history, with references beyond the artwork itself irrelevant. Interpretation of the poem thus must suppress any reference to the intentions of the author ("intentional fallacy") or the affect on the reader ("affective fallacy"). Its "content" cannot be abstracted from the specific words and structures that make it up ("the heresy of paraphrase").

This American formalism was reacting against a tradition of criticism that was more chatty, more essayist, taking the shape of general reflections on the work and its author and period. Certainly New Criticism introduced more rigor into literary studies. Nevertheless, such formalism represents, as M. H. Abrams traces in his opening chapter of *The Mirror and the Lamp* (New York: Oxford University Press, 1953), only one of several possible approaches to poetry and conceptions of what poetry is. Instead of being seen as an independent, closed art object, poetry can be approached through its effect on the reader, as a didactic teaching or rhetorical persuasion. It can be studied in historical, biographical, or philological terms. In the last decades, poetics has returned to these other approaches, in a number of different ways. Structuralist treatments

of poetry remain highly formalist, rigorously analyzing the struc-
tures and components of the poetic object. But in Structuralism
the poem is not self-enclosed. Instead, poetic language is analyzed
through the discipline of linguistics, in terms of linguistic struc-
tures that extend beyond and condition poetic language. Post-
Structuralist methods include philosophical and theoretical
understandings of the very conditions of language and meaning
as this bears on poetic interpretation, as in Deconstruction; the
affect of the poem on the reader, as in Reader-Response criticism;
and the way broad cultural, social, and historical conditions and
ideologies frame the understanding of any text, as in the New
Historicism. In this study, I attempt to combine these different
critical approaches into a multidimensional poetic.

Among works that review this critical history and discuss major
movements and terms are V. B. Leitch, *American Literary Criticism
from the Thirties to the Eighties* (New York: Columbia University Press,
1988); Frank Lentriccia, *After the New Criticism* (Chicago: University of
Chicago Press, 1980); and Lentriccia and T. McLaughlin, *Critical
Terms for Literary Study* (Chicago: University of Chicago Press,
1990).

I. INDIVIDUAL WORDS

Diction, the selection of individual words in a text, has been
generally treated as an historical question of the poetic norms
during specific periods, particularly in terms of kinds, or levels
of poetic genres. This is the case in Donald Davie's *Purity of
Diction in English Verse* (London: Chatto and Windus, 1952), and
in Geoffrey Tillotson's *Augustan Studies* (London: Athlone Press,
1961). Diction is thus traditionally seen as a matter of exclusion, a
gate-keeper for language appropriate to specific generic catego-
ries, with modern experiment a breakdown in decorum.

A more dynamic view of diction is implied in William Empson's
The Structure of Complex Words (Detroit: University of Michigan
Press, 1967 reprint), which examines words through their different
textual uses. The frame of investigation, however, remains form-
alist and internal to the text. This is equally the case in Winifred
Nowottny's *The Language Poets Use* (London: Athlone Press, 1962),
which discusses diction in terms of different fields of speech but
within the framework of formalist stylistics.

A more open, historicized sense of verbal invocation, interaction,
and reference beyond the enclosed textual frame is implied in Mikhail
Bakhtin's notion of "microdialogue" in *Problems of Dostoevsy's Poetics*,
trans. Caryl Emerson (Minneapolis: University of Minnesota Press,

1984). The individual word becomes a point of intersection between multiple historical uses. Although Bakhtin refers his work to fiction, his historicized sense of the permeable text is extended here to poetry. Diction comes to invoke the range of language-contexts to which words belong, and which they then import into the text, bringing these contexts into confrontation or congruence (while implicitly excluding others). Each word thus takes place within wider fields of language uses.

2. SYNTAX AND THE POETIC LINE

Analysis of poetic syntax has mainly been a topic in stylistics, but its study has important theoretical implications. For it is in syntax that the logic, or order of language relationships is manifested—or rather, it is through syntax that they are structured. Syntax has therefore played a pivotal role in discussions of Symbolist and Modernist aesthetics, and particularly in the notion of the art-object as standing in opposition to referential or mimetic functions.

William Empson undertakes stylistic, or as he calls it, "verbal analysis" of syntax in his 1930 book *Seven Types of Ambiguity* alongside other types of ambiguity (New York: New Directions, 1966 reprint). The writings of Leo Spitzer, *Linguistics and Literary History* (Princeton: Princeton University Press, 1948) and *Essays on English and American Literature* (Princeton: Princeton University Press, 1962), analyze syntax, along with diction and many other features, as part of his attempt to "bridge the gap between linguistics and literary history" with stylistics. Donald Davie in *Articulate Energy* (London: Routledge & Kegan Paul, 1955) elaborates the implications of syntactic experiments in Modernist poetics, which he sees as closing the artwork off from exterior reference, throwing attention instead back onto the art-object. See also Cristanne Miller's *A Poet's Grammar* (Cambridge, Mass.: Harvard University Press, 1987).

Essays by poets tend to throw the best light on poetic practice and theory. Modernist poets such as T. S. Eliot, Ezra Pound, and T. E. Hulme have written seminal essays on syntax as well as other features of poetic composition. See especially Ezra Pound's "A Retrospect" and "The Hard and Soft in French Poetry," in *Literary Essays of Ezra Pound* (New York: New Directions, 1968 reprint); T. E. Hulme's *Speculations* (1924); and "The Music of Poetry," by T. S. Eliot, in *On Poetry and Poets* (New York: Noonday Press, 1957). Joseph Frank's *The Widening Gyre* (Bloomington: Indiana University Press, 1963) examines these Modernist attitudes to syntax in aesthetic and historical contexts. Hugh Kenner's *The Pound Era* (Berkeley: University of California Press, 1971) brilliantly treats modernist syntax.

In structuralist treatments of stylistics, syntax is seen as a continuous linguistic structure joining poetic with ordinary discourses. It is from this background of formalism and structuralism that the notion of deviation, or foregrounding, derives (see Victor Erlich, *Russian Formalism* [New Haven, Conn.: Yale University Press, 1981]). In structuralist discussion, syntax tends however to be assimilated to other verse-structures, most notably metric and sound patterns, themselves generally treated under the category of rhythm as patterned repetition. Significant structuralist treatments of syntax include Roman Jakobson's *Poetry of Grammar and Grammar of Poetry*, ed. with a preface by Stephen Rudy (The Hague: Mouton, 1981); J. M. Lotman, *The Structure of the Artistic Text* (Ann Arbor: University of Michigan Press, 1977). Roger Fowler also works from this tradition of stylistics in *Essays on Style and Language* (Oxford: Blackwell, 1976).

Grammar on the one hand presents a technical opportunity for analyzing verse. But it also has powerful theoretical implications concerning how language orders rather than merely re-presenting experience, with poetic language bringing to view, examining, and extending this general involvement of language in experience. This power of language is provocatively proposed in works by Friedrich Nietzsche, especially in *Twilight of the Idols* (in *The Portable Nietzsche*, trans. Walter Kaufman [New York: Penguin, 1966]); and in *On Truth and Lying in an Extra-Moral Sense* and in writings from the course on rhetoric Nietzsche conducted at Basel in 1872–1873, collected in *Friedrich Nietzsche on Rhetoric and Language*, ed. and trans. Sander L. Gilman et al. (New York: Oxford University Press, 1989). The implications of Nietzschean language theory and its claims for the role of syntax are pursued by Paul De Man in his essays "Rhetoric of Tropes (Nietzsche)" and "Semiology and Rhetoric" in *Allegories of Reading* (New Haven, Conn.: Yale University Press, 1979), where De Man, however, sees this exposure of the work of syntax as one that strips rather than confirms its power, a position I do not take.

3. IMAGES: SIMILE AND METAPHOR

Literary analysis of metaphor begins, at least in the twentieth-century Anglo-American tradition, with I. A. Richards's *The Philosophy of Rhetoric* (New York: Oxford University Press, 1936, reprint 1967). Richards formulated the terms of metaphorical comparison as "vehicle" and "tenor." These terms, however, are exceedingly clumsy, and I do not use them. For one thing, it is quite difficult, if not theoretically impossible, to tell which term is the vehicle and which is the tenor. Such subordination of one term of a metaphor to another is, from a later theoretical perspective, highly questionable. In any event, terms developed in linguistics by Structuralists are much clearer and neater: signifier and signified. The extent to which this terminology still entails subordination of the first term to the second (signifier to signified) may be argued; but at least it does so with precision. And using this model of signification allows further analysis of metaphor within a whole range of figures, where 'signifier' can refer to 'images' or tropes that are not based in comparison. This in turn opens toward a broader theory of representation.

The terms signifier and signified derive, in modern discourse, from the work of Ferdinand de Saussure, whose 1906–1911 course given in Geneva was then edited as *Course in General Linguistics* (New York: McGraw Hill, 1966). That the terms have a history, especially within theological tradition, is very germane. Their function in the writings of St. Augustine are traced, if also duplicated, in Kenneth Burke's *The Rhetoric of Religion* (Berkeley: University of California Press, 1970). A critique of sign-theory as theological and metaphysical is one fundamental project of Jacques Derrida's writings, from his early article "White Mythology" *New Literary History* 6 (1974): 5–74, through his *Of Grammatology* (especially the first chapter), trans. Gayatri Spivak (Baltimore: Johns Hopkins University Press, 1976). I substitute the term signifier as it evokes the general impetus of figuration in place of the more traditional "literal" and "figurative"—terms that also raise questions about what is a "proper" and an "improper" use of language, which prove extremely cumbersome and which do not apply to other tropes, such as those involving word order. This study investigates a continuity in figural language, toward a more comprehensive theory of the arts of representation.

There are many studies of metaphor, both in literary and in philosophical contexts. More philosophical are Paul Ricoeur, *The Rule of Metaphor*, trans. Robert Czerny (Toronto: University of Toronto Press, 1977); and Carl Hausman, *Metaphor and Art* (New York: Cambridge University Press, 1989). Literary studies of metaphor in particular contexts include C. S. Lewis, *Studies in Words* (Cambridge: Cambridge University Press, reprint 1990); J. A. Mazzeo, *Renaissance and Seventeenth Century Studies* (New York: Columbia University Press, 1964); A. J. Smith, *Metaphysical Wit* (Cambridge: Cambridge University Press, 1991); and J. Sitter, *Arguments of Augustan Wit* (Cambridge: Cambridge University Press, 1992).

In this book, I have mainly used the term "figure" for metaphor and simile, referring to their component elements as "terms." In the chapter on incomplete figures, I have had recourse to the more theoretical term "signifier." In my discussion of John Donne's sonnet "I Am a Little World" in Chapter 4, I do refer to "physical" and "spiritual" terms of comparison, since these metaphysical meanings are central to Donne's own figural enterprise.

4. METAPHOR AND THE SONNET
5. VERSE FORMS: THE SONNET

Rosalie Colie's *The Resources of Kind* (Berkeley: University of California Press, 1973) approaches the sonnet as a complex historical site in which various genres have combined and realigned, in ways that have deeply influenced these chapters. For a concise history of the sonnet, with chronologies of development and discussions of specific authors in historical sequence, see, for example, Michael R. G. Spiller, *The Development of the Sonnet* (New York: Routledge, 1992). For the Troubador and Italian antecedents to the sonnet, see Peter Dronke's monumental *Medieval Latin and the Rise of the European Love Lyric* (Oxford: Clarendon Press, 1968). Leonard Forster's *The Icy Fire* treats the Petrarchan tradition (Cambridge: Cambridge University Press, 1969). Hallet Smith in *Elizabethan Poetry: A Study in Conventions, Meaning, and Expression* (Cambridge, Mass.: Harvard University Press, 1952) discusses the sonnet as a mode of psychological reflection. Daniel Javitch, *Poetry and Court-liness in Renaissance England* (Princeton: Princeton University Press, 1978), places the sonnet within the context of courtly culture. C. S. Lewis's *Allegory of Love* (New York: Oxford University Press, 1969) is a classic discussion of the trope of love in the Renais-sance. See also T. P. Roche, Jr., *Petrarch and the English Sonnet Sequences* (New York: AMS, 1989). Other discussions of romance structures with implications for the sonnet include Mark Rose, *Heroic Love* (Cambridge, Mass.: Harvard University Press, 1968), and Patricia Parker, *Inescapable Romance* (Princeton: Princeton Univer-sity Press, 1979).

Paradigmatic structuralist discussions of the sonnet were con-ducted by Roman Jakobson and Claude Levi-Strauss "Les Chats de Charles Baudelaire," *L'Homme* 2 (1962): 5–21; and Roman Jakobson and Lawrence Jones, *Shakespeare's Verbal Art* (The Hague: Mouton, 1970).

There are of course many commentaries on Shakespeare's sonnets, including sonnets I have discussed here. Helen Vendler's *The Art of Shakespeare's Sonnets* (Cambridge, Mass.: Harvard

University Press, 1997) offers a monumental, sustained reading, deeply embedded in poetics, of the sonnets as a sequence. Stephen Booth's annotated edition of *Shakespeare's Sonnets* (New Haven, Conn.: Yale University Press, 1977) is an indispensable tool for investigating the etymology and history of Shakespeare's language.

6. POETIC CONVENTIONS

Poetic conventions, or topoi, have been transformed by recent theoretical discussions from dry, philological research into psychologically and conceptually complex structures. Harold Bloom's *The Anxiety of Influence* (New York: Oxford University Press, 1979) and his many other writings ruptured the methods of literary history with the claim that relationships between texts can be charted not only through positive allusion but also through repressed references and influences, in a cultural psychology of poetic creativity.

The relationship between imitation and creativity in Renaissance literature is explored in both historical and theoretical terms in Thomas Greene, *The Light in Troy* (New Haven, Conn.: Yale University Press, 1982). Louis Martz's *The Poetry of Meditation* (New Haven, Conn.: Yale University Press, 1954) discusses the conventions of *Ars Moriendi* and the traditions of meditation in Renaissance lyric. Rosemund Tuve's *Elizabethan and Metaphysical Imagery* (Chicago: University of Chicago Press, 1947, 1972) is a classic study of seventeenth-century poetic conventions, as are various works of Barbara Lewalski, including *Protestant Poetics of the Seventeenth Century Religious Lyric* (Princeton: Princeton University Press, 1979). Exemplary discussions of the ways in which a motif may shift meanings in the visual arts are found in Erwin Panofsky, *Meaning in the Visual Arts* (Garden City, N.Y.: Doubleday, 1955) and *Studies in Iconology* (New York: Harper & Row, 1972).

The whole question of conventions touches on what has come to be called intertextuality, a term introduced by Julia Kristeva in *La Revolution du langage poetique* (Paris: Seuil, 1974), pp. 388–89. Compare "Revolution in Poetic Language," *The Kristeva Reader*, ed. Toril Moi (New York: Columbia University Press, 1986), p. 111. Kristeva's discussions emerge from her early Bakhtinian exposure, as is clear in "Word, Dialogue, Novel," *Desire in Language*, trans. Thomas Gora et al. (New York: Columbia University Press, 1980), pp. 64–91. But her use of the term tends to absorb intertextual relationships into a structural system, as does Michael Riffaterre in *Semiotics of Poetry* (Bloomington: Indiana University Press, 1978). Bakhtin's own theory in, for example, *Rabelais and His World*, trans. Helene Iswolsky (Bloomington: Indiana University Press, 1984), and

Speech Genres and Other Late Essays, trans. Vern W. McGee (Austin: University of Texas Press, 1986), emphasizes instead open inter-change, permeability, and reproduction of cultural and literary types in an ongoing literary-cultural interchange, without closure or finalization.

7. MORE VERSE FORMS

An overview of kinds of verse forms, which I have not attempted here, is available in various handbooks, as for example, the *Princeton Encyclopedia of Poetry and Poetics* (Princeton: Princeton University Press, 1993). There have also been works that systematize a broad range of literary types through classifications of their component features, most prominently Northrop Frye's *Anatomy of Criticism* (Princeton: Princeton University Press, 1957) and Alistair Fowler's *Kinds of Literature* (Cambridge, Mass.: Harvard University Press, 1982). Typologies of genre tend to offer taxonomies that classify features rather than trace historical relationships. As Rene Wellek and Austin Warren generalize: "Theory of genres is a principle of order: it classifies literature and literary history not by time or place (period or national language) but by specifically literary types of organization or structure," *Theory of Literature* (New York: Harcourt, Brace & World, 1956), p. 226. This ahistoricist approach I have resisted. Enumerations of features, while useful, evades the development of the artwork in interaction with the processes of cultural transformation.

An excellent study of one specific verse form is Peter Sacks's *The English Elegy* (Baltimore: Johns Hopkins University Press, 1987). Donald Davie's *English Hymnody of the Eighteenth Century* (Berkeley: University of California Press, 1980) offers a rare discussion of hymns. Hugh Kenner's *The Pound Era* (Berkeley: University of California Press, 1971) provides a foundational discussion of modern verse forms and their characteristic commitments. Stephen Greenblatt's work, notably *Renaissance Self-Fashioning* (Chicago: University of Chicago Press, 1980), has generally redirected critical attention, including genre theory, back into history (of particular relevance is the chapter on the poetic forms of Sir Thomas Wyatt). Works that provide a sense of the histories of verse forms include Philip Davies Roberts, *How Poetry Works* (New York: Penguin, 1986), and Barry Spurr, *Studying Poetry* (Melbourne: Macmillan Education, 1997). For postmodern verse forms, there is H. T. Kirby Smith, *The Origins of Free Verse* (Ann Arbor: University of Michigan Press, 1996), and Joseph Conte, *Unending Designs* (Ithaca, N.Y.: Cornell University Press, 1991). Mark Strand and Eavan Boland offer an anthology of verse forms in *The Making of a Poem* (New York: Norton, 2000).

In place of a taxonomy of poetic kinds, this chapter approaches verse forms as ever-changing historical sites in which a range of historical antecedents combine and re-form with each other, within a complex negotiation between poets and their specific audiences under particular conditions.

8. PERSONIFICATION

Personification is generally treated as a subset of metaphor or simile, in which the comparison involves some human term. Or it is treated in terms of the development of allegory or of mythological imagery. Here instead I develop personification in a more theoretical direction, not only as a pervasive image structure but also as a foundation for poetic language (and perhaps all language) generally.

Angus Fletcher's *Allegory* (Ithaca, N.Y.: Cornell University Press, 1964) includes marvelous discussions of allegorical personification. Jonathan Culler's "Apostrophe" in *The Pursuit of Signs* (Ithaca, N.Y.: Cornell University Press, 1981), pp. 135–54, broaches questions of personification and poetic address. Some implications for personification are contained in Paul DeMan, "Tropes (Rilke)," in *Allegories of Reading* (New Haven, Conn.: Yale University Press, 1979), pp. 20–56, and "Autobiography as Defacement," *The Rhetoric of Romanticism* (New York: Columbia University Press, 1984), pp. 67–82. See also S. Knapp, *Personification and the Sublime, Milton to Coleridge* (Cambridge, Mass.: Harvard University Press, 1985).

9. POETIC VOICE

Poetic voice, narrowly defined, denotes the persona, or speaking character, in a poem, with the dramatic monologue the limit case of this sort of impersonation. But in fact many poetic elements are structured through poetic voice, seen in broad terms of relationship of poet/speaker to reader/audience in varying circumstances and with a variety of rhetorical intentions. Robert Langbaum's *The Poetry of Experience* (New York: Norton, 1957) offers an excellent discussion of the speaking character or persona in the dramatic monologue form, as it is structured through and toward reader and audience. T. S. Eliot's "The Three Voices of Poetry," in *On Poetry and Poets* (New York: Noonday Press, 1943), proposes a variety of positionings of poetic voice through several poetic modes. A repression of audience, however, seems to be deeply ingrained in discussions of lyric voice. Northrop Frye defines lyric in

Anatomy of Criticism (Princeton: Princeton University Press, 1971) as the genre in which the poet "turns his back on his audience" (p. 271). Winifred Nowottny declares in *The Language Poets Use* (London: University of London, 1962): "A poem, in so far as it is a fiction uttered by a poetic 'I,' is not tied to any context save the context the poet himself articulates in the poem" (p. 42). Mark Strand writes in the *New York Times Book Review*, Sept. 1991: "The context of a poem is likely to be only the poet's voice: a voice speaking to no one in particular and unsupported by a situation or character, as in a work of fiction."

Roman Jakobson's work is fundamental in relation to poetic voice as to other topics. His mapping of the functions of language identified and placed both the speaker and the addressee as constitutive elements of linguistic action (see "Linguistics and Poetics," in *Style in Language*, ed. Thomas A. Sebeok [Cambridge, Mass.: Massachusetts Institute of Technology, 1960], pp. 350–77). Jakobson tended, however, to treat these as fixed formal structures. It was Bakhtin who, working out of formalist models, nevertheless broke through their static formations to reconceive the elements of linguistic action and literary structure as dynamic, mutually informing, and shaping interaction. His analysis of multiple voices through a range of stylistic techniques opens the literary text into social-histories which formalism tended to seal off and situates the speaker as actively anticipating and intending his audience of readers, as well as recalling, responding to, and addressing past authors and a wide range of other cultural discourses. See especially Bakhtin, *Problems of Dostoevsy's Poetics*, trans. Caryl Emerson (Minneapolis: University of Minnesota Press, 1984); "Discourse in the Novel," *The Dialogic Imagination*, trans. Caryl Emerson and Michael Holquist (Austin: University of Texas Press, 1981); and *Speech Genres and Other Late Essays*, trans. Vern W. McGee (Austin: University of Texas Press, 1986).

10. GENDER AND POETIC VOICE

It would be impossible to cite here the burgeoning literature of gender-criticism. Nina Baym offers a historically informed feminist poetics in her studies of American women writers, *Women's Fiction* (Ithaca, N.Y.: Cornell University Press, 1978), and *Feminism and American Literary History* (New Brunswick, N.J.: Rutgers University Press, 1992). Barbara Lewalski's study of early English women writers, *Writing Women in Jacobean England* (Cambridge, Mass.: Harvard University Press, 1993), similarly integrates historical and literary analysis. Treatments of American women's poetry include

Alicia Ostriker's *Stealing the Language* (Boston: Beacon Press, 1986), and Sandra Gilbert and Susan Gubar's more psychologically oriented *Madwoman in the Attic* (New Haven, Conn.: Yale University Press, 1979). Elaine Showalter's *A Literature of Their Own* (Princeton: Princeton University Press, 1977) sets forward many of the issues of feminist literary theory. Her "Feminist Criticism in the Wilderness" in *Contemporary Literary Criticism* (New York: Longman, 1986), pp. 51–71, summarizes many discussions to that date. Theories of female language(s) such as Helene Cixous's "The Laugh of the Medusa," trans. Keith and Paula Cohen, *Signs* 1 (Summer 1976) are provocative. Nevertheless, in my view, attempts to define a female language threaten to be prescriptive and restrictive.

There are many studies and essay collections available on women poets, as well as much writing on cultural, anthropological, psychological, and biological questions of gender. Especially excellent in its analysis of how Renaissance women transformed inherited verse forms is Anne Rosalind Jones, *The Currency of Eros* (Bloomington: Indiana University Press, 1990). Texts not explicitly related to poetics but of immediate interest and application to literary analysis of women's voices include Shirley Ardener, ed., *Perceiving Women* (London: Dent and Sons, 1977), which introduced an anthropological model analyzing dominant as against subordinate voices; and Carol Gilligan *In a Different Voice* (Cambridge, Mass.: Harvard University Press, 1982).

II. POETIC RHYTHM: METER

There are many handbooks that offer definitions and examples of metrical schemes. The writings of John Hollander, however, provide a theoretical foundation for thinking about meter as well as technical instruction. Hollander's approach to metric places it within a broader consideration of poetic language as figural expression. I have strongly relied on Hollander's notion of the metrical contract, which itself has antecedents in formalist studies of versification that describe the individual poem's deviation from strict metrical form. See Victor Erlich's *Russian Formalism* (New Haven, Conn.: Yale University Press, 1965). John Hollander's studies on metric (as well as verse forms) include *Vision and Resonance* (New York: Oxford University Press, 1975); *Melodious Guile* (New Haven, Conn.: Yale University Press, 1988); and *Rhyme's Reason* (New Haven, Conn.: Yale University Press, 1981).

Structuralist analysis deepened understanding of rhythmic language in general. *Style in Language*, ed. Thomas A. Sebeok (Cambridge: Massachusetts Institute of Technology Press, 1960),

offers a section on "Metrics," including Seymour Chapman's
"Comparing Metrical Styles," pp. 149–72. Wimsatt and Beardsley's
"The Concept of Meter: An Exercise in Abstraction," *PMLA* 74
(1959): 585–98 is an important essay on the relationship between
metrical norms and deviations.

John Thompson's *The Founding of English Metre* (New York:
Columbia University Press, 1961) studies the origins of metric in
English. A useful overview of metrical technique (as well as
forms) is Paul Fussell, Jr.'s *Poetic Meter and Poetic Form* (New York:
Random House, 1965). Harvey Gross's *Sound and Form in Modern
Poetry* (Ann Arbor, University of Michigan Press, 1964) discusses
metric as well as syntactic and other constitutive features within the
period extending from Walt Whitman to e.e. cummings. See also
Harvey Gross, ed., *The Structure of Verse: Modern Essays on Prosody*
(Greenwich, Conn.: Fawcett, 1966); and W. K. Wimsatt, *Versification:
Major Language Types* (New York: Modern Language Association,
1972). Derek Attridge's *The Rhythms of English Poetry* (London:
Longman, 1982) remains a standard work. See also Clive T. Probyn,
English Poetry (London: Longman, 1984); Barry Spurr, *Studying Poetry*
(Melbourne: Macmillan Education, 1997); and Alfred Corn, *The
Poem's Heart's Beat* (Ashland, Ore.: Storyline Press, 1998).

An exemplary discussion of Eliot's meter, especially in *Four
Quartets*, is Helen Gardner's *The Art of T. S. Eliot* (London: Faber
and Faber, 1949). Eliot's own essays on metrical features include
"The Beating of the Drum," *Nation and Atheneum* 34, no. 1 (Oct. 6,
1923): 11-12; "Reflections on *Vers Libre*," in *New Statesman* 8 (Mar. 3,
1917): 518–19; and "The Music of Poetry," in *On Poetry and Poets*
(New York: Noonday Press, 1943).

12. POETIC RHYTHM: SOUND AND RHYME

Roman Jakobson's studies of the sonnet highlight the grammatical
and other linguistic interrelationships between rhyme words and
other sound repetitions (Roman Jakobson and Claude Levi Strauss,
"Les Chats de Charles Baudelaire" *L'Homme* 2 [1962]: 5–21; and
Roman Jakobson and Lawrence Jones, *Shakespeare's Verbal Art* [The
Hague: Mouton, 1970]). This formalist-structuralist approach yields
elaborate charts of relationship, which are also highly suggestive
and revealing regarding the kinds of connections that sound repeti-
tion create in a poem. W. K. Wimsatt's "One Relation of Rhyme to
Reason," *The Verbal Icon* (Lexington: University Press of Kentucky,
1954), pp. 153–68, likewise investigates the relationships between
rhyme words and their functions. See also Donald Wesling, *The
Chances of Rhyme: Device and Modernity* (Berkeley: University of

California Press, 1980), and, more recently, Robert Pinsky's *The Sounds of Poetry* (New York: Farrar, Straus, Giroux, 1998).

Of great theoretical interest is the relation of poetry to nonsense, by way of sound and other material shapes or organizations of poetic material. Elizabeth Sewell's *The Field of Nonsense* (London: Chatto and Windus, 1952) remains a classic study. See also Jean-Jacques Lecercle, *Philosophy of Nonsense* (New York: Routledge, 1994).

13. RHETORIC: MORE TROPES

Rhetoric, the core of the original humanities curriculum, has re-emerged in twentieth-century criticism and theory in a number of guises. Roman Jakobson's essay, "Two Aspects of Language and Two Types of Aphasic Disturbances," in Roman Jakobson and Morris Halle, *Fundamentals of Language* (The Hague: Mouton, 1956), pp. 55–82, seemed to fulfill a dream of literary mastery and system, with metaphor and metonymy dividing between them almost every feature of poetry and prose. Kenneth Burke's writings, especially his *Grammar of Motives* (Berkeley: University of California Press, 1969), also introduced rhetorical figures into literary discussion, focusing on four "master" tropes. W. K. Wimsatt's "Rhetoric and Poems: Alexander Pope," in *The Verbal Icon* (Lexington: University Press of Kentucky, 1954), pp. 168–87, begins to explore the theoretical implications of rhetorical tropes. Rosalie Colie's *Paradoxica Epidemica* (Princeton: Princeton University Press, 1966) is an exemplary study of the specific figure of paradox within Renaissance culture. Paul DeMan has featured a number of different rherical figures through a series of essays, including chiasmus in his essay "Tropes (Rilke)," in *Allegories of Reading* (New Haven, Conn.: Yale University Press, 1979), pp. 20–56, and anthropomorphism in "Anthropomorphism and Trope in the Lyric," in *The Rhetoric of Romanticism* (New York: Columbia University Press, 1984), pp. 239–62. DeMan, however, as always interprets them as modes of their own undoing. Friedrich Nietzsche radically poses broad questions of tropes and representation in "On Truth and Lie in an Extra-Moral Sense" and other essays in *Friedrich Nietzsche on Rhetoric and Language*, ed. and trans. Sander L. Gilman et al. (New York: Oxford University Press, 1989).

Discussions of the relationship between rhetoric and literature are offered in B. Vickers, *In Defense of Rhetoric* (Carbondale: Southern Illinois University Press, 1989); Michael Shapiro and Marianne Shapiro, *Figuration in Verbal Art* (Princeton: Princeton University Press, 1988); and P. Bizzell and B. Herzberg, *The*

Rhetorical Tradition: Readings from Classical Times to the Present
(Boston: St. Martin's, 1990). A convenient list of rhetorical tropes is
provided in Richard Lanham's *A Handbook of Rhetorical Terms*
(Berkeley: University of California Press, 1969). Heinrich Lausberg's
Handbook of Literary Rhetoric (Boston: Brill, 1998) gives a thorough
overview of rhetorical tropes.

14. INCOMPLETE FIGURES AND THE ART OF READING

This chapter broaches a number of different but related issues.
Figural structure is investigated against a cultural background of
reading and audience relationships, as well as in theoretical terms.
The notion of figural structure as an open chain of signifiers finds its
basis in the theories of Jacques Derrida in, for example, *Of
Grammatology* (Baltimore: Johns Hopkins University Press, 1974),
and of Harold Bloom and Geoffrey Hartman in, for example,
Deconstruction and Criticism, ed. Bloom et al. (New York: Con-
tinuum, 1979). But the way both reader and text are placed within
literary and cultural contexts effects and shapes the unfolding of
figural chains, and therefore fundamentally penetrates figural
structure.

However, while insisting on the power of poetic figures as
operating within broad cultural contexts, I have not attempted to
theorize a poetics of reading—that is, I have not tried to draw clear
lines between where the text ends and interpretation begins. Such an
undertaking in my opinion soon arrives at a quagmire of unanswer-
able epistemological questions about relationships between mind and
text, and the role of the mind in perceiving or constituting a text. It
remains caught in epistemological problems that Derridean theory
of interpretation rejects.

Within literary discussion, reader-response theory has been
mainly cognitive and/or psychological, studying how the mind in
the reading process responds to, recalls, and anticipates structural
features of the text. The work of Wolfgang Iser (notably *The Implied
Reader* [Baltimore: Johns Hopkins University Press, 1974] and *The
Act of Reading* [Baltimore: Johns Hopkins University Press, 1978])
charts such cognitive responses and activities in the act of reading,
as the text invokes and then fulfills or defeats expected and remem-
bered patterns. Although Iser's work mainly addresses fiction, his
approach can be extended to poetry. Stanley Fish's interpretation of
Milton's *Paradise Lost* in *Surprised by Sin* (Berkeley: University of
California Press, 1971) charts a reading experience of poetry, mainly
through narrative sequences of suspense, expectation, and self-

reflective revision. He discusses the epistemology of readers' roles in *Is There a Text in This Class?* (Cambridge, Mass.: Harvard University Press, 1980).

Structuralist theorists have variously incorporated the reader within the terms of textuality. One succinct overview of semiotic and structuralist theories of reading can be found in Susan Suleiman's "Introduction" to *The Reader in the Text* (Princeton: Princeton University Press, 1980), pp. 3–45. These, however, tend to reduce the reader to a kind of textual function.

How cultural-historical matrices generate particular figural systems and their interpretation is an immense topic. Eric Auerbach's *Mimesis* (Princeton University Press, 1953) remains a classic discussion of figural changes in the development of prose fiction. W. K. Wimsatt's "The Structure of Romantic Nature Imagery" in *The Verbal Icon* (Lexington: University Press of Kentucky, 1954) explores the phenomenology of Romantic image-structure, as does Frank Kermode in *The Romantic Image* (London: Routledge and Kegan Paul, 1957). This area has been richly expanded in works by Geoffrey Hartman such as *Wordsworth's Poetry* (New Haven, Conn.: Yale University Press, 1964); many works by Harold Bloom; and in Thomas Weiskel's *The Romantic Sublime* (Baltimore: Johns Hopkins University Press, 1976). Paul DeMan takes up the question of Romantic image-structure in essays such as "Symbolic Landscape in Wordsworth and Yeats," in *The Rhetoric of Romanticism* (New York: Columbia University Press, 1984) and "The Rhetoric of Temporality" in *Blindness and Insight* (Minneapolis: University of Minnesota Press, 1971), pp. 122–44.

Interpretation of poetic sign-structures in terms of historical contexts has also been undertaken by Marxist critics, such as Raymond Williams in *Culture and Society* (New York: Harper and Row, 1958). Julia Kristeva, "The Bounded Text," in *Desire in Language* (New York: Columbia University Press, 1980), pp. 36–63, discusses the progress of symbolic representation. Ernst Hans Josef Gombrich's discussion of Cubist painting in *Art and Illusion* (London: Phaidon Press, 1962) provides a model for discussing sign-structure in Modernist poetics, developed by Marjorie Perloff in *The Poetics of Indeterminacy* (Princeton: Princeton University Press, 1983) and Hugh Kenner in *The Pound Era* (Berkeley: University of California Press, 1971). Other literary scholars whose work combines literary with historical, political, and theological analysis are Sacvan Bercovitch in, for example, *The Puritan Origins of the American Self* (New Haven, Conn.: Yale University Press, 1975) and *The Rites of Assent* (New York: Routledge, 1993); Christopher

Ricks in, for example, *The Force of Poetry* (New York: Oxford University Press, 1995); and Richard Poirier in *The Renewal of Literature* (New Haven, Conn.: Yale University Press, 1987). The theory of figures and figural chains proposed in this chapter owes much to the writings of John Hollander, Harold Bloom, Geoffrey Hartman, and Sacvan Bercovitch, whose works variously consider the generation of figures and their complex cultural and theoretical meanings.

Index of Poems

Index of Poets

Index of Terms and Topics